£10.00

C000216457

Rails in The Valleys

The best remembered Great Western locomotives in the South Wales valleys were the 56xx class 0-6-2Ts, sturdy, compact, reliable, and equally at home on freight or passenger duties. Here No 5613 stands at the unusual coal stage at its home shed of Ferndale on 1 March 1963.
(D. K. Jones)

RAILS IN THE VALLEYS

JAMES PAGE

DAVID & CHARLES
Newton Abbot   London

The quintessential valleys passenger train. GWR 56xx class 0-6-2T No 5688 of Treherbert shed near Llwynypia in the Rhondda valley, with an up Treherbert train on 12 May 1956. (S. Rickard)

British Library Cataloguing in Publication Data

Page, James
   Rails in the valleys.
   1. South Wales. Railway services, to 1979
   I. Title
   385′.09429′4

ISBN 0-7153-8979-3

© James Page 1989

All rights reserved. No part of this
publication may be reproduced, stored
in a retrieval system, or transmitted,
in any form or by any means, electronic,
mechanical, photocopying, recording or
otherwise, without the prior permission
of David & Charles Publishers plc

Book designed by Michael Head
Typeset by Typesetters (Birmingham) Limited
Smethwick, West Midlands
and printed in Great Britain
by Butler and Tanner, Frome, Somerset
for David & Charles Publishers plc
Brunel House   Newton Abbot   Devon

CONTENTS

INTRODUCTION

Pontypridd was one of the bustling hubs of the railway network within the South Wales valleys, cut into the hillside at the junction of the Taff and Rhondda valleys its multifaced island platform once dealing every day with well over 10,000 people arriving and departing, together with many more changing from one valley service to another, and over one hundred passenger trains. North of here such services threaded through the coal traffic of the Taff, Cynon and Rhondda valleys which at one time amounted to over 17 million tons annually, which if it is assumed that this traffic was in train loads of sixty 10 ton wagons, meant that a loaded coal train or an empty return working passed Pontypridd every eight minutes day and night. Although this is an extreme example, life was only slightly less hectic elsewhere in the valleys at this time for as a whole some 50 million tons of coal was being raised annually. But, despite this density of traffic, passengers passing through, say, Maesteg in the Llynfi valley could once admire the fountain maintained there by the stationmaster, or if in the Sirhowy the hanging baskets at Hollybush station. Railwaymen never lost their love of natural beauty despite the pressures of the job. Neither too did they ever forget their sense of duty to the public. Stations were manned at all towns and villages, and many were the services provided, and to give but one example, at Llangonoyd, again in the Llynfi valley, it was once the stationmaster's duty to also act as local postmaster. The business of valley towns revolved around their stations. All their necessities, and luxuries, came through them, either across the platform as mail or parcel, or via the goods yard through which, except for mineral and heavy industrial products, all the manufactured merchandise of a town passed. Even as late as the nineteen-fifties, included in the daily loads from Tonypandy would be steel furniture, shoes, nuts and bolts, life rafts, cutlery or waterproof clothing.

The story of the railways of South Wales can, and has, been told in hard statistics, of companies founded, lines built, dates of openings, stock owned and coal carried. The area was uniquely rich in competing railways and there were few areas of the country where towns could boast so many railway companies serving them. Cardiff once had six (Taff Vale, Barry, Great Western, Rhymney, Cardiff, and London & North Western), Swansea four (Great Western, London & North Western, Midland, and Rhondda & Swansea Bay), and Merthyr had five (Taff Vale, Rhymney, Brecon & Merthyr, Great Western, and London & North Western). Not that size was necessarily the criterion for such an embarrassment of riches, as evidenced by Cymmer in the Afan valley which was served by the Great Western, Rhondda & Swansea Bay, and South Wales Mineral railways. But little has been written of their social effects or their methods of operation. They were responsible for the shapes of the towns that grew up around them, and in many cases they determined the separation of the various classes of the population within them. The local railways were responsible for the relative ease with which immigrants could arrive in the valleys, it being a rather surprising fact that emigration from England at the turn of the century to the South Wales valleys was second only to that to the United States. For decades they were also the sole means of leaving the valleys for the seaside, today's holiday business being a direct successor, as elsewhere, to this traffic. Expectations were not as high then, day trips to the coast, from Penarth to the Gower, being the high spot of the year, with Barry Island the principal destination. On bank holidays the railway staff would be worked off their feet as every available locomotive and coach was pressed into service. All this extra traffic was accommodated on a system where station layouts were often restricted, which could inhibit the length of excursion trains, so that their frequency had to be increased to cope with the demand. This in turn meant operating headaches on the approaches to Barry from both the valleys and Cardiff directions, both of which were only double tracked with few passing loops at any of the intermediate stations.

South Wales was richly blessed with the minerals that were the basis of Great Britain's industrial growth and one-time world leadership. The operational practices introduced to cope with this traffic were of paramount importance, for if techniques had not been devised to cope with this enormous traffic the industrial development of South Wales, and its importance in the British economy, would have been severely limited. But such practices were devised and honed for over a century. Sophisticated control methods were put in place, for on a daily basis sudden demands for traffic to be moved could occur anywhere in the valleys due to the nature of the coal-ordering system then in operation, and compounded by the region's geography that precluded the construction of holding sidings at the mines to act as a buffer to these fluctuations. No system is infallible however and delays did occur which could force short-time working at certain mines if empty wagons did not arrive back in time from the docks. Rightly this caused great annoyance to the coal owners; they were not altogether blameless, however, as the state of their wagons was partially responsible for the delays, as the railways frequently pointed out, but to little avail.

Times have now changed and the need for such practices for both excursion and freight traffic has now largely disappeared. But before documents vanish and memories fade I have tried to tell some of the story of those times as a tribute to the railwaymen who devised and operated those practices, whether in control office, siding or signal box, or on footplate or platform. Not forgotten either are the dock operations which were no less vital; as can be understood if it is recalled that at Cardiff to ship the tonnage offered when the port was at its peak meant that daily throughout the year somewhere in these docks a wagon was tipped, and coal dropped into a ship's hold, every half a minute.

And there are other stories to tell, of the locomotives that worked in the valleys, and the sheds and works that served them. Not forgotten is the LMS, drawn to the Eldorado that was South Wales via Craven Arms, Hereford or Abergavenny. But although a great railway, it and its predecessors were never to dominate the region as did the Great Western. Finally there were the 'country' branches. Yes, they did exist and they too were a part of the railway scene in South Wales. All this and much more was part of the endlessly fascinating story of the valleys railways that I have attempted to narrate.

JAMES PAGE
Machen, Gwent

The 56xx class 0-6-2T No 5697 heads an excursion into platform 3 of Cardiff General station on 17 March 1953. This working was from the Newport valleys. (S. Rickard)

Cardiff Queen Street station in 1953. On 6 October 56xx class 0-6-2T No 5603 is seen at the head of a Rhymney valley working. (S. Rickard)

1
JOURNEYS IN THE VALLEYS

Nine hundred and eighty-five square miles of hill and vale, twenty major valleys crowded with more than three hundred towns and villages, with nearly one million seven hundred thousand inhabitants. These are the valleys and their immediate surroundings. Within them a mineral wealth, second to none in its day, spawned one of the densest rail networks in Great Britain, with up to fifteen railways operating within their confines. Such was this mineral wealth that for years it was the most important, and profitable, commodity moved. For generations merchandise and people were secondary. But this state of affairs was modified as social attitudes changed and the population exploded, so that by the turn of the century all major and most minor valleys had a much improved passenger service.

Today few memories can reach this far back, and it is from the thirties onward to the end of steam in the sixties that are now most likely to be recalled. To those who remember these years steam in the valleys meant an 0-6-2T and a rake of five or six non-corridor coaches that, depending upon the period, or the valley one was obliged or perhaps chose to travel in, could vary in hue from Great Western chocolate and cream or LMS lake, to the British Railways shade of the latter colour. Exceptions of course abounded. The 0-6-0PT with up to three auto coaches was common on lightly used services or lines, both in the valleys and elsewhere, and a 14xx class 0-4-2T was at home for many years on the Llantrisant to Penygraig line. Ex-Midland Railway 0-6-0Ts could be seen in the Swansea area, while ex-LMS 2-6-2Ts and 2-6-4Ts ran the Sirhowy valley services from the fifties. Notwithstanding these exceptions however, the most common sight as one arrived on the platform of a South Wales station, from Aberbeeg to Aberdylais, or Resolven to Risca, was an 0-6-2T at the head of five or six non-corridor coaches. Stepping into such a train one could if one wished make two journeys. In reality to one's destination, and in imagination much further afield as one studied photographs of Penzance or Paignton, Weymouth or Weston, that beckoned from the group of photographs set either side of a central mirror that adorned the compartments of such stock. One could always find a little sunshine here, even if outside it was a typical South Wales day of penetrating rain.

The 6.50am Cardiff (Queen Street) to Aberdare (Low Level) – change at Abercynon for Merthyr – was one such train in the summer of 1957. Beneath the cavernous roof of Queen Street station it would stand shadowed and brooding, as even in the summer months sunlight could not easily penetrate the station interior at this hour. Queen Street, in steam days, was always dark and smoky, for with the exceptions of Merthyr, before its Brunel roof was dismantled, and the early years of the Taff Vale station at Aberdare (later known as Low Level) which had an awning extending over its single platform line, it was the only station with an all-over roof in or serving the valleys. The engine, frequently blowing off, stood alongside the old Taff Vale Railway offices that backed onto the main up platform

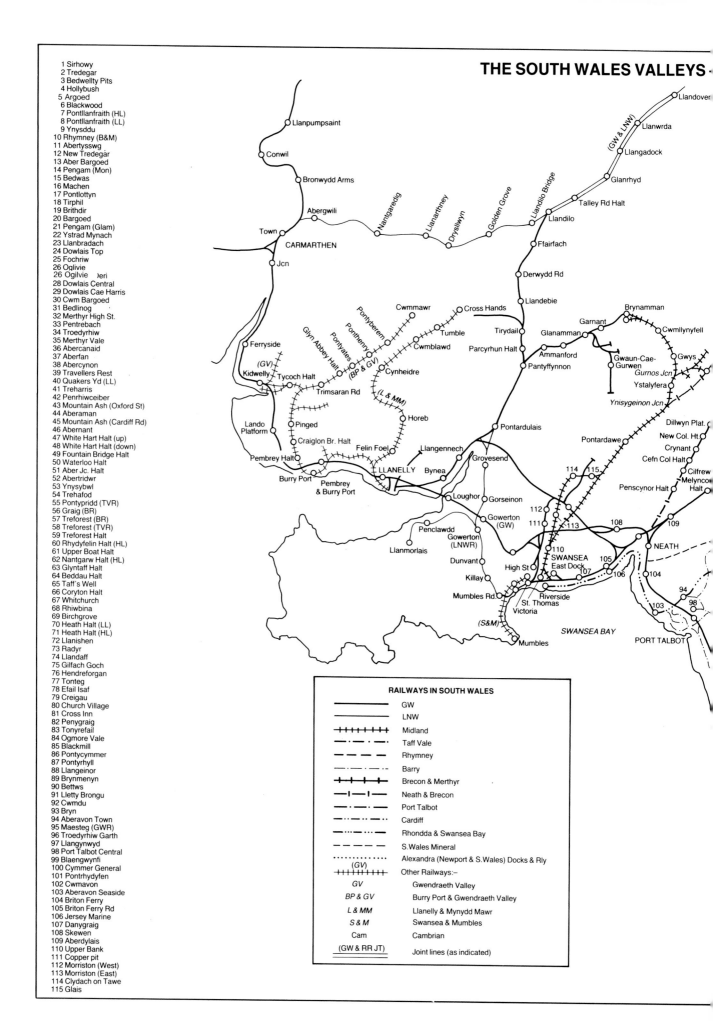

THE SOUTH WALES VALLEYS

1 Sirhowy
2 Tredegar
3 Bedwellty Pits
4 Hollybush
5 Argoed
6 Blackwood
7 Pontllanfraith (HL)
8 Pontllanfraith (LL)
9 Ynysddu
10 Rhymney (B&M)
11 Abertysswg
12 New Tredegar
13 Aber Bargoed
14 Pengam (Mon)
15 Bedwas
16 Machen
17 Pontlottyn
18 Tirphil
19 Brithdir
20 Bargoed
21 Pengam (Glam)
22 Ystrad Mynach
23 Llanbradach
24 Dowlais Top
25 Fochriw
26 Oglivie
26 Ogilvie   )eri
28 Dowlais Central
29 Dowlais Cae Harris
30 Cwm Bargoed
31 Bedlinog
32 Merthyr High St.
33 Pentrebach
34 Troedyrhiw
35 Merthyr Vale
36 Abercanaid
37 Aberfan
38 Abercynon
39 Travellers Rest
40 Quakers Yd (LL)
41 Treharris
42 Penrhiwceiber
43 Mountain Ash (Oxford St)
44 Aberaman
45 Mountain Ash (Cardiff Rd)
46 Abernant
47 White Hart Halt (up)
48 White Hart Halt (down)
49 Fountain Bridge Halt
50 Waterloo Halt
51 Aber Jc. Halt
52 Abertridwr
53 Ynysybwl
54 Trehafod
55 Pontypridd (TVR)
56 Graig (BR)
57 Treforest (BR)
58 Treforest (TVR)
59 Treforest Halt
60 Rhydyfelin Halt (HL)
61 Upper Boat Halt
62 Nantgarw Halt (HL)
63 Glyntaff Halt
64 Beddau Halt
65 Taff's Well
66 Coryton Halt
67 Whitchurch
68 Rhiwbina
69 Birchgrove
70 Heath Halt (LL)
71 Heath Halt (HL)
72 Llanishen
73 Radyr
74 Llandaff
75 Gilfach Goch
76 Hendreforgan
77 Tonteg
78 Efail Isaf
79 Creigau
80 Church Village
81 Cross Inn
82 Penygraig
83 Tonyrefail
84 Ogmore Vale
85 Blackmill
86 Pontycymmer
87 Pontyrhyll
88 Llangeinor
89 Brynmenyn
90 Bettws
91 Lletty Brongu
92 Cwmdu
93 Bryn
94 Aberavon Town
95 Maesteg (GWR)
96 Troedyrhiw Garth
97 Llangynwyd
98 Port Talbot Central
99 Blaengwynfi
100 Cymmer General
101 Pontrhydyfen
102 Cwmavon
103 Aberavon Seaside
104 Briton Ferry
105 Briton Ferry Rd
106 Jersey Marine
107 Danygraig
108 Skewen
109 Aberdylais
110 Upper Bank
111 Copper pit
112 Morriston (West)
113 Morriston (East)
114 Clydach on Tawe
115 Glais

RAILWAYS IN SOUTH WALES

────────	GW
────────	LNW
┼┼┼┼┼┼┼	Midland
─·─·─·─	Taff Vale
─ ─ ─ ─	Rhymney
───────	Barry
┼─┼─┼─┼	Brecon & Merthyr
─┃─┃─┃	Neath & Brecon
─·─··─··	Port Talbot
─·─··─··	Cardiff
─ ─ ─ ─	Rhondda & Swansea Bay
─ ─ ─ ─	S. Wales Mineral
··············	Alexandra (Newport & S.Wales) Docks & Rly
┼┼┼┼┼┼┼ (GV)	Other Railways:-
GV	Gwendraeth Valley
BP & GV	Burry Port & Gwendraeth Valley
L & MM	Llanelly & Mynydd Mawr
S & M	Swansea & Mumbles
Cam	Cambrian
(GW & RR JT)	Joint lines (as indicated)

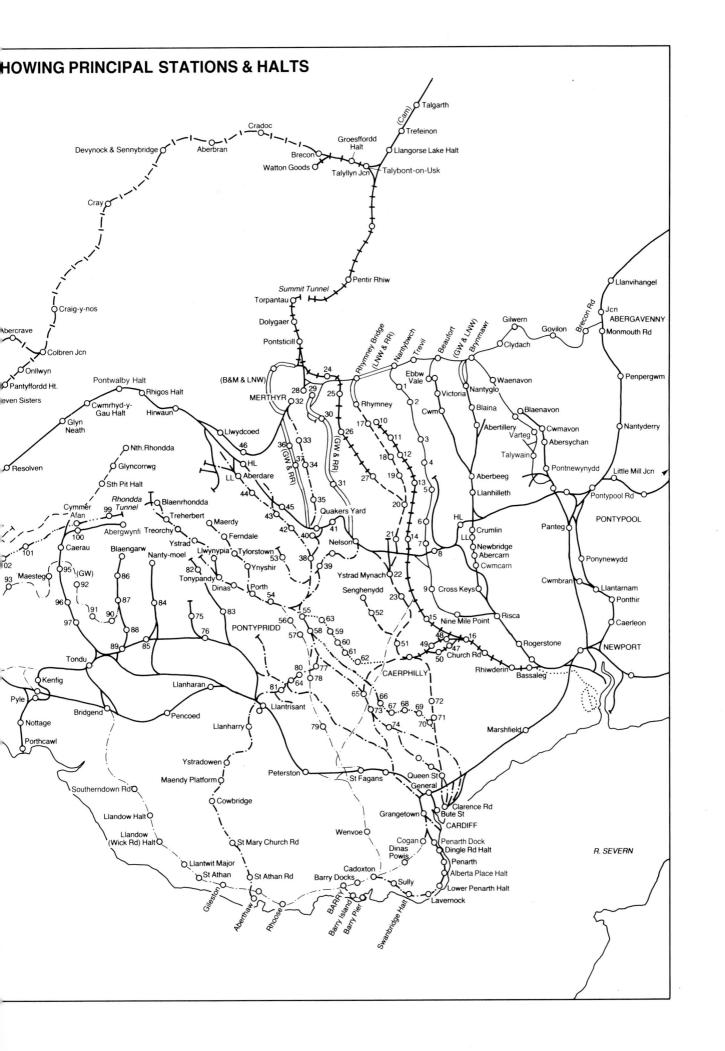

(up at Queen Street was northwards into the valleys), clear of the austere gable at the end of the steeply pitched roof, as its crew started yet another turn.

The dying cries of a shrill whistle screech followed by the first sharp exhaust blasts that heralded movement, accompanied the train out across the ornately decorated bridge that spanned the Newport Road and on past Queen Street North Signal Box, set in the vee of the Taff and Rhymney valley lines. Shortly after, Crockherbtown sidings slid past on the right as the straight four-tracked line headed towards Cardiff's northern suburbs, and passed behind the rear gardens of once well maintained Victorian houses; solid three-storeyed upper middle class on the left or up side, somewhat smaller and cheaper on the right between the diverging lines to the two valleys. Running beneath the overbridge immediately beyond the single platform of Cathays Halt, a little to the north of the present day twin platforms of Cathays station, Cathays engine shed on the up side, and carriage and wagon works on the down, came into view. Situated at the north eastern corner of Cardiff's renowned Civic Centre, the shed, wedged between the back of a row of three-storey terraced houses and the running lines, was discreetly hidden from view, the smoke nuisance inevitably associated with such premises being abated by the fact that the prevailing wind direction is generally from the south west. The largest running shed in the Taff Vale Railway system, it housed between fifty and eighty engines at various times between 1950 and late 1957 when the shed was closed to steam. Remodelled and partially truncated by the Great Western, at this time in the morning it would usually sport both GWR and

Not all excursions in South Wales were to the seaside. In this view taken on a wet 17 January 1953, 56xx class 0-6-2T No 5638 is seen standing at platform 4 of Cardiff General station at the head of a rugby international excursion from the Newport valleys. (S. Rickard)

British Railways 2-6-2Ts alongside the ubiquitous 56xx class 0-6-2Ts and assorted pannier classes. The last locomotives of its original owners were about to be withdrawn following banishment in their later years to the valley sheds.

Beyond the next overbridge at Maindy, immediately in front of which was another single-platform halt of the same name, the sidings to shed and carriage works have terminated apart from one on the up side to a wagon works. From here the four running lines, first straight then curving to the west, are hemmed in by an embankment on the down side until shortly before the fan of sidings at Roath Branch Junction, which trailed into the freight lines, which were the right-hand pair of the four, and via a double crossover into the passenger lines, to form a northward-facing junction. Approximately two and a half miles from Queen Street this large array of sidings was set in a deep eastward-facing cutting, the running lines to the Roath Dock bisecting the loops, for like all storage sidings on this and other valley lines they were open at both ends to minimise shunting movements and interference with through traffic.

Once past the junction the line ran along a shelf with falling ground to the up side and Llandaff Cathedral a prominent feature three-quarters of a mile away to the south west, and soon steam was shut off as the first stop was reached at Llandaff (for Whitchurch) at about 6.55am. Following a brief halt, the timetable calling for a departure at 6.56am, and with few of the good folk of Llandaff abroad at such an hour, a smart start, so typical of the 56xx class was always made. Almost immediately the junctions that brought the goods lines from the down

Valleys terminus at Maerdy in the Rhondda Fach. The photograph dates from the early 1950s. Behind the Taff Vale signal box the mineral-only line to Maerdy colliery is visible. (L&GRP)

side across to the up were crossed, and those lines swung westward across the River Taff to run past the sidings at Radyr, on the Radyr to Penarth line, before reappearing alongside again, but now on the up side of the passenger lines, just short of Radyr station, about three-quarters of a mile beyond Llandaff. Our train however continued north west on a low embankment to also cross the Taff, and as it did first Radyr running shed and then the northern end of the large group of sorting sidings, set beneath the high ground that bordered the western bank of the river, came into view. Although by this date it was a shadow of its former self, the yard and shed still had a busy air about them as shunters bustled to and fro, and coal from the Rhondda, Rhymney, Taff and Cynon valleys – then still busy – pits eased into the yard for sorting and onward dispatch. Radyr station was now reached in a few minutes, and departed equally as quickly as Llandaff.

From here to Taff's Well was the most attractive part of the whole journey to Merthyr. Working hard in the morning sunlight as the climb into the hills continues unbroken, the train is first wedged between the steep curving bluff close to the left and the river below to the right, then runs across open fields and heads towards the narrow gorge at Taff's Well that separates the Taff valley from the plain on which Cardiff stands. Once across this last piece of relatively open ground with its views of the woods above the gorge, with Castell Coch, the second Marquis of Bute's ornate folly set amongst them, the main towering sandstone cliffs rapidly dominate and restrict the view. The train is now dwarfed as it heads northwards. Crossing the river again, where concrete road intersections now dominate the scene, one could see the outline of the Glamorganshire canal, and the – by then – disused line of the old Cardiff Railway, in cutting, tunnel or on its ledge. Both these features together with the main road, which was then of a discreet size and in scale with its surroundings, were on the down side. But as one hurried north the whole scene was dominated by one of South Wales' outstanding engineering landmarks, the Barry Railway's Walnut Tree viaduct. Standing 120ft above the valley floor, with seven lattice girder spans, and a total length of 1,548ft, it imperiously stood above all, a triumph of Victorian engineering and enterprise. Once beneath, steam would again be shut off, and drifting past Walnut Tree Junction, where the line from the Rhymney valley made a connection that was controlled by a tall ex-Taff Vale Railway signal box, Taff's Well station was entered a few minutes after seven o'clock. Curiously the signal box bore the name of the junction and not the station even though it stood at the end of the latter's up platform. A busy little station at the edge of the village whose name it bore, it could usually be relied upon to add to the train's load, and from now on the relative quiet of one's compartment would frequently be broken as the day began in earnest and one's travelling companions enquired as to one's well being as they recognised a regular on the train.

With what now sounded like a cheerful crow of the whistle rather than the screech that heralded the journey's start, the valley proper was entered as the now hard working locomotive treated us to the rhythmic surging of a two-cylinder tank engine. The line to Nantgarw colliery headed off on the down side soon after the station was left; (a short connection which took this mineral line to the ex-Cardiff Railway metals that ran to the mine, and which was opened as late as 1953).

Soon the train was above Treforest Trading Estate, built in the 1930s to bring work to the area and once more fulfilling this primary function, and slowing to a halt at the little wooden station of Treforest Estate which was set amongst trees

14

half way along the estate's western edge, giving the impression that one was in rural rather than industrial surroundings. But soon the estate was in view again, dominated by the power station at its northern end. As one now glanced from the windows to left or right one was soon, and repeatedly, reminded of the valley's frenetic past. In quick succession one passed, on the up side, the junction with the ex-Taff Vale line to Llantrisant, and the Barry Railway's junction to its own system, while immediately before the latter were – and still are – the enormous earthworks by which the Cardiff Railway sought unsuccessfully to connect with

On a dull afternoon 64xx class 0-6-0PT No 6433 departs for Hirwaun from the slender central platform at Merthyr High Street. Originally the Brunel designed terminus of the Vale of Neath Railway, High Street later played host to five companies, and advantage was taken of the space provided following the introduction of the standard gauge in 1872, to squeeze in an, albeit narrow, extra platform to cater for the extra traffic of the later years of the nineteenth century. (M. Hale)

A local practice

To work the South Wales valleys was to work on steep gradients, which generated local practices not applicable elsewhere on the system. Passenger-train working at Pantywaun Halt was a case in point. Situated on a 1 in 37 between Fochriw and Dowlais Top, drivers of up trains would come up the climb from Fochriw at full regulator until the engine was alongside the platform ramp and then quickly shut off. The train would then come to a halt within the platform length, which was barely the length of the train. Then and only then would the brakes be applied, *not* to stop the train, but to hold it on the gradient.

Auto-train working in the valleys; the 11.00am Aberdare to Abercynon enters Abercynon on 3 August 1957. The locomotive sandwiched between the three trailers is 64xx class 0-6-0PT No 6431. The line in the foreground is the up line to Merthyr Tydfil. (S. Rickard)

the Taff Vale Railway. These three junctions were all within the space of only 72 chains, and Treforest station was reached 15 chains after the connection to the Barry line had been passed.

A neat, compact station, the main buildings of which were on the down platform, it was typical of the many fully staffed valley stations at this time. It had two platforms flanking the passenger lines, while the mineral lines passed behind the up platform, which was essentially therefore of the island type. The station buildings were, in 1957, of dressed stone, locally quarried, with window and door surrounds of yellow brick. A short and rather ornately supported awning was provided on the down side as a protection against the often atrocious weather with which South Wales can be afflicted. Connection between the platforms was, as elsewhere in the area, by an open iron foot-bridge, and despite the provision of an awning on the down side none was provided on the up. A little before quarter past seven the station would come to life with the arrival of our train, as it coasted past Treforest Junction, rattled over the girder bridge just to the south of the station, and came to a halt.

16

Once more we were dispatched with speed and were soon not only well above the valley floor, but also the rooftops of the houses on the down side too, while in a short distance those on the up side were soon over thirty feet above us. We climbed steadily up the 1 in 277 around the long left-hand curve past PC&N Junction, where the line from Newport of the ex-Pontypridd, Caerphilly & Newport Railway, trailed into ours on the down side from a tall embankment that crossed the valley at this point, then swung sharply to the right and entered Pontypridd station, once the hub of the Taff Vale system, at 7.18am.

Set on a right-hand curve, Pontypridd station, which in its present form dates from the early years of this century, is a masterpiece of compact design which even in 1957, shorn of some of its services, stood as a monument to the sheer ingenuity of our forefathers. The station is situated on the lower slopes of a hill and when enlargement was needed as the volume of traffic grew, sideways expansion was limited, not to mention expensive. In fact for seventeen years following the quadrupling of the main line to Cardiff in 1885, the station remained a double-track bottleneck. At the turn of the century however the Taff Vale Railway finally bit on the bullet and excavated the hillside on the western side and laid a double mineral line clear of the station which was completed in 1902. At least now the problem of moving the coal past the bottleneck had been solved. However a few years later the TVR introduced new local passenger services starting and stopping at Pontypridd, which created problems with the Merthyr, Aberdare and Rhondda through trains. With no room for further sideways expansion one of the most imaginative stations ever designed came into being. Up and down platforms were replaced with one immense island platform with access from a booking hall below at street level. The island had a unique combination of stepping and bays to give a total of seven platform faces. There were two bays at the northern end for Aberdare, Nelson and Ynysybwl, and one at the southern end for Llantrisant and Cowbridge. Rebuilding in this form took from 1907 to 1912 to complete, the single-storey station building being finished in a glazed red brick beneath a single awning of no less than 7,370 square yards.

On our arrival there is noise and bustle and many leave the train for connections to the Rhondda; doors slam, whistles blow, porters and passengers shout across

Valleys junction. Porth in the early years of the century. At the far platform a Taff Vale Railway steam railmotor trailer can be seen on a Rhondda Fach train. (L&GRP)

*A section from the Newport
Traffic District Service Time
Tables, July 1960.*

the platform, and up and down the wide stairway to the street below the early morning travellers scurry. We rapidly refill, and having just said goodbye to one set of travelling companions, we wish others good morning as they enter. Promptly at 7.22am we are away again accelerating past the Rhondda platform face, inset beyond ours, and swing north east across the complex junction where the Taff and Rhondda lines divide, and are soon across the river on Brunel's viaduct and continuing above the rooftops once more.

We have left the four-tracked section behind us now and once having passed, on the up side, Pontypridd North Junction, where the North Rhondda loop joined the Taff valley line, then about half a mile beyond, Pont Shon Norton Junction, where the Nelson branch once bore away on the down side, settle to the rhythmic surging of the train as on the right open fields and the river come into view with the Albion colliery beyond. On the up side Clydach Court Junction, at the start of the Ynysybwl branch, is passed about a mile further on, then Stormstown Junction leading to Abercynon colliery on the down side, before we swing left and then right between a high retaining wall on the up side and woods on the down. This short stretch was typical of many in the Taff valley where for a few moments sights and thoughts of industry could be forgotten as green foliage briefly closed in and shut out all other sights. But soon these thoughts were brushed aside as the curve was rounded and the trees fell away as we arrived at Abercynon station, junction for the Cynon valley, and it was time to change trains for the remainder of the journey to Merthyr.

With the spirited departure of our train at 7.29am around the curve towards Aberdare, one was always struck by the quietness that followed, despite the fact that Abercynon running shed was only a few yards away beyond the down side of the single island platform. Usually only a few passengers changed trains at this hour, although in the interval before the arrival of the Merthyr train there would be a continuous trickle on to the platform from the entrance at the northern end. On a fine morning the ten minutes or so one had to wait could be pleasantly spent

*The simple layout and minimal facilities provided on the Burry Port & Gwendraeth Valley Railway, where passenger services always seemed even more of an afterthought than on many other South Wales railways, is captured in this photograph of Pontyberem station. Despite this, however, the train appears to be well loaded, judging by the numbers watching the photographer. Passenger traffic commenced on the BP & GVR on 2 August 1909 and the station layout was altered in October 1912, so the photograph would appear to have been taken between these two dates.
(L&GRP)*

Incline Situated between	Length of Incline	Ruling Gradient 1 in.	Falling Towards	Modifications of, or Additions to, the General Instructions for Working Inclines
BLAENAVON L.L. TO DOCK STREET				
Terminus and Blaenavon L.L.	17 ch.	40	Blaenavon L.L. ...	—
Blaenavon L.L. and 10¾ m.p.	4 m. 10 ch.	46	10¾ m.p.	—
10¾ m.p. and 10½ m.p.	5 ch.	42	Snatchwood ..	—
10½ m.p. and Pont-newynydd Station	35 ch.	74	Pontnewynydd Station	—
Pontnewynydd Station and 10¼ m.p.	20 ch.	120	Pontnewynydd Junction	—
Pontnewynydd Jn. and 9¾ m.p.	14 ch.	154	Pontnewynydd Junction	—
9¾ m.p. and Trevethin Junction	14 ch.	54	Trevethin Junction	—
Trevethin Junction and Pontypool Crane St.	25 ch.	131	Trevethin Junction	—
Pontypool Crane Street and Panteg & Coedy-gric Junction	1 m. 46 ch.	54	Panteg & Coedy-gric Junction	—
Panteg & Coedygric Jn. and Panteg & Coedy-gric Jn. Up Home signal	20 ch.	56	Panteg South Ground Frame	—
Panteg & Coedygric Jn. Up Home Signal and 6 m. 70 ch.	50 ch.	88	6 m. 70 ch. ..	—
6 m. 70 ch. and 6½ m.p.	28 ch.	112	6½ m.p.	—
6½ m.p. and Upper Pontnewydd	40 ch.	131	Upper Pontnewydd	—
Upper Pontnewydd and Cwmbran Sidings	43 ch.	116	Cwmbran Sidings	—
Cwmbran Sidings and overbridge at 3 m. 18 ch.	1 m. 75 ch.	95	Tunnel	—
Overbridge at 3 m. 18 ch. and 1¾ m.p.	1 m. 60 ch.	105	Crindau	—
1¾ m.p. and Mill Street South	70 ch.	116	Mill Street South	—
Mill Street South and Shaftesbury St. Bridge	10 ch.	44	Shaftesbury Street Bridge	—
Shaftesbury St. Bridge and Moderator Sidings	20 ch.	110	Moderator Sidings	—
BRANCHES FORK JUNCTION TO PONTNEWYNYDD JUNCTION				
Branches Fork and Pontnewynydd Jn.	41 ch.	65	Pontnewynydd Jn.	—

Interlude at Tredegar. 57xx class 0-6-0PT No 7787 stands at the head of empty stock in Tredegar yard. A working to Risca, headed by 0-6-0PT No 9644 of the same class can be seen standing at the station platform. Tredegar engine shed is on the left, and the coach next to No 7787 is ex-Burry Port & Gwendraeth Valley Railway stock. (R. E Toop)

stretching one's legs and viewing, perhaps, what there was to see on shed, although it was generally as quiet as the station itself at this hour of the morning. Directly opposite the station the yard, coaling line, and shed itself were in clear view. In 1957 it was the final resting place for the remaining ex-TVR A class 0-6-2Ts, the last two, 373 and 390, being withdrawn in late August. A few members of the 56xx and 57xx classes were always in the yard at this time, and occasionally one of the heavier 94xx class 0-6-0PTs; what movement there was was quite leisurely, usually being between the coal line and the shed throat and then back along a shed road, by an engine that had arrived shortly before, having come off an early duty. This early morning perambulation was soon over as our train to Merthyr bustled in. On this leg of the journey no 56xx class side tank was provided but a 64xx class 0-6-0PT and two old auto coaches. One of these had vertical matchboard sides and the comfort of its seats left a lot to be desired.

At 7.40am we were away, and what a start this was for the diminutive pannier; straight up a one-mile-long 1 in 40 incline right off the end of the platform. Whatever silence there had been a few moments before was completely destroyed as the bank was tackled in ear-splitting fashion. In modern political parlance there was no alternative. Brunel in his wisdom laid out the Taff Vale Railway as he had both the Great Western and the South Wales Mineral railways; maintaining the road on as easy gradients as possible for as long as possible, and confining the steepest inclines to one short stretch. Originally a cable-worked incline of between 1 in 19 and 1 in 22, complete with a tunnel at its upper end, it was later opened out to the present day longer incline, to allow locomotive haulage along its length. It is a good job that all loaded mineral traffic has always worked down the incline and not up it. The incline ends almost as abruptly as it starts, but in a cutting from which one suddenly emerges to be projected across another Brunel viaduct high above the River Taff as it twists through a narrow curved defile. The poor pannier is still working like a Trojan, its presence audible for miles around, but

20

soon its labours ease as Quakers Yard (Low Level) is approached, where it and the fireman can catch their breath.

Once away from Quakers Yard (Low Level) station which is situated a little way below the village, and to which it was connected in 1957 by a long and multilevel foot-bridge via the High Level station, the junction with the Pontypool to Neath line trailed in from the right. As the pannier gathered speed up the eastern side of the Taff valley along which side it continued to Merthyr, we soon passed beneath one of the more unusual railway sights of South Wales. The line from Pontypool to Neath crossed the valley here on a masonry viaduct, alongside which was a second which carried the ex-Great Western Railway-Rhymney Railway joint line up the western side of the valley to Merthyr. The proximity of two viaducts would not in itself be unusual except that for decades both had been shored up by heavy timbers, with the exception of the arch over the Cardiff to Methyr line, to combat the effects of mining subsidence. Both had a distinctly fragile air about them, but they were in regular use until their closure, which was as late as 1964 in the case of the one on the Neath line, some thirteen years later than that on the Merthyr branch.

Twisting along the side of the hills, contour hugging in fact, one now runs parallel and, until Merthyr Vale, above and to the right of the course of the famous Penydarren tramway along which Trevithick's historic journey took

The 4.55pm Llantrisant to Penygraig auto-train working stands in the bay at Llantrisant station on 7 June 1958. 14xx class 0-4-2T No 1471 worked this and similar services to Pontypridd and Cowbridge for twenty years. (S. Rickard)

place, although too close to be viewed from the train until just before its course runs into the siding area south of Merthyr Vale colliery. But as the train heads up the valley the gossip of fellow travellers, be it of politics or ailments, the two most common topics of conversation, was more likely to claim one's attention than trying to spot a much overgrown pathway. The valley is at its narrowest near here and dominated by the Merthyr Vale colliery flanked by the twin villages of Merthyr Vale itself and, across the river and once served by the GWR/RR joint line, Aberfan. Beyond here as the train begins climbing again after a brief halt, the surroundings become much more barren as the original industrial heart of the valley, now two centuries old, is approached. After Troedyrhiw reclamation has today improved the appearance of the area considerably, although trees still have

From the Appendix to Section 9 of the Service Time Tables, *March 1950.*

LIST OF HALTS.

Name of Halt.	Situated between	Under supervision of Station Master at
Cathays (Woodville Road)	Cardiff and Llandaff	Cardiff (Queen Street).
Maindy (North Road)	Cardiff and Llandaff	Cardiff (Queen Street).
Dingle Road	Penarth and Penarth Dock	Penarth.
Alberta Place	Penarth and Lower Penarth	Penarth.
Lower Penarth	Alberta Place and Lavernock	Penarth.
Swanbridge	Sully and Lavernock	Sully.
Trerhyngyll and Maendy	Cowbridge and Ystradowen	Cowbridge.
Tonteg	Treforest and Church Village	Treforest.
"	" " Efail Isaf	"
Church Village	Tonteg and Llantwit Fardre	Llantwit Fardre.
Beddau	Llantwit Fardre and Cross Inn	Llantwit Fardre.
Gelli	Llwynypia and Ystrad	Ystrad (Rhondda).
Pentre	Ystrad and Treorchy	Ystrad (Rhondda).
Clydach Court	Pontypridd and Ynysybwl	Pontypridd.
Ynysybwl (New Road)	Pontypridd and Ynysybwl	Ynysybwl.
Robertstown	Pontypridd and Ynysybwl	Ynysybwl.
Old Ynysybwl	Above Ynysybwl Station	Ynysybwl.
Pontcynon Bridge	Abercynon and Penrhiwceiber	Penrhiwceiber.
Matthewstown	Abercynon and Penrhiwceiber	Penrhiwceiber.
Abercwmboi	Mountain Ash and Aberaman	Mountain Ash.
Ninian Park	Grangetown and Radyr	Cardiff (General).
Heath (High Level)	Cardiff and Llanishen	Llanishen.
Cefn-On	Llanishen and Caerphilly	Llanishen.
Aber Junction	Caerphilly and Penyrheol (On Main Line)	Caerphilly.
Penyrheol	Caerphilly and Abertridwr	Caerphilly.
Gilfach Fargoed	Pengam and Bargoed	Bargoed.
Trelewis Platform	Nelson and Llancaiach and Bedlinog.	Bedlinog.
Heath (Low Level)	Cardiff and Whitchurch	Llanishen.
Birchgrove	Cardiff and Whitchurch	Whitchurch.
Rhiwbina	Cardiff and Whitchurch	Whitchurch.
Coryton	Whitchurch and End of Branch	Whitchurch.
Llandow	Southerndown Road and Llandow Wick Road	Llantwit Major.
Llandow Wick Road	Llandow Halt and Llantwit Major	Llantwit Major.
St. Athan	Llantwit Major and Gileston	St. Athan.

Permanent staff at Trelewis and Heath (High Level) Halts.

Halts used solely for Colliery Workmen.

Nantmelyn	Bwllfa Branch	Aberdare.
Gadlys Road	" "	"
Penydarren	Dowlais and Cwm Bargoed	Dowlais.
Bedlinog	Cwm Bargoed and Bedlinog	Bedlinog.
Taff Merthyr Colliery	Bedlinog and Nelson and Llancaiach	"
Windsor Colliery	Abertridwr and Senghenydd	Abertridwr.

A quiet evening at Dowlais (Cae Harris), the terminus of the GWR/RR joint line from Nelson & Llancaiach. The 56xx class 0-6-2T is on working K1 from the nearby shed, a daily sixteen-hour turn that included workmen's trains to Hengoed, shunting at Dowlais, and colliery turns to Bedlinog and Fochriw. (L&GRP)

a hard time in establishing themselves. In 1957 however the remains of the past were unmistakable. The Plymouth Ironworks once stood near here, and the collieries associated with it were also close by.

About a mile beyond Abercanaid the outskirts of Merthyr are reached and the train has now, after a continuous pull from Quakers Yard, to make one last effort as at Brandy Bridge Junction we leave the original line of the Taff Vale Railway and run up the connection to Mardy Junction along what was a section of joint GWR/TVR track. Here we join the line from the Aberdare valley that has pierced the intervening mountain and now sweeps us past the goods yard and running shed, both on the down side, across a road on a girder bridge, and into High Street station in the centre of Merthyr.

Brunel designed, and until 1953 sporting an all-over roof, it was a much more prepossessing affair than the cramped Plymouth Street station of the TVR. At first having only three platforms it was perhaps fortunate that when the original broad gauge was replaced by standard, sufficient room was left to build a narrow wooden platform centrally between the main arrival and departure platforms. Even so the facilities were never adequate for the five railway companies that once had access to this famous town.

Our arrival at 8.08am cuts short the chatter of the journey, and we stream along the platform past the diminutive pannier whose fireman is now usually busy trimming the firebox while the driver maybe has climbed down to the tracks for a brief inspection of the engine.

Such was a journey through the valleys some thirty years ago. At the time an unremarked-upon event and repeated daily by thousands as it had been for generations. Yet no two valleys were the same, and each could offer something different to the traveller.

To journey up the Rhondda Fawr was to never be out of sight of a colliery, many of which had their own internal rail systems characterised by uneven track,

23

sharp curves, and steep inclines all half buried beneath small coal; or the towns that grew up around them. In fact from Trehafod to Treherbert it was sometimes difficult to judge where one town ended and the next began. To continue out of the Rhondda, along the ex-Rhondda & Swansea Bay line through the long single-bore tunnel at the end of the Rhondda Fawr and into the Afan valley one was immediately struck by the difference, for between Blaengwynfi and Pontrhydyfen the villages were now much smaller and more isolated. Only Cymmer was of any appreciable size, and was for many years an important junction between the railways of the Afan, Corrwg and Llynfi valleys. The Rhymney valley would give one broad views below Bedwas, which contrasted with the narrow, bare, and steeply sided defile, of doubtful stability, above Bargoed. Both the Swansea and Neath valleys were broad and always retained a distinctly rural atmosphere in certain isolated pockets, although the lower Swansea valley could remind one of the surface of the moon.

Just as no two valleys were the same, the rail services within them could also vary markedly, particularly before the GWR, and to a lesser extent the LMS, introduced their standard stock into the area in the twenties and thirties. Both companies however did little by way of alteration to the services, except to reduce them as the economic climate deteriorated and forced these unpalatable changes upon them. Before this period, though, not even the GWR itself was above reproach in the standards of its stock in the valleys in which it operated. Six-wheelers, transferred from more prestigious services elsewhere on the system had for decades been the norm. In fact both their six-wheel and clerestory stock survived the thirties, and examples of the latter could still be found in the valleys well after nationalisation.

Travellers on the Taff Vale, Rhymney or Barry railways were the most fortunate as, latterly at least, each of these companies had some quite respectable coaching stock, even if the Barry Railway never went as far as heating its coaches. Perhaps the most unfortunate were those obliged to travel by the Brecon & Merthyr Railway whose motley collection of carriages, even as late as 1922, could not rise above six-wheelers, and second hand at that. In fact it was said that some of the colliery companies' workmen's stock was better.

On a valleys journey, wherever it was taken, one's view of the surroundings was to some extent restricted by the enclosing hills. A complete contrast however was the journey from Pontypool to Neath. An initial pull up the narrow, steeply sided Glyn valley and through the tunnel at Hafodyrynys led one into the Ebbw valley and across that marvellous example of Victorian engineering, the Crumlin viaduct. Beyond, a descent via Penar and a junction with 'Hall's' tramroad (actually a railway, but the old name remained in use) led to Pontllanfraith. Here lay the complex but delightfully named junction known as 'Bird-in-Hand', where the Sirhowy lines were met. Another climb brought one through a short tunnel from the Sirhowy to the Rhymney valley, spanned this time by the masonry Hengoed viaduct. Beyond, another watershed was passed as the line continued westward by way of Nelson & Llancaiach to Quakers Yard in the Taff valley. Here the river crossing was made on the timber-shored viaduct referred to earlier, naturally at a restricted speed. In this case it was 10mph, which was higher in fact than that allowed over the Crumlin viaduct, which was restricted to 8mph. Once through the tunnel beyond this alarming structure the Cynon valley was entered and followed to Aberdare. A final climb from here to Hirwaun took one to the bare moorland at the head of the valley before the steep descent of Glyn

In this undated, though obviously Edwardian photograph, a Great Western 0-6-0ST is seen approaching the Brecon & Merthyr Railway station at Bassaleg, over the Rumney Railway viaduct that dates from 1826, on a through Newport to Pontypridd working. These services ran over B & M metals from Bassaleg Junction to Caerphilly East Junction, thence via the Rhymney Railway to Penrhos Junction, the ADR to PC&N Junction immediately south of Pontypridd, and for the last few yards of the journey over the metals of the TVR. The tall B&M somersault signals are a delight, while behind the chimney of the saddle tank can be seen Bassaleg Junction signal box on the Great Western's Western Valleys line. (L&GRP)

Neath bank was undertaken, to be followed by an easy run down the valley to the town of Neath itself.

This switchback east-west journey was one of the most scenically varied in South Wales, and the views as one crossed high above the valleys of the Ebbw, Rhymney and Taff were impressive. On such a journey too the working locomotive types were much more varied also. The train engine for instance was likely to be a GWR large Prairie of the 41xx or 51xx series, successors to generations of saddle and pannier tanks. 28xx 2-8-0, 42xx 2-8-0T, and 72xx 2-8-2T classes, rare or unheard of in certain valleys, regularly worked this line. LMS, and at an earlier date LNWR, locomotives and stock were often passed at Pontllanfraith.

That there was variety in the South Wales valleys was undeniable, although for years it was largely overlooked. Stemming from its earliest beginnings the independence of the individual systems gave each line a character of its own which even standardisation, introduced firstly at the grouping, then extended following nationalisation, failed to eradicate completely.

Timetables based on those developed by the pre-grouping companies remained largely unchanged over the years. The one major revision occurred in the Cardiff Valleys Division in 1953 when the services were completely recast and, it must be said, greatly improved. Over the years following the grouping even the locomotive workings retained more than a few idiosyncrasies. Pre-grouping locomotives were, for instance, frequently retained on the same service long after more modern engines had been introduced. Nor was the working of the coal traffic always straightforward either. At Swansea docks, for example, certain coal sidings could only be reached directly by loads from the specific valleys they were built to serve fifty years or more before.

It was this individuality that gave the valleys their charm and interest. True, the valleys could not be called beautiful, although small isolated pockets of countryside survived, and on the extensions of the pre-grouping companies' lines into Breconshire to the north, and the coastal region to the south, industry intruded hardly at all. Similarly they could not be called dull, the sheer intensity of the mineral traffic handled saw to that. The valleys had a dynamism that survived two centuries. Only now is it being stilled.

2
MOVING THE COAL

For those who recall the times when the 0-6-2T at the head of a rake of non-corridor coaches reigned supreme on valleys' passenger services, what would their memories be of that mainstay of South Wales' freight – the coal train? Perhaps not as many, nor as vivid, unless of course one was involved with such traffic. It is a fact of life that it is the memory of places visited, or those of early pleasures that tend to remain in the mind, rather than the repeating, commonplace, everyday sights. But if anything survives it is of the ubiquitous tank engine, again most commonly the 0-6-2T type, at the head of a rake of up to perhaps fifty wooden wagons before World War II, or afterwards of similar numbers, but now of anonymous rusting steel. One has to go back many years to recall the names of *Ocean, Ferndale, Glamorgan* or *Cambrian*, and the host of others that told of the hundreds of collieries that once existed in the South Wales valleys.

The valleys are all but silent now, but for year after year, generation after generation, train upon train headed fully loaded to the sea, and hurried home again either empty or with pitwood from Scandinavia. As their numbers increased single lines were doubled, then quadrupled, and in one case even sextupled. When storage sidings that already spread over hundreds of acres within dock precincts were saturated, others grew up at the entrances to many valleys, such as those at Rogerstone, Bassaleg, Radyr, Llantrisant, Tondu, Duffryn Yard, and Neath & Brecon and Sandy Junctions. In time even these were not sufficient and forced the construction of yet further storage sidings within the restricted valleys themselves, often requiring difficult and expensive feats of civil engineering. Aberbeeg, Coke Ovens (near Pontypridd), Stormstown (near Abercynon), and Aber (near Caerphilly) are some that come to mind. Generations of engines, each vastly more numerous than the last, worked these once bustling valleys, manned by enginemen who themselves, in many cases, were the current generation of families that had faithfully served the railways before them, and were the fathers of those to come.

While all this was the visible manifestation of the traffic handled, there had grown up behind the scenes a large and complex system of train control which matched an equally complex system of purchase. The demand for coal ensured that large tonnages would be moved but the methods of sale meant that delivery times were frequently short and, since trainloads and ship capacities were vastly different and the available numbers of wagons and storage space were limited, close liaison between colliery, railway and docks was vital. Without such a system, only a fraction of the potential traffic could have been handled, which would have strangled the development of South Wales' export coal trade almost at birth.

So, in steam's heyday a loaded train whistling for the road at the colliery exit of say, Bedwas in the Rhymney valley, Lewis Merthyr in the Rhondda, or Caerau in the Llynfi, was nearly at the end of an intricate process that, quite likely, began weeks before on the floor of the Cardiff Coal Exchange in Mountstuart Square

The Rhonnda Fawr in the nineteenth century. The wagons belong to the Ocean Coal Company, whose owner David Davies was instrumental in the construction of the Barry Railway and Docks. The scene is believed to be just north of Ystrad station (looking north westwards) and for reasons unknown the trains and the workers have posed for the camera. (Welsh Industrial & Maritime Museum)

Radyr Yard, May 1943. In this wartime photograph an unidentified and extremely disreputable Mogul stands at the head of a down coal working, probably to an inland destination, while a Taff Vale Railway A class 0-6-2T and a GWR pannier work the yard. The water tank and coal stage at Radyr shed are visible in the right background. The duties of the lady carrying the bucket (in the middle of the group of assembled guards, shunters, etc) is not known. (Welsh Industrial & Maritime Museum)

27

in the heart of Cardiff's then flourishing business quarter, or in one of the many coal companies' offices nearby. At this time an export order could be placed by, say, an agency maintained by a foreign government, a state railway or a coal or bunkering station company; or, alternatively, by an agent acting on behalf of a private steel, railway, gas or electricity company. Such an agent would approach representatives of coal companies, or their sales agents, on the floor of the Exchange, where, obviously, much hard bargaining would be done. Alternatively they could also deal directly with a company's sales office, if, like say North's Navigation, Ocean Coal, or Powell Duffryn, they maintained such offices nearby. Once a tonnage and a price had been agreed, which would frequently be 'fob' (free on board: the seller being responsible for all charges on the coal until it is delivered into the ship's hold, hence the colliery companies' keen interest in competitive railway rates), then the question of chartering a vessel could arise. This was undertaken by the purchaser who was responsible for making all the arrangements regarding charter, including rates, insurance and harbour dues. Such arrangements would be made with ship brokers who also operated in the Exchange, as did insurers, enabling if needed, all business to be arranged under one roof. They would offer a suitable ship, or ships, that would arrive at a given South Wales dock on a specific date, into which the coal could be loaded.

One of the many connections between the valley lines and that between Pontypool and Neath, was between Ystrad Mynach (Penalltau Branch Junction) and Penalltau Junction. 56xx class 0-6-2T No 5636 hauls a load of empties from Cardiff Docks to the Ocean colliery at Treharris along this connection on 24 April 1957, climbing towards Penalltau Junction.
(S. Rickard)

SHUNTING OPERATIONS AT SIDINGS.

From Instructions affecting LMS servants working over the Great Western Railway, *published by the LMS in 1939.*

At the following Sidings no Up train must perform any shunting or stop to attach or detach traffic unless there is an engine at the Swansea end of the train :—

Name of Siding.	Situate between
Penwyllt Brick Works	Colbren and Craig-y-nos.
Abercrave Colliery Siding (north end)	Colbren and Ystradgynlais.
All Sidings at Abercrave Station and adjacent thereto	,, ,,
International Colliery Sidings and Gwaunclawdd Colliery Siding ...	,, ,,
Penrhos Brick Works Siding	Abercrave and Ystradgynlais.
Ystradgynlais Colliery	,, ,,
Lower Cwmtawe Colliery and Varteg Brick Works	Ystradgynlais and Ynisygeinon.
Ynisci Colliery Sidings and Cwmtawe Colliery	,, ,,
Varteg Colliery Sidings	,, ,,

The engine or wagons must not be detached from down trains before the van brake has been put on, and brakes on a sufficient number of the wagons next to the van and on leading wagons left on the main line have also been applied by the guard, and sprags used where necessary.

It was at this point, when the purchaser could inform the seller that he required a certain tonnage to be delivered at a certain date to a named vessel which would have arrived at a specific dock, that a firm order would be taken. On the closure of the Exchange at 3.00pm, the day's orders, all of which had been entered on what was known in North's Navigation Collieries sales office as a 'STEM' sheet, would be collated. When this was completed the order clerk would telephone the weigher at the appropriate colliery and advise him of the tonnage, delivery dates, and delivery points of the day's orders. He would also enquire the position of the previous day's orders too, for any delays could have quite serious repercussions which would have to be allowed for since the entire process from mine to dock was nothing less than a balancing act between many factors; a delay anywhere in the chain caused chaos unless quickly identified and corrected.

Armed with the instructions from the order clerk the colliery weigher now went into action. It was his responsibility to arrange for sufficient coal of the right grade to be lifted at the correct time. He then ensured that sufficient wagons were available, and if there were not he would contact the Cardiff (or Swansea) office manager who would arrange with the railway the return of outstanding empty wagons, or hire additional ones either from one of a number of local wagon-hiring businesses such as Hall, Lewis & Company, or perhaps from a neighbouring colliery. The wagons would then be filled and dispatched on the weigher's order in time to meet the specific loading requirements of the vessel or vessels chartered to export the coal. Delivery times could be days or weeks ahead and each day's orders had to be dovetailed into existing schedules. Perhaps the most difficult part of the balancing act to be performed would be when the tonnage ordered to fill a particular vessel required maybe ten or twelve or even more trainloads. The restrictions on siding capacity at the docks would preclude the whole tonnage being ready nearby when the vessel docked, since dozens of collieries would be competing for space at any one dock. Thus only a fraction of the load would be waiting and the remainder had to be dispatched on a schedule to refill the sidings as quickly as they were emptied until loading was complete, which could be as little as two tides (about twenty-four hours). It must be remembered that while vessels were independent of the tide once inside the dock, they could only enter or leave at restricted periods each side of high tide, because of the exceptional differences in depth of water at high and low tides in the Bristol Channel, which

As important as the loaded coal train to the various South Wales docks was the return of empty wagons to the collieries. Taff Vale Railway A class 0-6-2T No 373 returns along the Roath branch, around the eastern and northern sides of Cardiff, destined for Stormstown Junction sidings with such a load on 25 June 1957, a few weeks prior to withdrawal. (S. Rickard)

were of the order of 10 metres (32 feet).

It was also the colliery weigher's responsibility to prepare the necessary weighbills and to inform the local railway traffic control office of his intended dispatches, the tonnages involved, wagon totals and identity numbers and of course their destinations. Similar details were also supplied to the docks from which shipping was to take place. The return of empty wagons was, of course, the responsibility of the railway company. Their system was not infallible however, and it was not unknown for wagons to become lost, particularly those that had to be removed from a train en route because of, say, a hot axle box. Such wagons were frequently discovered at a later date languishing at the end of a sorting or dock storage siding, usually after the railway company had been 'reminded' of the coal company's loss.

Such then were some of the behind-the-scenes activities at the colliery that were undertaken before a loaded train of coal could turn a wheel on its journey to the coast. But equally complicated activities had also occurred at the railway traffic control office, to enable an engine and brake van to arrive at the correct time to

30

work this coal train to the docks, via a vacant path in the timetable. Traffic control offices were situated across South Wales each controlling and co-ordinating movements within their boundaries as well as between them. Newport control office handled the traffic in the Eastern and Western valleys of Monmouthshire, the Brecon & Merthyr line as far as Brecon itself, and LMS traffic off the Sirhowy valley line. Cardiff (Queen Street) supervised the territory of the pre-grouping companies that centred on it or Barry. The Tondu control office regulated the Llynfi, Ogmore, Garw and Ely valleys, while further west that at Swansea (High Street) controlled the lines converging on it, including the Rhondda & Swansea Bay line, and in addition those centred on Port Talbot, Llanelly and Burry Port. There were also control offices in both Swansea and Barry docks, whose workings are explained in more detail in Chapter 8.

Probably the most complex control area was that of the Cardiff Valleys, which was divided into three 'valley' sections (there was also a fourth, the main line from St Brides to Pyle). The largest of these three over which Queen Street control office held sway was the Taff Vale Section. This included the lines from Cardiff to Merthyr; Pontypridd to Rhondda & Swansea Bay Junction and the Fernhill branch, both at the top of the Rhondda Fawr; the Porth to Maerdy line, the Eirw branch and the Pwllyrhebog Incline. Further north the Abercynon to

Indian summer. September 7 1957 and Rhymney Railway R class 0-6-2T No 38 works back along the Cylla branch with a Penalltau colliery to Cardiff docks turn. The last of the South Wales railway companies main line engines to remain in service, it soldiered on alone for another month and was withdrawn on 5 October, having worked right up to the end on colliery workings in the Rhymney valley. Its final turn was to Bargoed pits, its driver that day having fired the engine when new in 1921. In the foreground can be seen a Rhymney Railway somersault signal, and crossing the branch in the background is the Pontypool to Neath line. (S. Rickard)

Aberdare and Dare valley lines, together with the Cilfynydd and Ynysybwl branches came within its scope. Finally to the west were the branches to Llantrisant and Cowbridge, and the Radyr Junction to Penarth Dock line. The Rhymney Section encompassed the line to Rhymney itself, and the sections from Ystrad Mynach to Dowlais (Cae Harris), Penallta Junction to Cyfarthfa Crossing, together with the Senghenydd branch. The Barry Section was centred on Cadoxton and radiated to Peterston, Trehafod and Aber Junctions, and to Cardiff.

The controller had to maintain contact with a variety of staff whose duty it was to report conditions within their locality, usually these were signalmen at important boxes, yard inspectors, shunters and foremen. He also liaised with his opposite number in other control areas, principally those adjacent, to be informed of arising traffic for his area from sections of the system outside his control. It was his duty to ensure that traffic from collieries, works or junctions etc, was cleared promptly, once having been advised of their readiness to be moved. Trains had to be loaded as nearly as possible to their full capacity, light engine mileage avoided as far as possible, and excessive shunting eliminated. Also trains directed by control had to be scheduled so as not to cause delays to other traffic. As if this were not enough the controller was enjoined that as far as possible overtime working was to be avoided. He also had to determine priorities among the traffic to be moved. Highest would be coal for immediate shipment and the return of urgently needed empty wagons or loads of pitwood to collieries if shortages of wagons or pit props had been reported. Such workings were given priority over all others.

On 12 June 1956, Taff Vale Railway A class 0-6-2T No 398 shunts at Maritime colliery, Pontypridd, while working the 11.00am Llantrisant to Coke Ovens mineral turn.
(S. Rickard)

Problems with sheep

The antics of the sheep that live on the hills of South Wales are notorious and stories of them are legion. Those that inhabited Cwmbargoed in the days before oil axleboxes were introduced on the humble coal wagon, however, should be offered a prize for ingenuity. Colliery sidings here still sprawl unfenced across the moorland, and the wagon examiner stationed here had one extra duty; perhaps ritual would be a better word, to perform. Not more than half an hour before a loaded train was to depart he had to refill most, if not all, the grease boxes on the wagons, for these wily woolly denizens of the uplands had learnt to lift the lids of these axlebox covers with their noses and lick out the grease inside. Such was their appetite for this delicacy that to leave the wagons much longer than a half hour would result in empty axleboxes again, and the inevitable 'hot box' en route to the docks.

More problems with sheep!

The problems of sheep on valley lines has been referred to more than once, but there was one occasion in the Rhondda Fach during World War II when the random wanderings of one of their number was put to someone's advantage. Early one morning a permanent way ganger at Ferndale enquired of the crew of a Radyr based 56xx class 0-6-2T at the head of a load of empties, whether they had seen any sheep on the way up the valley, as some had been reported straying over the line between Ynyshir and Tylorstown. 'No', replied the driver. 'Haven't seen any', said the fireman, backing him up. With a shrug the ganger walked away to report that there were now no sheep on the line, relieved no doubt that he had been saved the job of having to walk down to Ynyshir to see for himself and chase them off. However he failed to notice the significance of the driver's and the fireman's grins, and the fact that the cab side door was shut. That evening, and for some days afterwards, the families of the driver and fireman had no need of the meat coupons in their ration books!

To discharge these duties successfully a continuous flow of information passed to and from the control office. Among that received on a regular basis were what were termed the 'Special Advices' telephoned to the controller. These were sent to the control office from throughout the Cardiff Valleys area. In all some eighty-three locations regularly sent information to Queen Street, of which forty-eight were signal boxes. Typical of the items of information sent by signalmen were those required from Ocean Navigation Signal Box, Treharris, with particulars of traffic from the Ocean and Taff Merthyr collieries, the position of outwards traffic standing in the sidings, and the colliery requirements for empty wagons and pitwood. The task of the signalman at Tyn-y-caeau Signal Box was somewhat simpler, his contribution being to report the passing of all down freight trains en route to Barry. From Treherbert Junction inspector's cabin at 6.00am, 2.00pm, and 10.00pm came information regarding the state of the sidings, departure and loading of all down trains, and also the departure of all freight workings advised from Port Talbot together with details of the load and estimated time of arrival at Treherbert Junction. Interestingly one of the contributors to this regular flow of information was the LMS controller at Abergavenny who advised his opposite number at Queen Street of freight traffic from his area destined for the Rhymney Section.

Important as these Special Advices were, they represented but a fraction of the information received both day and night at Queen Street. Additionally a Daily Advice showing the state of all colliery and works sidings, giving particulars of traffic waiting clearance, empty wagons on hand, and requirements for the night and the following day's work, had to be sent to the control office at 3.00pm daily, or as near to that time as possible. Besides these, notice had to be given of all traffic immediately it was ready for clearance. Furthermore the loading and departure of all freight trains had to be notified from the starting point and all points where the trains picked up. The arrival times at destinations had also to be forwarded. Exceptional delays, and their cause, either in running or in

In the Rhymney valley the gradient approaching Machen from Caerphilly often required motive power somewhat heavier than an 0-6-2T. On 2 September 1957, 42xx class 2-8-0T No 5237 heads past White Hart halt on its way to Newport (Michael Hale)

connection with yard working had to be reported immediately. Having received all this information, digested it and ordered the necessary traffic movements, it was then the controller's duty to advise the destination point, the junction signal boxes to be passed, and the storage sidings in the neighbourhood of the docks of the departure time from the colliery and particulars of the load. If it was a returning train of empties the colliery signal box would be notified of the departure time from the docks.

When train departure or passing times were reported, the target number had to be stated, or failing that the engine number. This target number was an important feature of freight-train operation in the South Wales valleys where, daily, hundreds of trains were run in accordance with the varying demands of the coal trade, and to a lesser extent those of the steel and other industries. They also applied to passenger workings, for some engine diagrams could include these mixed with the freight workings. Target numbers were the means by which specific trains under the direction of control could be easily identified, since frequently they were not shown in the service timetable, apart from a note of their departure times from various sidings in a table at the rear of such a document. How many target numbers were used in South Wales it is impossible to say with any accuracy; certainly in 1938 there were 292 identifiable mineral diagrams covered by target numbers, while in addition they also applied to certain ordinary goods and some passenger workings.

The target number, which was usually a single letter and number combination, was painted on a metal disc (black letters on a white background) and, in the Cardiff Valleys Division, fixed to a lamp bracket above the right-hand front buffer of the train engine when running chimney first, or to a similar bracket on the bunker when travelling in the reverse direction. However, instructions for the Newport Division stated that when travelling chimney first the target number had to be carried on the lamp bracket below the chimney.

34

The letter denoted the starting point of the working, which often identified the home shed of the locomotive working that particular train. In the Cardiff Valleys Division twelve letters in all were in use in the late thirties. 'J' denoted an Abercynon working, 'D' a Cardiff East Dock, 'T' a Treherbert, and 'Y' a Radyr Junction. Of the remainder, workings from Aberdare carried the letter 'A', Barry 'B', Cathays 'C', Dowlais (Cae Harris) 'K', Coke Ovens 'X', Ferndale 'F', Merthyr 'M', and Rhymney 'R'. In the Newport Division 'H' or 'P' were workings from Cardiff Canton, 'U' from Tondu, 'Z' from Llantrisant, 'A' from Aberbeeg, and 'PR' from Pontypool Road. The remainder were 'E' for the Eastern Valleys, which were usually worked by a Pill engine, 'W' for the Western Valleys, 'R' for Rogerstone, 'B' for Bassaleg, and 'N' for West Mendalgief, all of which were normally worked by Ebbw Junction engines.

The number following the letter denoted an engine diagram, which may have been a single working, or a series of them, perhaps repetitive, throughout the day. In the late 1930s, J16 from Abercynon was an afternoon coal working to Roath Branch Junction Sidings, D7 worked from Cardiff East Dock to Bargoed pits and return, while A12 from Aberdare worked to Cadoxton. In contrast to these straightforward engine diagrams, H4 from Cardiff Canton at 5.00am worked first to Tonyrefail and then Penygraig where the locomotive shunted at both goods yards. It then returned to Llantrisant, where it was remanned by a

Heading into the Rhymney valley on 2 May 1959, the original member of the 56xx class 0-6-2Ts No 5600 is near Energlyn sidings, on the outskirts of Caerphilly, on D7, working from Cardiff Docks to Bargoed pits. (S. Rickard)

Llantrisant crew, following which it worked the Brofiskin branch and shunted at Cross Inn. Returning to Llantrisant Yard at 11.45am, it once more departed at 1.35pm with empties for Cil-Ely colliery. Here it picked up a full load for Cardiff Docks, and stopping to reman once again with a Canton crew at Llantrisant Yard, at last departed at five minutes past four. The routine of Z8, an all-day working from Llantrisant over the Cowbridge branch altered little over many years. In 1938 it started from Llantrisant Yard at 5.20am on the first of four return trips to the Llanharry Iron Ore Mine, returning for the last time at 7.20pm. In between these trips it also fitted in two goods workings to Cowbridge, calling if required at the Glamorgan Quarry and Ystradowen goods yard. There was also a separate quarry trip just before midday, following which Z8 was remanned. Altogether it shuttled up and down the Cowbridge branch fourteen times a day in 1938, a schedule which some fifteen years later was basically unaltered except that the evening working to the mine was no longer required, and the quarry trip had been deleted following its closure.

Such then were some of the activities that had occurred for example, before,

57xx class 0-6-0PT No 5617 banking the 11.00am Llantrisant to Coke Ovens mineral working at Cowbridge Road Crossing (near Llantrisant) on 3 May 1958. (S. Rickard)

Steep climbs

Rogerstone to Barry coal trains, which like many in South Wales had their own bell-code to identify them to each signalbox en route, had one steep bank to climb; that up to Cardiff General station. To assist these trains the signalman at Newtown West Signal Box would do his best to ensure that they had clear signals so that they could get a run at the bank and not need to stop for assistance. If no clear run could be obtained he would signal the boxes to the east to halt the train before it reached him, which could be as far back as Roath Signal Box, until a 'line clear' from there up the bank and through the station could be obtained.

CONTROL ARRANGEMENTS FOR THE WORKING OF FREIGHT TRAINS AND ENGINES.

From the Appendix to Section 9 of the Service Time Tables, *March 1950.*

Control Offices.—The Control Offices are situated at Cardiff (Queen Street) and are open continuously.

Post Office Telephones :—
8100 Extensions 321, 322, 323, 324, 325.

EXTENT OF CONTROL AREA.

Main Line.   St. Brides to Pyle.   See Appendix to No. 7 Service Book for instructions relating to this Section.

Taff Vale Section.
Cardiff to Pontypridd.
Pontypridd to R. & S.B. Junction.
Fernhill Branch.
Eirw Branch.
Pwllyrhebog Incline.
Porth to Maerdy.
Pontypridd to Merthyr.
Abercynon to Aberdare.
Dare Valley Branch.
Cilfynydd Branch.
Ynysybwl Branch, as far as Windsor Colliery.
Llantrisant Branch.
Penarth Dock to Radyr Junction.

Rhymney Section.
Cardiff to Rhymney.
Ystrad Mynach to Dowlais (Cae Harris).
Penalltau Junction to Cyfarthfa Crossing.
Aber Junction to Senghenydd.

Barry Section.
Cadoxton to Peterston.
Cadoxton to Trehafod Junction.
Cadoxton to Penrhos Junction and Aber Junction.
Cadoxton to Cardiff.

or would be set in motion after, the engine for the Y15 goods and mineral working from Radyr Junction to Treherbert and return, left Radyr shed at 9.10am each weekday morning (except Monday when it departed at 8am), to begin its turn of duty. Coaled, watered and oiled, and with a freshly prepared fire, it would move across to the up sidings to pick up its load of mixed goods and empty mineral wagons for the Rhondda valley. Booked away from the sidings at 9.25am it would ease its partially vacuum-fitted load out on to the up relief road and head steadily north. Up the continuously rising gradients it would steam, putting off wagons firstly at Treforest and then perhaps Pontypridd, the latter often being cattle wagons. Swinging through the long reverse curve that took the relief lines past the west side of the station it entered the lower Rhondda valley immediately beyond and shortly afterwards eased to a halt at Coke Ovens sidings. Here it was booked to stop and put off empty mineral wagons for the nearby collieries, pilot engines stationed here working them forward to the mines later in the day. The next halt would be made at Porth where Gordon Chard, a regular driver on this turn in the fifties, remembers that wagons would be put off here for Dan Jones, a local fruit importer with a number of retail outlets in the Rhondda valleys. The gradients became steeper now as Dinas was passed, although this was compensated for as the train was now lighter. This continuous lightening continued as further wagons and vans were dropped off at Trealaw Goods Station, Ystrad (cattle wagons for the nearby abattoir), and Cwmparc, where a foundry was served as well as the Ocean collieries. Following a final stop at Treherbert Goods the sidings at Treherbert Junction were booked to be reached at 12.50pm. Not that this meant a respite for the crew, since no meal break was allowed. Food was taken en route, when conditions permitted, using the traditional methods of

The triangle at Pontllanfraith, where London & North Western and Great Western railways crossed and exchanged traffic, was one of the many complex junctions in the valleys. In fact three junctions existed within a matter of yards, consisting of Sirhowy Junction, Tredegar Lower Junction and Bird-in-Hand Junction. Here ex-LNWR 'G2a' 49121 passes Bird-in-Hand Junction West signal box at the head of a Tredegar to Ystrad Mynach freight on 18 May 1957. In the left background Tredegar Lower Junction signal box is visible. (R. O. Tuck)

railwaymen. As Y15 worked into the valleys its progress was reported to the traffic control office at Queen Street from a number of locations, so that the controllers were constantly aware of the location of the train. Details of its load, and time of departure were first given from the traffic office at Radyr Junction. Next the signalmen at Rhondda Cutting, Dinas Junction, and Ystrad boxes reported the times of its passing, while finally the inspector at Treherbert Junction reported its arrival time there.

The engine, now under the orders of Queen Street, would, after completion of shunting of any remaining wagons or vans, pick up a rake of loaded coal wagons. The load of this return working, depending on whether they were 10, 12 or 16 ton wagons, could be up to sixty, if the engine was a 56xx class 0-6-2T, or up to fifty wagons if it was a Taff Vale Railway A or O4 class 0-6-2T. The wagons would be from the Bute Merthyr, Tydraw, Fernhill and Blaenrhondda collieries and destined for Roath Reception Sidings or perhaps Radyr Yard if they needed re-forming or combining with other loads before shipment. The train would have been made up by Treherbert engines, on such turns as TP1, TP3, TP7 or TP9, which worked throughout the day to these collieries, and would bring out the full wagons and assemble them into trainloads at Treherbert Junction. Shortly after 2 o'clock with one third of the wagon brakes pinned down by the guard, and with water tanks fully replenished, Y15 would ease out of the sidings to begin its long downhill journey to the sea.

Control of such a load, which at sixty 10-ton wagons would be of the order of 960 tons, relying solely on the engine's brake supplemented by the guard's van and a limited number of wagon brakes, was no easy job. Trains such as these did not have the glamour of the main line expresses, their workings were almost totally unrecorded in the literature, but they demanded no less a level of skill and judgement from driver and fireman than their better known brethren. Apart from controlling such a load on a continuously falling gradient, water too was another problem. The fire could not be allowed to die down and the engine coast since the fall-off in steam pressure would have an adverse effect upon braking, so a good head of steam had to be maintained. Conversely too large a fire, resulting in blowing off at the safety valve, would waste steam and therefore water. This balance was delicate at the best of times for any loaded mineral train making its return run from the valleys to a port, but on this downhill run water could only be taken from the down main line at Dinas Junction, and if that were missed there was no more until Radyr was reached.

It might seem odd that a crew could miss the only water column on the journey, but it was situated on a curved stretch of the line where the falling gradients continuously changed over short distances, and even the best of drivers could find their train pushing them inexorably past, with no hope of reversing such a load uphill back to the water column even if they missed by only a few feet. Such water columns are now a thing of the past, and it should be remembered that their reach was very restricted and a driver had to halt his engine directly opposite them. It was a movement ranking in precision with stopping the correct door of a royal train directly opposite the red carpet. Water was therefore always taken at Treherbert, no matter how full the tanks were on arrival. In fact one driver was well known for filling his tanks at every conceivable opportunity when travelling up the valley, in which direction water columns were plentiful, just in case there was trouble at Treherbert.

Such then were some of the problems facing the crew of Y15 as it accelerated past Treherbert station and on down the 1 in 100, the steepest main line fall in the upper part of the valley, towards Treorchy. Past the sidings for Ynisfeio colliery, and the long disused connection to Abergorki, on to Cwmparc then past Maendy colliery at Ystrad the train would roll under careful control to avoid a runaway. At Llwynypia the downhill gradient, which had eased considerably once Treherbert was cleared, steepened significantly, although not uniformly, and a halt was made at the Stop Board to pin down extra brakes, the number depending upon the judgement of the driver. All goods and mineral trains had to halt here, and a banksman was employed here to assist in the pinning-down operation. The next four and a half miles to Gyfeillon Upper Junction were the most difficult to work on the whole journey, and included the stop, or perhaps the attempt to stop, at the infamous water column at Dinas Junction. For the first three miles the gradient was never easier than 1 in 126, and contained sudden short dips, some a matter of a little more than a hundred yards in length, of 1 in 90, 85, 80 and near Trealaw, shortly after the stop to pin down extra brakes, a nasty stretch of a quarter of a mile at 1 in 67. This initial fall was the most tricky to negotiate. Too many brakes pinned down and you could stall as the gradient levelled beyond, too few and there was the danger of running away until the gradients eased beyond Porth. It was therefore always with a certain amount of relief that

Gyfeillon Upper Junction was at last reached where a halt could once again be made, this time to raise all the brakes for the run past Coke Ovens and beyond. As with the morning up journey the position of Y15 would be reported to the traffic control office at Queen Street. However, unlike that leg of the journey it was now the turn of the signalmen at Naval Colliery Junction (near Trealaw), and Gyfeillon Upper to telephone Cardiff, the signal boxes referred to previously only having to report the passing times on the up journey.

Soon the train would be entering the Taff valley and once again snaking along the relief lines past Pontypridd. Rattling steadily south the only likely interruptions to its journey would be at Treforest, Taff's Well or Pentyrch, if traffic were crossing the junctions here, or Maesmawr. Depending upon the time and the make-up of the load it would either put in or bypass Radyr Yard, although a stop was usual. Here any wagons that had to be re-sorted would be put off and if the working was running late the crew would be relieved. Once this was done Y15 would continue on around the Llandaff loop line. This diverged from the Penarth branch beyond the west side of Radyr shed, curved behind it, crossing the Taff as it did so, and rejoined the main line just north of Llandaff station. At this point the mineral lines crossed those of the passenger on the level, and continued on the east side of them for the remainder of the distance to Queen Street. At Roath Branch Junction the train swung first east and then south along the branch for the final few miles to its destination at Roath Marshalling or Tidal Sidings. Having delivered its train there the inspector would tell the crew where to pick up a return load of empties. These would normally be assembled at the nearby Swansea Street Sidings, and they would have to be returned to Radyr or perhaps the storage sidings at Roath Branch Junction. So after perhaps a round trip of some nine hours the locomotive that had worked Y15 would come on shed

One of the valleys' most arduous duties were the iron ore trains between Newport and the Ebbw Vale steelworks. In the early 1950s the new British Railways Standard class 9F 2-10-0s were allocated to Ebbw Junction shed for this work. On 6 May 1954 No 92001, seen here at Park Junction, heads unassisted into the valley with twenty-one loaded ore wagons. The equivalent load for a GWR 72xx 2-8-2T was sixteen such wagons. (S. Rickard)

Running past Llanbradach colliery 56xx class 0-6-2T No 5687 heads a Cwm Bargoed to Cardiff docks freight on 27 April 1957. In the colliery sidings a National Coal Board saddle tank is busily at work. (S. Rickard)

again at Radyr, having hauled yet another of the countless heavy loads of coal that have found their way to the sea from the dark mines of the Rhondda.

Lest one get the wrong impression it must be said that not all the coal traffic was worked in this way, that is, using target numbers as a means of identification, and working under the daily instruction of the traffic control department. In the Swansea area colliery workings were not as intensive as in east Glamorgan and Monmouthshire. Target numbers were not used and mineral-train timings appeared in the service timetable. In the thirties on the Burry Port & Gwendraeth line, Pentremawr colliery was cleared three times daily at just after 4.13pm, 5.19pm, and 7.37pm by the 3.20pm, 4.42pm, and 7.00pm goods trains from Cwmmawr, while further down the valley at Carway colliery full wagons were removed once a day at 11.00am by a direct working from there to Burry Port. In the Dulais valley Brynteg and Dillwyn collieries were also cleared once a day by the 11.40am from Onllwyn, and on the Port Talbot Railway's line from Cwmdu, North's colliery was cleared six times a day by three workings starting from Duffryn Junction at 7.30am, 1.25pm, and 3.30pm, each of which made two trips into the Llynfi valley.

Workings to inland destinations also appeared in the service timetables and an important group of these were to numerous Great Western sheds carrying locomotive coal. Daily from Aberdare, via the Sirhowy valley and Newport, or from Rogerstone sidings, they travelled to Old Oak Common, Bristol Bath Road, or Reading, etc. The loads they carried were of top-quality Welsh locomotive coal around the steam-raising qualities of which Great Western fireboxes were designed, and upon the performances subsequently achieved more than one reputation was founded.

Thus was the industrial wealth of South Wales moved to dock or works. An intense traffic, varying in its method of direction as experience and order patterns dictated, as one travelled across the coalfield. Here only the surface of such workings has been skimmed and only an inkling given of the amount and complexity of the work carried out daily in colliery, control office, or on footplate, by hundreds of men across the coalfield. Men who successfully, and without the modern aids today's generation would deem indispensable to make such a system operate, ran what was, in all probability, the most complex and intensive freight service in the world.

The full impact of the industrialisation of the South Wales valleys is caught in this turn of the century photograph taken at Llwynypia in the Rhondda Fawr. The extensive workings and sidings of the Glamorgan Coal Company are amply displayed, while in the background the buildings of the Llwynypia Brick Company, and its chimneys, dominate the scene, and the terraces of the valley houses rise behind them up to the wooded slopes of Llwynypia Mountain. Through all this the Taff Vale Railway squeezed itself along the valley floor, and a down coal train can be seen approaching, headed by what appears to be one of their fleet of 0-6-2Ts. (L&GRP)

3
THE VALLEYS AWAKE

Although the working steam locomotive is now banished from the everyday valley scene, it is fitting that the few that have managed to survive, through the efforts of dedicated enthusiasts, should be found in a corner of the Caerphilly Works of the ex-Rhymney Railway, and that one of this elite band should not only be an ex-Taff Vale Railway locomotive, but also one of the limited number built in Cardiff by that company. Here are also to be found industrial locomotives with connections to the iron and steel industry. Thus preserved together are the last remaining examples of the thousands of locomotives that for a hundred and thirty years or more served the railway system of the South Wales valleys, a railway system called into being by the twin forces that fuelled the region's economy for more than two centuries: iron and coal.

In today's world, following decades of uniformity and a constant cutting back of the system, it is difficult to imagine the sheer number of individual railways, coal mines, iron, steel and other manufacturing works that once flourished in South Wales. It was not unusual for valleys to be served by at least two railway companies for all or part of their length. In the Cynon valley the Taff Vale and Great Western ran parallel to one another. Always in sight of each other, often only feet apart, they only separated any distance to skirt either side of a once seemingly endless succession of collieries. In the Afan, the Rhondda & Swansea Bay, the only railway to run along its full length, was shadowed firstly by the Port Talbot Railway, then beyond Pontrhydyfen by the South Wales Mineral Railway, and finally above Cymmer by the Great Western. Similar examples could be quoted throughout the region. It is true that this resulted in duplication, but the market could stand it, and oh! what a delicious variety of services, operating practices and sometimes the near impossible condensing of multiple tracks into confined spaces this led to. Many legal and parliamentary battles were also fought, as when the Brecon & Merthyr and Rhymney railways both claimed the same land in the lower Bargoed Rhymney valley, or when the Taff Vale Railway attempted to obtain powers for a terminus at Barry for its branch from Penarth, right in the middle of the Barry Railway's proposed No 2 dock!

Frequently double tracked throughout, these lines clung to hillside shelves in the upper reaches of the valleys, and climbed fearsome banks to pass from one valley to the next. Bottlenecks were common and great inventiveness, and expense, was lavished in overcoming them. A classic case was the Barry Railway's crossing of the Taff valley at Nantgarw, soaring 120ft and crossing the Taff Vale, Rhymney and Cardiff railways, together with a private line and the Glamorganshire canal in a matter of yards. Only slightly less enterprise was shown in devising the complex layouts, complete with exchange sidings, south of Pontypridd where successively the Pontypridd, Caerphilly & Newport and Barry railways joined the Taff Vale (and where the Cardiff Railway would also have done so had it been allowed). In the same context one can also cite the lines from

Treherbert at the head of the Rhondda Fawr in 1911. The Lady Margaret colliery dominates the foreground, while behind is the Taff Vale Railway's terminus, complete with carriage sidings and unique semi-roundhouse engine shed. The open field on the right of the photograph was later the site of the GWR engine shed built in 1931. A TVR 0-6-0 can be seen at the shed coal stage adjacent to the carriage shed. (L&GRP)

43

Trouble with the navvies

The following is an extract from the writings of Mrs Jennette Cribb, dated 5 February 1935:

'The Rhondda and Swansea Bay Railway was opened on 14 March 1895, the first tickets were issued to my grandmother, Jennette Morgan, my father and myself to Blaenrhonddda. The engineer surveyor was Mr John Cribb, my father-in-law. He had done a remarkable piece of engineering in bringing the two sections of borings in the tunnel to within an inch of each other in the centre, one section starting at the Blaengwynfi side and the other across the mountain at the Blaenrhonddda side.'

She then recalls how the villagers in Cymmer lived in terror from the Irish workmen, called the navvies, who were working on the Gelli tunnel between 1885–90. She writes: 'During the year that the railway was being built the navvies employed thereon, and the villagers had some very lively times each viewing the other as enemies, so that when the wine flowed, especially on Saturday nights, they clashed, and many were the pitched battles fought in the one and only village street. Cymmer in those days consisted of the village inn, the Farmers' Arms, and a handful of cottages. There was also a small chapel called Hebron, where the few farmers gathered on the Sabbath, and I have heard my uncle relate many times how on one Sunday evening in mid-summer, one of the villagers had burst in upon the worshippers shouting, 'Come at once, the navvies are killing John the Farmers,' and all, including the preacher, had rushed to the scene. The navvies it seems had come to seek vengeance for the insults of the night before, but they were beaten off successfully this time, again my great-uncle, Thomas Griffiths, Llest farm, a very big man with a terrible blow and strength of an ox, had lifted one of the enemy and carried him a distance of twenty yards and thrown him over the bridge into the stream below, luckily it was summer and the water shallow, or there may have been serious consequences, but it was not allowed to finish there. The following Saturday night again saw them on the warpath and this time the navvies had decided to lie in wait on the Abercregan road for my uncle Thomas Morgan who lodged with his cousin Eliza Davies. Behold us then this night, I a baby of seven weeks being carried by Modryb Mari also carrying a basket of groceries, walking along with Mary and Sara, little girls of ten and five years respectively and Mam, Uncle Tom, and John Davies bringing up the rear, when like a bolt from the blue, within a hundred yards of our destination, Abercregan farm, about a score of navvies surrounded us and beat the women and children unmercifully. Mam ran back to Cymmer for help and brought the whole village with her and the onslaught was terrible. In the melée Modryb Mari and I were thrown into the brook, the Cregan, and were pulled out by Dafydd y Cymmer who took us safely into the farm where seven weeks previously I had been born, he then rushed back to the fray. The navvies were howling for their lives and were glad to get away. Needless to say, they never troubled Cymmer again and the company had to get a new lot of employees. Mary and Sara, poor little terrified girls, for years afterwards when relating the scene would say, 'Mam wedi cael blackeye, Modryb wedi cael bonclyst,' no doubt imagining bonclyst (box on the ear) to mean something dreadful.'

(Bygone Railways in the Afan – Clive Smith)

the Llynfi, Ogmore and Garw valleys that converged on the triangle at Tondu before diverging again to Port Talbot, Porthcawl and Bridgend. Almost unheard of elsewhere were fans of storage sidings or loops where one end could be up to ninety degrees to the other, as at the exchange sidings at Port Talbot and Llantrisant, and the storage sidings at Cadoxton.

Normally deadly rivals, on occasions politics, finance or local geography conspired to force companies to unite or concede running powers. The Rhymney Railway for example built jointly with both the Great Western and London & North Western to reach Merthyr and Dowlais as well as to give themselves a direct northern outlet from the coalfield. Mention of the line to Dowlais is a reminder of a unique characteristic of this RR/GWR joint line from Llancaiach. From the time of the earliest tramroads the problem to be overcome was the climb to Dowlais, high on the eastern hills at the head of the Taff valley. This joint line had the distinguishing feature however that having struggled manfully up the valley of the Bargoed Taff, it found itself *above* the town, and had to descend via a series of zigzag lines to the ironworks. Only South Wales could give the observer of the railway scene so much variety in so limited an area of the United Kingdom.

Such then were some of the features of over a century of expansion, the end result of a story that began before the railway, as we know it, came into being.

The industrial prosperity of South Wales was founded in the late eighteenth century with the establishment of the iron industry whose furnaces formed a flaming necklace in the hills from Hirwaun to Blaenavon along the northern borders of the counties of Glamorganshire and Monmouthshire (now mid-Glamorgan and Gwent), at the heads of the South Wales valleys where their then clear and sparkling waters flowed down from the rolling uplands of the Brecon Beacons. The industry grew and prospered to become the principal iron manufacturing and exporting district not only of Great Britain but for a period, of the entire world. With the introduction of the steelmaking processes of first Bessemer and later Siemens and Gilchrist Thomas, the iron industry declined. The most foresighted of proprietors however invested in the new technology, ensuring that South Wales retained a major stake in this new industry, but for a variety of technical and economic reasons, the steelmaking centre of the United Kingdom moved to the north east, and in South Wales, with the notable exceptions of Dowlais and Ebbw Vale, steelmaking moved to the coastal areas.

The decline in the ironmaking industry of the valleys, which began in the late 1850s and accelerated after about 1870, concentrated the minds of local proprietors and landowners to look for alternatives, and one was found immediately to hand, coal. As coke, coal had been used from the earliest days of large-scale ironmaking in the area, together with a modest export trade, particularly through Newport and Swansea, and a negligible local household use. However, with the development of railways, steam shipping and gas lighting, and most importantly the advancement of deep mining techniques, since the best coal for these purposes lay in the main at depths below about 125yd (114 metres), its full potential could now be exploited. Little could they have realised, those proprietors who sought to develop new trade, that they were to bring South Wales, for the second time in one hundred years, world-wide leadership, this time in coal exporting, and in doing so establish one of the densest and most competi-

Brecon & Merthyr 0-6-0ST, either No 17 or 18, heading a rake of four-wheelers from Dowlais Central, circa 1912. (Locally Dowlais Central was known as 'The Tip' station, since it was built on an embankment jutting out of the steep hillside.) (Dowlais Library)

45

tive railway networks the world has ever seen. A measure of this density can be gained from the fact that when the Great Western Railway Group was set up following the Railways Act of 1921, no less than fourteen South Wales railway companies became constituents or subsidiary members of this group, a figure that rises to seventeen if one includes the independent companies that were worked by their neighbours. In addition the London Midland & Scottish Railway absorbed another two by virtue of its take-over of the Midland and London & North Western railways. Further the original Great Western Railway itself, between the years 1860 and 1903 had already taken over seven companies, and all this in a compact area no more than fifty-five miles by twenty-five miles.

The first railways of the South Wales valleys, in the accepted sense of a company set up by Act of Parliament for the carriage of goods and passengers and whose motive power was the steam locomotive, were the lines of the ironmasters. The Taff Vale and Rhymney railways in the east of the region, the Vale of Neath & Llanelly in the west, and the Llynfi Valley Railway sandwiched between, were called into existence at their behest. Of these early railways in South Wales only one held itself aloof from this trade. It had its mind on higher things. The South Wales Railway – godchild of the GWR – was on its way to Ireland and points west, South Wales was merely to be crossed as quickly as possible.

Railways in the form of tramroads or tramways, however, are known to have existed in South Wales from around 1780, although in the interests of strict accuracy one should claim Sir Humphrey Mackworth's wooden waggonway at Neath, circa 1698, as the true forerunner. However, it was not until the building of the great canals of South Wales from 1794 that the tramroad system developed and grew to any significant size. For nearly four decades from the mid 1750s the output of the Glamorganshire and Monmouthshire ironworks, slung across the backs of mules and horses, plodded the lonely ridgeways southwards to the sea, or eastwards to the lowlands. This slow and increasingly uneconomic method of transport was finally swept aside, mainly between 1794 and 1799, when the impetus to demand of the Napoleonic wars necessitated finding a faster, more reliable and cheaper outlet. Between these years were opened four of the five great canals of South Wales: the Glamorganshire in 1794, the Neath in 1795, the Swansea in 1798 and the Monmouthshire in 1799. (The fifth, the Brecon and Abergavenny, opened over the fifteen years between 1797 and 1812.)

Each of these four canals stretched from the sea to as near the ironworks they were built to serve as was economically feasible. This meant some miles, as for example the five or so that separated the Monmouthshire canal from the Blaenavon Iron Works, or merely a few yards as in the case of the Glamorganshire

---

CEMETERY SIDING AND "TOP OF THE RUN" SIDING.

The hand levers working the points leading to these sidings are secured by padlocks. The keys are kept in Tyndall Street Junction Box.

The Guard or Shunter, as the case may be, must obtain the key of the padlock from the Signalman at Tyndall Street Junction to unlock the points and, when the work is complete, he must lock the lever in the normal position, i.e., right for through trains on the main line, and return the key to the Signalman.

The Down Home signal must be kept at " Danger " while the key of Cemetery Siding is out of the Signalman's possession, and the Up Home Signal must be kept at " Danger " while the key of the " Top of the Run " Siding is out of the Signalman's possession.

The keys are labelled with a brass label, and are not interchangeable. The Signalman at Tyndall Street Junction must enter in the Train Register the times at which the keys are taken from and returned to the Signal Box, and the Guard or Shunter must see that this is done.

From the Appendix to Section 9 of the Service Time Tables, March 1950.

canal and the Cyfarthfa Iron Works. The final connections however, be they long or short, were made by tramways built either by the canal company itself, as was the line from Pontnewynydd to Blaenavon; by local industrialists under the four- or eight-mile clause in the appropriate canal's Act of Incorporation (which allowed them to build their own tramways to connect with it), as for example the famous Penydarren; or like the somewhat later Sirhowy Railway, by a separate Act incorporating a tramway, often of considerable length. By their very nature these tramways were only a series of separate and largely independent concerns. By far the largest system was that connected to the twin arms of the Monmouthshire canal, but even that only served the valleys of the Ebbw, Afon Llwyd, and by way of the railway of that name, the Sirhowy.

Nevertheless despite this and the fact that South Wales was not amongst the earliest users of tramways, two notable firsts may be claimed. South Wales saw the first fare-paying railway passengers in the world when the Oystermouth Railway, later known as the Swansea & Mumbles Railway, commenced a passenger service on 25 March 1807. However a much more important event occurred some three years earlier when, on 21 February 1804, Richard Trevithick's locomotive ran from the Penydarren Ironworks near Merthyr to Navigation House near Abercynon, starting a chain of events which the correspondent of *The Cambrian* could but have dimly perceived when he wrote, '. . . the machine . . . will be made use of in a thousand instances never yet thought of for an engine.' This momentous journey was made for a one hundred guinea wager between two prominent Merthyr ironmasters, Samuel Homfray and Richard Crawshay, but it was never honoured.

Some twenty-five years were to pass though before the next successful use of

The TVR station at Pontypridd with its distinctive island platform has been well known for nearly eighty years. As a contrast this view shows its predecessor, with a line up of staff, and four-legged station 'shunter'. The photograph is believed to be circa 1879. (Pontypridd Library)

47

Line-up at Aberdare Low Level in 1919. The tender locomotive is a K or L class 0-6-0, while the tank locomotive is probably one of the O3 class 0-6-2Ts. Behind them can be seen the roof and water tank of the Taff Vale engine shed. (Actually the shed here was two separate buildings, the second shed being situated to the right of the photograph.) (Aberdare Library)

the steam locomotive is recorded in the area, when the Sirhowy Iron Company's Stephenson-built locomotive *Britannia* ran to the Tredegar Wharf on the River Usk at Newport from the Iron Company's works at the head of the valley, a distance of approximately twenty miles. It was a journey not without incident as the locomotive lost its chimney en route and which had to be repaired before the journey could be completed. Following this event the Sirhowy Company's locomotives, and others, became regular visitors to Newport.

For nearly forty years canal and tramway monopolised freight haulage in South Wales, but by the mid 1830s the canals had reached saturation, their tolls were considered to be extortionate, and frost and drought could cause disruptive and expensive delays for days or maybe weeks. The owners became rich and complacent, and a vested interest that fought hard to resist the next, inevitable phase of development, the steam railway. These restrictions to the expanding iron trade of the area, particularly at Merthyr, were instrumental in forcing the majority of the leading ironmasters of that district, assisted by Bristol financial interests, through which presumably Brunel became associated with the scheme, to propose the construction of a railway from Merthyr to Cardiff – the Taff Vale Railway. Incorporated on 21 July 1836, it was opened from Cardiff to Newbridge, as Pontypridd was then known, in 1840, and throughout to Merthyr the following year.

There then followed a pause for reflection of some four years, after which the Taff Vale Railway sought authorisation for its first major extension, and the Monmouthshire Canal Company, also with Parliamentary approval, began the process by which it was to become the only such company in South Wales to establish a railway system. The former adopted what was to become its favourite ploy – supporting the establishment of a nominally independent company. In this case it was the Aberdare Railway incorporated in 1845 and opened between Abercynon and the ironworks at Aberdare and Abernant in the following year. The latter, though it did not know it, began a long and laborious metamorphosis; a process that was to last a decade and one that would bring this once prosperous company to its knees, although it managed to retain its independence for a further twenty years. 1846 also saw the handiwork of Brunel for the second time in the South Wales valleys, when the broad-gauge Vale of Neath Railway was authorised to Aberdare and Merthyr from Neath. Here it made a junction with the South Wales Railway, Brunel's major work in the area. Incorporated the previous year, this latter railway was to provide South Wales with a main line to England and, while never conceived to serve local industrial interests, was ultimately connected to all the major valleys.

These early lines were to be instrumental in the commencement of the expansion of the South Wales coal trade, particularly those in the Cynon valley, but it was not until 1852 that new railways, or branches from existing ones, were promoted to tap new mining areas. However, for many years, and long after Merthyr had reached its zenith and begun its long decline, the very name retained a cachet that continued to draw railways to its ironworks. Directly or indirectly the London & North Western Railway was behind two such railways. A lease of the Merthyr, Tredegar & Abergavenny Railway, incorporated in 1859, and the assistance, willingly or otherwise, of the Rhymney and Brecon & Merthyr railways, finally brought it to that town in 1879. However, it had originally gained

Treherbert station 1873. The reason for the impressive line-up of station staff is not known but the number present underlines the numbers employed on such duties in the late nineteenth century. The locomotive is a Sharp Stewart 0-6-0, and was one of four delivered to the Taff Vale Railway in that year. They were later rebuilt as 0-6-0STs. (Gordon Coles Collection)

access to Merthyr by running powers over the Newport, Abergavenny & Hereford Railway's Taff Vale Extension and the Taff Vale Railway itself in 1858, when the former company's line from Pontypool reached Quakers Yard. Not to be outdone the Great Western, which from 1865 had rather awkwardly gained access from the west following the absorption of the Vale of Neath Railway, joined forces with the Rhymney Railway, reaching Dowlais from Llancaiach in 1876, and finally Merthyr from Quakers Yard and along the west side of the Taff valley ten years later.

In 1852, having recognised the potential of the top-quality coal mined in the Cynon valley, the Vale of Neath Railway promoted the Dare Valley branch, and three years later an extension of its own main line down the valley under the name of the Aberdare Valley Railway. These broad-gauge lines were opened between 1854 and 1857. Following hard upon the heels of the Vale of Neath the South Wales Mineral Railway was incorporated in 1853 to tap the nearby Corrwg valley, although this eccentrically routed broad-gauge line, engineered once more by Brunel, did not reach its destination until 1863. In 1854 the Rhymney valley was opened up with the founding of the Rhymney Railway. Arguably a line built to tap the iron trade from the works at the head of that valley, coal almost immediately became its principal commodity following its opening in 1858 to a junction with the Taff Vale Railway at Taff's Well. The Swansea valley featured for the first time, officially that is, in 1855 when the privately promoted Swansea Vale Railway regularised its existence and took off in a somewhat half-hearted fashion up the Tawe valley reaching Yniscedwyn in 1859 and Brynamman five years later, to exploit the anthracite of that region. Brynamman had in fact been reached from the west by a branch of the Llanelly Railway as early as 1842. The Llanelly company was absorbed jointly by the Great Western and London & North Western in 1873, which gave the LNWR access to Swansea over the Central Wales line, while the Swansea Vale Railway was purchased by the Midland in 1874 thus ensuring that company's entry to the South Wales coalfield. The development of the anthracite trade with its specialist uses, for example in

Aberavon station on the Rhondda & Swansea Bay Railway looking northwards in 1906. In the background is the engine shed, to the right of which can be seen the three-road carriage shed. Careful examination of the engine shed shows that there are actually two buildings, one behind the other. That nearest the photographer is the original gable roofed timber shed, dating from 1885, and which was demolished shortly after this photograph was taken. Behind this wooden building is a later stone built shed with a saw tooth roof which survived until 1922. (L&GRP)

The frugal B&M

The desire to reduce expenditure led the Brecon & Merthyr to strive for the fullest economies, and to record their efforts in this direction in the records of the Committee of Directors, and those of the Traffic and Works Committee.

The evidence of these drives is often most diverse in character.

August, 1869. – A minute stating that the Engineer had arranged to take from the Dowlais Iron Works, as ballast, 'scoriae from their tips . . . at the rate of two pence per truckload'.

January, 1870. – An order 'that the Engineer do report upon the comparative advantages of purchasing break blocks ready cut and of purchasing poplar for the purpose.'

December, 1870. – A report 'that a Cheese had been found in the van of Wm. Williams acting as extra guard on Brecon Fair Day, November 17th. Ordered, that he be kept under observation'.

January, 1872. – A claim from Messrs Woodruff for £33 representing the value of twelve sheep which a Brecon & Merthyr train ran down on 28/12/1871 – 'the remnants of the sheep had been sold for £3.7.7.'

April, 1873. – David James, signalman, was found 'taking ale from a cask in transit' and, preferring discretion to defiance, 'absconded'.

November, 1873. – The Traffic Manager noted that 'on Monday, the 17th November (Brecon Fair) 2,844 passengers were conveyed to and from Brecon'. The receipts amounted to £293.4.4.

January, 1882. – An application from the Midland Railway 'for means of supplying foot-warmers at Brecon station'. A minute of February, 1882, notes that the Midland had agreed to provide the boiler and other appliances required to produce hot water at Brecon.

February, 1883. – A recommendation that greatcoats should be obtained for 'the men employed in putting down fog signals.'

February, 1884. – A minute underlining the need to procure good coal for the engines of the Brecon & Merthyr – the Locomotive Superintendent reported that he had received 'five wagons of Hirwain coal' and that it was 'not suitable for the heavy inclines'.

April, 1884. – A minute recommending that 'small premiums of £3, £2, £1 each be given for the best kept station houses and gardens on the line'.

July, 1895. – A report about the failure, in June, of the 'electric train tablet' between Dowlais Top and Pantywaen – a failure 'caused by the great heat expanding the commutator wheel at the latter place'.

February, 1896. – A tablet failure between Talyllyn and Talybont 'causing a delay of 10 minutes to a passenger train. The failure was caused by rats or mice destroying the gutta percha around the wire'.

V. J. Parry

---

brewing, lime burning and later cement manufacture, was slower and never reached the levels achieved at the eastern end of the coalfield by the steam coals. It was coal for this purpose that was the reason for the phenomenal rate of growth and the dizzy heights reached by the coal trade in South Wales before World War I, and it is the steam-coal trade that now brings us back to the isolated – yes in 1855 the isolated – valleys of the Rhondda Fawr and Rhondda Fach.

It is true that the Taff Vale Railway had by 1849 penetrated the lower reaches of these valleys as far as Dinas in the Rhondda Fawr and Ynyshir in the Rhondda Fach, to serve the shallow pits and levels sunk to the bituminous seams. But industry had not yet reached beyond these places. They were still valleys of quiet beauty; of small farms watered by crystal streams. The death knell of this sylvan beauty was rung in the spring of 1853 when the Upper Four Feet seam, as it is known, was proved on the Marquis of Bute's land at Treherbert at the head of the Rhondda Fawr. The resulting mine was in production by the end of 1855, and was reached by the Taff Vale Railway in August of the following year. Three years later that railway's Rhondda Fach branch reached Ferndale, and the exploitation of South Wales' most productive valleys was underway.

Following the opening up of the Rhondda, railway promotion accelerated during the next decade reaching untouched valleys, seeing major extensions commenced to existing systems (either to increase traffic or safeguard strategic interests), and breaking monopolies in certain areas, although in truth this had already begun in the Cynon valley and to a lesser extent around Brynamman. In this period the Ely, Ogmore, Dulais and Gwendraeth valleys were entered. The Ely was tapped by the broad-gauge Ely Valley Railway, incorporated in 1857,

Mercifully, serious railway accidents were rare in the valleys. This one was the result of a collision with a coal train at Coke Ovens on 23 January 1911. There were eleven fatalities. (Pontypridd Library).

which branched northwards from the South Wales Railway at Llantrisant, and was opened to Penygraig by 1862. The Ogmore Valley Railway of 1863 built a standard-gauge line to join the broad-gauge Llynfi Valley Railway at Tondu in 1865, whereupon a complex marriage ensued, the offspring of which was the standard-gauge Llynfi & Ogmore Railway. Finally the Dulais Valley Mineral Railway, later to become the Neath & Brecon Railway, came into being in 1862, reaching its original terminus at Onllwyn in 1864. At the end of the decade the incorporation of the Burry Port & Gwendraeth Valley Railway, and the much smaller Gwendraeth Valley Railway, began the serious exploitation of the anthracite deposits of that area. The former was not completed until 1869, and the latter, never a serious contender for this traffic, fizzled out at a tinplate works a short way up the Gwendraeth Fach in 1871.

The monopoly of the Vale of Neath Railway in the Dare valley was broken in 1863 when the Taff Vale Railway promoted a branch under the name of the Dare Valley Railway which opened in 1866. This tit for tat was more than justified in the eyes of the Taff Vale company for by 1864 the Great Western Railway (as successor to the Newport, Abergavenny & Hereford and West Midlands railways) had extended from Quakers Yard to join the Vale of Neath at Middle Duffryn Junction, and a third rail was laid over the latter's system, thus posing a much greater threat to the Taff Vale now the break of gauge had been overcome, particularly since the Vale of Neath itself had been absorbed by the Great Western in 1865. To further safeguard itself in this period the Taff Vale, threatened by the Ely Valley Railway's proposals to build to Cardiff and into the Rhondda proper, backed the Llantrisant and Taff Vale Junction and the Cowbridge railways thus protecting its exposed western flank.

Falling into none of these categories was the Brecon & Merthyr Railway which was incorporated in 1859, but it did not enter the South Wales valleys proper until after 1863 when it acquired the Rumney Railway, an impoverished tramway that ran down the eastern side of the Rhymney valley to join the Monmouthshire Railway's line at Bassaleg. Rebuilt as part of the Brecon & Merthyr system it re-opened throughout from Rhymney to Bassaleg in 1866, although it was not connected to the northern section of its parent, via the Bargoed Rhymney valley, until two years later.

1866 saw this rapid and accelerating pace of railway development in South Wales suddenly brought to a halt with the collapse of the Overend and Gurney Bank, which shook confidence not only in railway speculation but also in mining itself. The three years from 1866 to 1869 saw no new pits sunk in the Rhondda Fawr, an unprecedented break in the almost continuous expansion over the twenty-five years from 1855 to 1880.

Recovery in new railway construction in South Wales did not recommence until 1875 when the Llanelly & Mynydd Mawr Railway was incorporated from Llanelly to Cross Hands in the anthracite region, and 1876 when the extension of the Llynfi & Ogmore Railway into the Garw valley was completed. These were the last railways built to serve untapped areas of the coalfield. All the railways promoted from 1878 onwards, with one arguable exception, merely took their traffic from the existing network. Between that year and 1897 five new companies were promoted, of which four were combined dock and railway undertakings, and their construction was only finally halted by the advent of World War I.

The first of these railways, the Pontypridd, Caerphilly & Newport, a nominally independent railway, but sponsored by the Alexandra (Newport & South Wales) Dock & Railway Company into whose fold it entered in 1897, was incorporated in 1878, and by a series of relatively short lines linked the Taff Vale Railway at Pontypridd to Newport via Caerphilly and Machen. Next came the Rhondda & Swansea Bay Railway, the only one of this group that was not a combined dock and railway system, although it certainly had the backing of the Swansea harbour authorities who desired a stake in the burgeoning export trade

At an unknown date in the Edwardian era staff and passengers pose at the Brecon & Merthyr Railway's Church Road station, between Machen and Rhiwderin. The original method of portrayal of the station name was a feature of this station. (L&GRP)

53

*Views of the Rhondda valley
end of the R&SB Rhondda
tunnel are very rare, whereas the
more easily accessible
Blaengwynfi end is well known.
This view of the Blaencwm
portal was taken in 1967.
(Derek Jones)*

in Rhondda steam coal. Piercing the mountain above Treherbert it ran down the Afan valley to the coast then swung along the foreshore to Swansea. Incorporated in 1884 it finally reached its goal in 1899.

Two years after the incorporation of the Rhondda & Swansea Bay the Barry Railway came into being and began three decades of continuous fighting between itself, the Taff Vale and the Cardiff Dock authorities. Opened between Barry and Trehafod in 1889, branches were built to Cogan, Bridgend (under the auspices of the Vale of Glamorgan Railway) and to the Rhymney and Brecon & Merthyr systems up to 1905. Further expansion into Monmouthshire although approved by Parliament was not undertaken before World War I intervened. 1894 saw the incorporation of the Port Talbot Railway which by 1898 had grown to tap the Ogmore, Llynfi, Afan and Pelena valleys. Like the Rhondda & Swansea Bay it was a sound company, much favoured by the Great Western, into whose system it became absorbed in 1908, together with the South Wales Mineral Railway, although both retained their separate identities until 1921, a similar agreement having been reached with the R&SB two years previously.

Not favoured by any company however, least of all the Taff Vale, was the last independent railway promoted and constructed into the valleys. This was the Cardiff Railway incorporated in 1897 as a reincarnation of the Bute Docks Company which owned the Cardiff dock complex. Too late into the field, even for the speculators' paradise of the South Wales coalfield, and outsmarted legally at every turn by the Taff Vale, its truncated 'main line' ran from the Rhymney Railway at Heath Junction, in the northern outskirts of Cardiff, to a junction, used but once, with the Taff Vale Company at Treforest via the congested Taff's Well gorge. A double-track monument to imprudence and greed, the westward abutment of its once impressive, but useless, crossing of the Taff river just short of its junction with the Taff Vale Railway still stands as a monument to Victorian folly – a bridge too far.

Thus ended the headlong expansion of South Wales' railway network. One final improvement to the system, the Swansea District lines, was begun but never completed by the GWR before the advent of World War I changed forever the political and economic climates that for two centuries had nurtured the industrial expansion of South Wales.

The events of 1921–4, when all the local railway companies became either constituents or subsidiaries of an enlarged Great Western Railway, are too well known to need repeating here, but perhaps before ending this brief résumé of the history of steam in South Wales, which now became a part of the history of the GWR, one should recall what that company attempted to achieve in a hostile economic environment. Despite the fact that the bulk of GWR advertising was aimed at the holiday traffic to the West of England, it was acutely conscious that its most profitable area of operations, both as regards freight and passenger traffic, was South Wales. Unfortunately the GWR was obliged to close two South Wales docks, Newport (Town) and Penarth; to abandon a number of passenger services including Black Mill to Hendreforgan and Gilfach Goch (1930), Pontypridd to Nelson (1932), and Maesteg to Blaengarw (1933); and to reduce the number of stations handling parcels from over 150 to 46 and later 11. Against these however, should be placed their investments in coal-handling facilities at all the major ports to allow them to handle larger wagons of 20 tons capacity; the rebuilding of Swansea, Cardiff and Newport stations; the enlargement of the marshalling yards at Rogerstone and Severn Tunnel Junction; and the enlargement and modernisation of Caerphilly Works (1926 and 1939), together with the provision of new engine sheds at Treherbert, Pantyffynon and Radyr. It is true that some of this investment was undertaken with Government backing, but it still indicates the faith the GWR had in South Wales even in the midst of deep economic troubles.

World War II brought much increased activity to the South Wales railway system. Afterwards it was attested that more than 4 million tons of American supplies were handled, and more than three-quarters of the D-Day supplies for the American forces passed through South Wales. But the events of 1939–45 finally saw the beginning of the end of the export coal trade, for although it carried on beyond the end of steam in the valleys its pre-eminence was finished. In early 1987, some twenty-two years after British Railways steam was eliminated in the area, only Swansea, whose days are limited, and Barry, see the small tonnages, principally anthracite duff, that are still exported.

Once more following a global conflict there again occurred a major upheaval in railway affairs with nationalisation, followed a few years later by the decision that steam traction was to be replaced by diesel. By 1965 the change-over in South Wales was complete. Only industrial steam locomotives now remained for a further twenty-one years before they too were finally silenced, and for the first time in 182 years, if one goes back as far as Trevithick, the valleys echoed no more to the sound of a working steam locomotive.

Like a Lowry painting workmen at Swansea North dock pause in their work in this interesting study in broad-gauge days. The standard-gauge wagons in the foreground contrast with the broad-gauge 'container' wagons in the sidings behind (four 'containers' per wagon). The broad-gauge saddle tanks are fitted with extended buffers for working both broad- and standard-gauge trains, a fascinating detail rarely seen in photographs. The primitive enclosed coal tippers are noteworthy. In the left hand background the viaduct carrying the Vale of Neath line to Wind Street Junction can just be discerned. (Welsh Industrial & Maritime Museum)

General View showing Graigwen, Pontypridd

4
CITY, TOWN AND SEASIDE

Maerdy station in the Rhondda Fach was opened on 18 June 1889, and a pamphlet of no less than four pages was printed to list the events of the opening ceremony. A brass band played, addresses and presentations were made, and a specially composed air of four verses, set to the tune of 'Men of Harlech' was sung. A donation was given by the local colliery company to 'various places of public worship', and local children were given a tea party, the programme specifically separating Sunday School children from those who attended Day School, the power of the Chapel being something to be reckoned with at that time. But until these later Victorian years the railway was quite definitely not for the masses, although even from the beginning it dominated their lives in ways now difficult to appreciate. In fact the revolution they brought to the lives of ordinary people far outweighs anything achieved by their successors: the motorway, the heavy lorry and the private car. The influence of the railways on the towns and cities of South Wales is perhaps not fully appreciated today, but it is true that not only did they allow the growth in population of towns, but also unprecedented mobility between them. Everywhere they were welcomed, and the services they provided applauded by all. The celebrations on the opening of a new railway in the middle years of the nineteenth century are well known, and while this was true of many South Wales lines (at the opening of the Vale of Neath there were seventeen toasts alone, with the one to Brunel well down the list incidentally), it has been largely forgotten that when some of the original mineral branches flourished sufficiently to be provided with a passenger service, this too was greeted with no less an outburst of enthusiasm, as evidenced by the rejoicing at Maerdy.

The railways were also responsible for the geography of South Wales towns and the population distributions within them. Travel around Cardiff, Newport or Swansea, and you will be surprised how the stamp of the railway network, even if now much reduced or totally abandoned, has affected the present day environment. The same is even more true in the valleys where the dominating feature of many of the towns there, of either parallel rows of terraced houses rising in tiers up a towering hillside, or the sometimes crazily steep streets linking them, are a direct result of the presence of the railway. It and the collieries arrived first and quickly occupied the majority of what little level ground there was available on the often narrow valley floor, forcing the community that grew up around them to live on the slopes above.

In Cardiff, along the main road from the city centre to Newport (the A4161), you will notice that the three-storey Victorian terraced houses to the south of the road stop abruptly and, following a short gap, are replaced by large retail and light industrial developments. At the extreme southern end of Butetown, beyond the flats of the rebuilt Tiger Bay, stand many magnificent buildings, in the one-time business heart of the city. The city's shopping centre, a mixture of both Victorian

Quiet afternoon at Cardiff Queen Street station. This photograph, taken in 1970 from platform 1 and looking in a southerly direction, well illustrates Cardiff's gateway to the valleys, which even as late as this is still largely unchanged, apart from the platform sign, from earlier days. (Jeff Morgan Collection)

Pontypridd looking towards the Rhondda valley, with the Taff Vale Railway station on the right. The Barry Railway line can be seen on the left climbing towards Graig tunnel. In the background are Coke Ovens sidings and Tymawr colliery. The date of the photograph is not known, but is probably in the 1930s.
(Pontypridd Library)

and Edwardian styles together with the latest developments, lies in a well-defined and compact area.

The route of the Glamorganshire Canal can be traced from the north east of Cardiff Castle until alongside its walls it swings beneath Kingsway (the tunnel is now an underpass). It then disappears and its course, which swung to the south immediately beyond here, can only now be identified some distance away as the curve of Mill Street, as it passes in front of the recently built Holiday Inn hotel. The distance from underpass to hotel can be comfortably walked, on a route parallel to that of the canal, in less than ten minutes. In 1794 these two points marked the approximate northern and southern limits of the town of Cardiff, the actual line of the canal between them identifying the eastern boundary, and the River Taff the western. By 1840 when the Taff Vale Railway opened from its Dock station to Pontypridd, the eastern boundary of the town was now delineated by the line of that railway whose terminus was actually over a mile to the south on the moorland which separated it from the estuary, and on which the Bute West Dock had been built. Ten years later, Cardiff's southern boundary had not altered, and it was to just outside this that the South Wales Railway built its line, separating town from dock area, a feature that has had a lasting effect upon Cardiff's development, and established its station alongside the Taff in the south-west corner of the town. So even as late as 1850 Cardiff was barely one mile square. But the foundation was laid for its present day shape. The business area developed well to the south near the dock. The rapidly expanding working class lived in the area between the dock and the South Wales Railway – Butetown. The residential area for the proprietors, managers, etc, remained within the town boundaries as delineated by castle, river and the two railways. As the town grew, and later became a city, it moved to the north, east and west of the central area leaving it to develop into the main shopping area which has now been well established for over a hundred years. As the population expanded, the split with the working class areas to the south of the South Wales Railway, and the remainder of the population to the north of it, continued as the town spread first east and then west. The westward expansion was not affected by the barrier of a railway until after the turn of the century when housing at last reached the Taff Vale Railway's Radyr to Penarth line which when it was opened in 1859 passed through open countryside well away from any urban development. The eastward expansion however was, after 1888, restricted by the construction of that company's Roath Dock branch, which although long closed and partially removed

Rivalry at Ebbw Vale

The railways were the only speedy route to other towns. On the London & North Western one could travel westwards to Merthyr and eastwards to Abergavenny, the Usk valley, Hereford and the north. Punctilious in its routine, the LNWR demanded that the station signalman should descend from his box and ring a handbell five minutes before a train was due and again before it left. The booking office was closed two minutes before a train left, and later arrivals had to wait fuming outside the locked gate until the train moved off in its leisurely way. LNWR locomotives were black 0-6-2T engines, but an 0-6-0 tender engine with a beautifully painted crest as large as a cauliflower would sometimes come to take a coal train to Crewe. The passenger carriages with their red upholstery and chocolate and white exteriors were always very clean. The Great Western was the route to Cardiff and West Wales, Bristol, Gloucester and London. Unlike the LNWR it provided Sunday trains; although its brown and cream carriages were cosier than the LNWR's, they never seemed quite as clean. The locomotives were 0-6-0 tank engines, smaller but more efficient than their LNWR rivals, and the first 2-8-0T goods engines with tapered boilers that appeared locally in 1908 were greatly admired and known as the 'Yankees'.

Arthur Gray-Jones

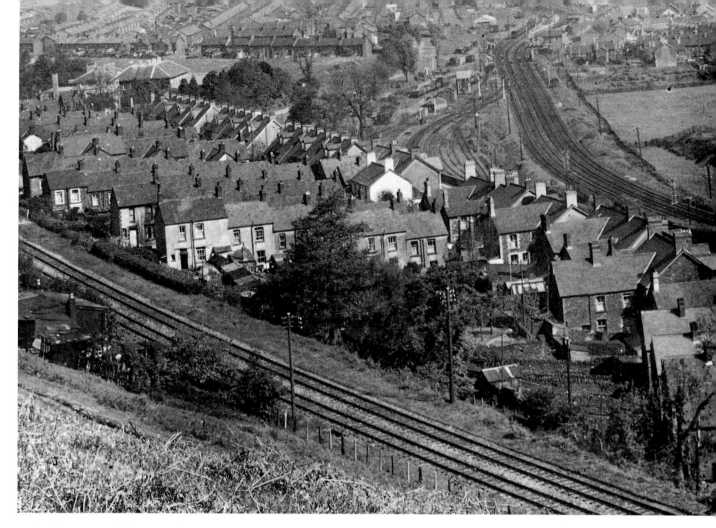

or built over, still has an effect upon its environs, since for many years, where it once crossed the Cardiff to Newport road (A4161), it effectively stopped the eastward expansion of the town, as evidenced by the abrupt end of the distinctive three-storey Victorian houses seen at this point.

These are just a few examples of how the physical shape of Wales' capital has been affected by the building of the railways which gave it birth and sustained its growth for nearly a century. Similar examples can be found in both Newport and Swansea. The layout of the streets in the Pillgwenlly area of Newport, and the sunken road opposite the Royal Gwent Hospital nearby, come to mind in that town. In Swansea one can cite the curve of The Strand, and the layouts of the large roundabouts near the end of Wind Street, around the southern, eastern and western sides of which once ran Swansea's once famous low-level docks lines.

The similar effects on the colliery towns of the valleys has already been mentioned for they, like the major coastal towns, grew up from negligible hamlets, or perhaps only a farm, under the influence of South Wales' industrial expansion. In complete contrast were the ironmaking towns strung along the north Glamorgan and north Monmouthshire borders. These were already long established and had large populations when the railways arrived. The ironworks dominated the town, and the houses of the population were already well established. In 1832, when Cardiff was an unknown town on a muddy, twisting tidal creek, Tredegar had been an ironmaking town for more than three decades, and supported drapers, grocers, hatters, clockmakers, shoemakers, a glover and a tailor. The railway when it arrived therefore had to fit into the existing set-up rather than the other way around as was the case when it was first upon the scene.

Valley complexities at Treforest. The line in the foreground is the Barry Railway main line from Trehafod to Cadoxton. In the background, at a lower level, are the four tracks of the Taff Vale Railway main line to Cardiff. Treforest Junction can be clearly seen, with the Barry Railway connection from the Taff valley rising to join its main line. The exchange sidings can be clearly seen, while behind the water tower is the goods yard at Treforest station. To the right of the Taff Vale main line, the earthworks that appear to end in the field are the remains of the abortive attempt of the Cardiff Railway to make a junction with the Taff Vale Railway. (Pontypridd Library)

59

Interview with Mr Edward Lake
General Manager, Barry
Railway

'I suppose, Mr Lake, the area of original docks has been increased, and other sources of dock revenue, apart from the shipment of coal, are catered for?'

'Certainly. Powers were obtained to construct an additional dock in 1893, which was opened almost simultaneously with a deep water lock, which was brought into use in January, 1898, and by means of this lock large-sized steamers can be dealt with at almost any state of the tide.

'Subsequently a pontoon was constructed within the break-waters, at which passenger steamers land or take in passengers. The pontoon is served by railway lines made from Barry through Barry Island, and it is now possible for passengers from Cardiff, and the districts containing the teeming population of South Wales, to travel by train to the pontoon, and embark for the various watering-places and towns in the Bristol Channel. To further assist in the development of business, the Barry Railway, by which name it has, by the authority of Parliament, been known since 1891, has obtained Parliamentary powers to work, or arrange for, steamers to ply in the Bristol Channel to and from this pontoon.

'Under these powers, arrangements have been made for a steamship service between Barry and Bristol, Clevedon, Weston-super-Mare, Minehead, Ilfracombe, Clovelly, Mumbles, and Tenby, and it is confidently anticipated that an increasing railway business will accrue from this service.'

(Railway Magazine – October 1906)

The Taff Vale Railway, for example, terminated near the Cyfarthfa Ironworks, to the south of Merthyr Tydfil, the Rhymney and the Brecon & Merthyr railways similarly stopped short of Rhymney. Thus the railways had a lesser impact on the established ironmaking towns, although it must be said that the local tramways that preceded them did leave their mark on town layouts.

Whenever they passed through or terminated in a town however, as well as their routes perhaps dividing the population or forcing it to less hospitable ground, the position of their stations determined the commercial centres of the neighbourhood. It is no accident that Cardiff's shopping centre remained and grew out from the site of the medieval town. When that site became enclosed by the town's first two major railways, and each established stations, the area became a natural focus as the first businessmen came to live nearby. With them came the demand for better shopping facilities, which remained conveniently near the railways, through which their goods arrived, long after the majority of their customers had prospered and moved further away. They now arrived by driving to the town centre in their own carriages or, if not that affluent, by horse bus and later by tram. Near the mid point between the Taff Vale's Queen Street station and what eventually became the Great Western's General station, the 'New' market was built, and nearby were also established two of Cardiff's principal multiple stores, the original proprietor of one (David Morgan) stating that his reason for choosing the site was because it was conveniently positioned between the two stations and therefore admirably situated for trade. Similarly it is not accident that, throughout the period that railways reigned supreme as the method of long-distance travel, all of Cardiff's hotels were built here too. Similar developments occurred in valley towns both large and small. Pontypridd, Risca, Port Talbot, Cymmer and Aberdare are but a few examples of where the main shopping streets can be found close to the railway station. Even Merthyr eventually fell into this category. High Street was the Great Western (as successor to the Vale of Neath Railway) station in the town centre, the advantages of which were so evident to the Taff Railway that they, like the Brecon & Merthyr and London & North Western railways, negotiated entry, and closed their original station to passengers.

60

Thus it was that the station became the hub of a town's activity, a fact no less recognised by the railways themselves. As the coal trains travelled to the docks they would pass stations with well-equipped goods yards full of the diverse products needed to sustain the life of the local population. To handle such traffic at, say, Pontypridd, were facilities for all manner of goods (to handle which a crane was provided), parcels, furniture vans, livestock (including prize cattle), horse boxes and, up to the early years of this century, private carriages. Even the diminutive Great Western station at Abergwynfi, before the drastic rationalisation of later years, had facilities for all these types of traffic, except the furniture vans and private carriages. In fact it shared the same level of facilities with nearby Blaengwynfi, the Rhondda & Swansea Bay station but a stone's throw away across the valley. When one considers the disparity in population between Pontypridd and Abergwynfi and its neighbour (in 1921 the former's was 34,819 and the combined total for the latter only 4,149) this is perhaps a little surprising, but it vividly illustrates the importance the railway station once had in the life of even the smallest communities. Though lacking in size they still required the full range of facilities to sustain themselves in the days before the lorry and car. The traffic once handled by these and countless other stations in the days of steam was enormous. Virtually no food was produced locally, so that all the staple commodities had to pass through the station. Bread was locally baked even after it had ceased to be common practice to bake it at home, so large quantities of flour had to pass through the goods yard. Meat was slaughtered locally, in fact as late as 1938 there was still a weekly service from Brecon to Merthyr for this traffic. Hence the provision at nearly all stations of cattle pens. Fruit would arrive from the Vale of Evesham, and as refrigeration techniques improved South Walians were introduced to more exotic fruits, from Britain's far flung Empire. Hops for the local brewery would also be handled, as well as perhaps some of the products for, what were then, the distant parts of the valleys. Shoes and boots were also regular items, for mass-produced footwear soon replaced the local

The Rhymney Railway terminus at Rhymney prior to the turn of the century. The photograph is looking southwards with the locomotive shed in the right background, and the goods yard clearly visible beneath the footbridge. (L&GRP)

61

shoemakers that once flourished in the valley towns. The list is almost endless.

To distribute all these goods and products, stations were hosts to local agents and carters. Horses reigned unchallenged in this work until the 1920s when lorries slowly began to replace them. But the horse did not disappear for many years, and to look after their welfare the Great Western employed veterinary surgeons to ensure their continued health. One of their number, a Dr Kirk, was extremely conscientious. Not only would he make his regular inspections, but between times would arrive at a station unannounced and carry out a spot check. He was also known to take a drive around the town to see the horses at work. A haulier seen using a sick animal, or mistreating one, would face prosecution and lose his contract with the railway. Horses were not the only animals to come under his gaze, for half a century ago the Great Western Railway had twenty-five sheepdogs on its payroll. No, they were not in the delivery business; straying sheep have always been a nuisance in the valleys.

The goods trains that worked this traffic wove their way between the enormous number of coal and passenger trains, on schedules which while they hardly appear demanding had of necessity to be flexible enough to allow for day-to-day variations in volume. One such working in the Western valleys of Monmouthshire in

The branch to Porthcawl was always a difficult one to work in summer; siding space was so restricted that the carriage sidings seen on the left were actually on the approach inclines to the long dismantled harbour coal tips. In this view taken on 5 June 1960 56xx class 0-6-2Ts 6634 and 6675 are shunting empty excursion stock. In the right foreground is the signal box that controlled not only the approach to the station but also a level crossing, a further headache for the operating staff. (S. Rickard)

Sully station on the Taff Vale
Railway's coastal line between
Penarth and Biglis Junction. A
delightful photograph taken
before World War I, which
illustrates the spacious goods yard
layout to great advantage. It is
unusual for a photograph to show
such a yard, but this one has it
all: goods shed, stores, loading
gauge, cattle pens, and road
approach in the background.
Even though the station has been
almost ignored by the
photographer the very tall signal
in the cutting beyond the road
bridge is of interest. (L&GRP)

1938 well illustrates this type of traffic. At 7.50am Maesglas sidings, on the outskirts of Newport, would dispatch a pickup goods (target number W15) to Llanhilleth. Shunting would be performed at Rogerstone Yard, which was left at 8.45am. W15 then called when required at Pontymister, Lime Kiln Siding and Halls Road Junction, and was booked to arrive at Cross Keys, about four miles from Rogerstone sidings, at 9.30am. Twenty minutes working Cross Keys goods yard followed, after which the train continued up the valley shunting the station yards at Abercarn (one hour allowed), Newbridge (35 minutes), and Crumlin (Low Level) (30 minutes), as well as calling when required at Abercarn, Celynen South and Crumlin Navigation collieries. Finally it would arrive and shunt at Llanhilleth, being booked to arrive at Llanhilleth North Box, which was opposite the station goods yard, at 12.25pm. The scheduled time for the journey of just under thirteen miles was 4hr 35min, of which no less than 3hr 3min was booked for shunting. W15 returned to Newport at 1.35pm as a coal working, calling again when required, to pick up loaded coal wagons at Crumlin Navigation and Abercarn collieries. It reached Rogerstone at 2.30pm and after half an hour's shunting of the mineral wagons, arrived at Maesglas sidings once again at 3.15pm.

Similar goods services ran in all the South Wales valleys. Typical of those in the Afan, which were accommodated around the frequent through mineral and goods services to and from Treherbert and Swansea, was the 7.20am from Aberavon which after shunting the yards at Cwmavon and the colliery at Duffryn Rhondda reached Cymmer just after 9 o'clock. In the Dulais the 10.15am from Neath Yard served Cilfrew, Crynant, Brynteg colliery, Ynisdawley and Seven Sisters, Onllwyn, and finally Colbren Junction, where it was timed to arrive at 1.58pm. It departed from Onllwyn at 3.30pm and with only two calls on its return journey eventually reached Neath Yard once again some two hours later, a round trip of some seven and a half hours. Towns along the main line through South Wales were not without local goods services either. Among their numbers in 1938 may be mentioned the 8.15am from Cardiff and the 6.45am from Tondu. The former, having called at Llantrisant and Llanharan yards to shunt, moved on to

Valley terminus at Abergwynfi, at the head of the Afan, dominated by the enclosing hills. 57xx class 0-6-0PT No 8740 waits at the head of the 2.33pm to Bridgend on 16 April 1960. The single line in the foreground continued to Avon colliery. (R. O. Tuck)

Llanharan colliery and returned to Cardiff with a coal working at 12.25pm, while the latter shunted at Pencoed, Llantrisant, Ely and Canton sidings before terminating at Cardiff Goods at 10.00am.

With hindsight it appears rather surprising that for so long the older valleys railways failed to develop passenger services, being content with a token number daily until about the last quarter of the nineteenth century. The Taff Vale Railway for some twenty-five years following its opening provided no more than three such trains daily to Merthyr, yet paradoxically ran Sunday trains from 1841. Similarly on the Rhymney Railway a thrice-daily service on its main line sufficed until as late as 1871. Even when these services were increased as a result of the population growth in the valleys, and the increase, when times were good, in disposable income, particularly by the middle class, there could be some remarkable imbalances in such services. The Barry Railway throughout its entire independent life never ran more than half a dozen passenger trains daily to the Rhondda valley, yet its passenger service on the 'Cardiff Branch' was over thirty such trains daily. Ever independent the Brecon & Merthyr Railway had its own idiosyncratic methods of working in that the passenger services from Newport to Rhymney and Brecon were run separately, even though they shared the same metals for nearly eighteen miles as far as Aberbargoed Junction. This method of working arose from the historical accident that the two sections of the Brecon & Merthyr were physically separated for a number of years. It took a landslide in 1930, which severed the Rhymney branch north of New Tredegar, to oblige the Great Western to reorganise things on a more logical basis. Similarly by another historical accident the passenger service from Gilfach Goch never ran to Llantrisant despite the fact that there was a direct connection, but to Bridgend. Such workings always had to reverse at the isolated station at Hendreforgan, whereas mineral traffic continued to Llantrisant by way of Gellirhiad Junction. This unique arrangement survived until the withdrawal of the passenger service in 1930.

Obviously the first passenger services, which remained the mainstay of such traffic down through the years, were those which shuttled up and down the valleys linking the developing towns within them, and providing access to the major towns along the coast and the South Wales main line. Had they remained independent of each other, as they did for many years, an isolation forced on them in large measure by the geography of the region, they would perhaps call for little comment. However, under the competitive pressures of the time that were responsible for connecting many valleys to more than one dock outlet, inter-valley connections were built, often at great cost and no little ingenuity. One such line was the Pontypridd, Caerphilly & Newport which was a useful outlet to Newport for the Taff and Rhondda collieries. Such links however were often fraught with operational difficulties, and the PC&N was one such. Between Caerphilly and Machen, to ease the gradients for loaded eastbound coal trains, the up and down lines separated into two single lines on opposite sides of the valley for a distance of about one and a half miles. However, as a result of links such as this a limited passenger traffic between many valleys grew up which had by the 1930s developed into some quite lengthy and complex services.

The obvious way to travel from Merthyr to Cardiff was down the Taff valley. In 1938 however, the 10.49am service ran via the GWR/RR Joint Line, down the west side of the valley to Quakers Yard, thence by way of Penallta Junction and Ystrad Mynach to Caerphilly and Queen Street. It arrived here at 11.52am, a very good time and well within what was then the normal range of journey times from Merthyr to Queen Street direct. There were also similar services from Merthyr to Newport via Pontypridd and Caerphilly which were extensions of the original Pontypridd to Newport workings of pre-grouping days. The 10.51am from Merthyr was in fact extended to give a through service to Pontypool Road,

57xx class 0-6-0PT No 7766 pauses at Brandy Bridge Junction on the ex-Taff Vale Railway south of Merthyr Tydfil; the pannier is standing on the original Taff Vale main line to Plymouth Street station which stands behind the bridge in the background carrying the ex-Vale of Neath line to Merthyr High Street station. The double track on the right was joint GWR/ TVR which gave the local company access to High Street station. (M. Hale)

arriving at 12.56pm, a very roundabout way to get there. Pontypool Road was also served at this time by a regular Saturdays only service from Barry Island, by way of Cardiff and Ystrad Mynach. This working was part of the weekend summer service to and from Barry Island, of which more later.

There were also regular services in the summer months from the valleys to destinations much further afield at this period. On Saturdays there were workings from Treherbert to Moat Lane, Barry to Llandrindod Wells, and Cardiff (Queen Street) to Aberystwyth. The Moat Lane train left Treherbert at 10.00am, travelled down the Rhondda Fawr to Rhondda cutting, thence continued via Merthyr, Pontsticill, Talybont and Tallyllyn Junction to Moat Lane. The return service was at 2.06pm, Treherbert being reached at 6.49pm. The Barry to Llandrindod Wells working also ran via Merthyr and the Brecon & Merthyr line, departing at 11.00am, and running under class A express headlamps, very rare on a valleys' train. The reverse working returned to Barry at 8.09pm having left Llandrindod Wells at 4.15pm. The Aberystwyth service from Cardiff (Queen Street) was however the odd man out. Once again heading into the heart of Cambrian Railways territory it did not do so via the B&M route, but ran by way of the Rhondda Fawr and then the Afan valley to join the South Wales main line at Briton Ferry. Taking the Swansea Avoiding Line it then ran to Carmarthen to reach the Manchester & Milford line, eventually arriving in Aberystwyth at 3.23pm, having started from Cardiff at 10.05am. The section from Carmarthen to Aberystwyth was run in a creditable 2hr 3min, nearly half an hour faster than the remainder of the passenger workings on this line. The reverse working departed from Aberystwyth at 3.25pm, eventually arriving once again at Cardiff (Queen Street) at 8.56pm. By far the longest of these valley workings in 1937 was the 24 December 3.10pm service from Paddington to Treherbert, with the return working at 3.25pm from Treherbert on the 27th. The route was via Newport, Caerphilly and Pontypridd, with of course an engine change at Newport.

The route of the Aberystwyth train, along the Rhondda Fawr and the Afan valley, was the most commonly used inter-valley link. It was originally a co-operative venture between the Taff Vale and Rhondda & Swansea Bay railways, which saw the inauguration of a Cardiff (Queen Street) to Swansea (Riverside) service. By the late 1930s the Great Western had enlarged the number of through passenger trains by increasing both starting and terminal points. Thus by 1938 there were comprehensive services to Swansea (High Street) via Queen Street from Bute Road, Penarth, and Cadoxton, together with separate workings to Briton Ferry and Neath (General). Altogether at this period there were half a dozen such workings daily in both directions.

As well as these regular services, excursion trains, assiduously promoted by the Great Western, featured prominently for many years. It is now almost forgotten that the valleys' railways gave the majority of the local population what was probably their only chance of a day trip to the seaside, or perhaps to a popular local event. In today's society where paid holidays are normal and expectations are much higher than they were even two decades ago, it is difficult to appreciate how, for over half a century, the prospect of a day out at Barry Island or Porthcawl was eagerly anticipated by those who lived and worked in the valleys. This was equally true of those who worked much further afield, and under the influence of good advertising, coupled with cheap rates, the Great Western drew traffic to Barry Island from as far away as Birmingham, the Black Country, Taunton, Reading and even London itself. But the majority of such traffic on

Valley crossing. This diminutive Taff Vale Railway signal box was situated some four hundred yards east of Mountain Ash (Oxford Street) station. The Abercynon to Aberdare line is in the foreground. Behind and to the right the winding gear of Nixon's Navigation colliery dominates the scene, while between the far buildings and the hillside beyond ran the river Cynon and the GWR Pontypool to Neath line. (J. Morgan Collection)

High summer at Barry Island. 56xx class 0-6-2T No 5645 heads an excursion into Barry Island station on 25 July 1959. An up working can be seen in the background alongside the lines descending to the level of the dock. Woodham's yard stood to the right of the underbridge. (S. Rickard)

On 16 May 1954 ex-LNWR G2 48921 arrives at Barry Island from Tredegar. This train would have run to Pontllanfraith, then via the Pontypool to Neath line, crossed to the Rhymney valley to Ystrad Mynach and the ex-Rhymney Railway, joined ex-Barry Railway metals at Penrhos Junction and continued via Tyn-y-caean Junction and Cadoxton to Barry. These excursions probably had the most tortuous route of any to Barry Island. (S. Rickard)

summer weekends was from the local valleys, and it reached enormous proportions in the late thirties, and from the end of World War II until almost the end of steam workings in South Wales. During these years it was not unusual for almost the entire population of a valley's mining town to descend upon Barry Island, such was its popularity.

The beginnings of this traffic though were modest enough. In the case of Barry Island it was the desire of the Barry Railway to develop the island as a resort for the middle classes of Cardiff, while also of course increasing their revenue. Porthcawl was slightly different. The opening of the Port Talbot Railway in 1897 destroyed Porthcawl's coal-exporting trade within a very few years. Faced with this fact the Great Western successfully built up a tourist traffic making use of Porthcawl's wide beaches, the only sheltered sandy beaches between Barry Island and the Gower. However, Porthcawl never achieved the level of popularity of Barry Island. This was just as well perhaps, considering its limited rail facilities, although there were plans immediately before World War II to improve the access to the branch at Pyle, on the South Wales main line, and to double it as far as Nottage. As with so much else after 1945 the changed conditions were such that this scheme was never finished. Only the improved access from the Swansea direction was ever completed.

The story of the founding and growth of the Barry Railway is too well known to warrant repetition here, but there is one aspect that is pertinent to its later popularity as a resort. The Barry's major passenger traffic was not on its main line, but on its 'Cardiff branch'. In fact the company's first revenue-earning trains were put into traffic on this line from Cadoxton to Cogan, and one of the Barry's major early battles was over the access of its passenger trains into Cardiff. It actually threatened that, if necessary, it would do so over its own metals if running power concessions over the Taff Vale Railway were not granted.

Looking at Barry after, say, the first decade of this century, it is difficult to believe the reason why this early passenger traffic was so important to the railway. At this period it was a fine modern town. The offices of the company proudly looked out over the property they administered. Behind them the town was one of the most prosperous in South Wales. Fine shops had been established, near the railway of course, and street upon street of new houses of all types covered the slopes to east and west above the docks. Yet some twenty years before Barry had been like a frontier town in the American west. It was a shanty town inhabited by the many who remained of the thousands of navvies that had built both dock and railway. It had few paved streets, and the small number of permanent buildings had been cheaply built. The public houses were rowdy and fights and

Long distance excursions to Barry Island were also popular. On 18 August 1963 Grange class 4-6-0 No 6856 Stowe Grange *stands ready for the return journey at the head of an excursion from Evesham. (S. Rickard)*

69

*Porthcawl 1960. On 5 June
51xx class 2-6-2T No 5169
arrives with an excursion from
Newport. Another such working
can be seen on the right of the
picture. This engine spent its time
working local services on the
Porthcawl branch before
returning (S. Rickard)*

Things that went bump in the night

At Llantrisant shed there was a boiler washer who was an exceptionally sound sleeper. He knew his problem and came to an arrangement with the 'call boys' that they would take his front door key from under the doormat, let themselves in, walk upstairs and actually shake him until he was awake. The system worked perfectly, except once. The young lad on call duty did as requested. He shook the sleeping figure only to be rewarded with an almighty scream that was quite obviously female, and reputedly woke half the neighbourhood, as well as the boiler washer who came rushing in from the next bedroom. The poor 'call boy' was as frightened as the woman in the bed! It transpired that the sleeper was the boiler washer's daughter, a nurse at a London hospital, who had come home unexpectedly and her father, forgetting he was on call, gave her his bed to sleep in!

56xx class No 6663 removing the empty stock of an Eastern Valleys' excursion from Barry Island on 16 May 1954. (S. Rickard)

woundings were commonplace, and of course the usual 'pleasures' offered to sailors the world over were also available here too. In its earliest years Barry was definitely an unsavoury place, being compared unfavourably with its larger neighbour's famed Tiger Bay. With this reputation the Barry company quite obviously had a difficult problem in attracting respectable people to work in the many responsible positions available. Working in Barry had its attractions, certainly, but nobody in their right mind wanted to live there at that time. Similarly businessmen, while realising Barry's potential, had no desire at that stage to move, or set up offices in the town. So the railway had the task of quickly developing what would now be called commuter traffic from Cardiff, and in the undertaking of which it was very successful. From these beginnings, which concentrated on a middle class market, the Barry company took the bold decision to exploit Barry Island as a seaside resort, in the manner of successful developments elsewhere in the country. In 1896 it opened Barry Island station, and by the following year had tunnelled beneath a headland and opened Barry Pier station, from which, in 1908, it instituted its own short-lived steamer services on the Bristol Channel. These services were almost immediately replaced by the paddle-steamer operations of P. & A. Campbell which continued in regular summer operation until the 1960s. The Barry Railway did all it could to encourage the growth of these new services to Barry Island, and soon ran its first excursion trains from the Rhondda valleys. The popularity of these excursions was immediate. Barry Island grew apace, and was soon drawing trippers from other valleys. This traffic increased to such an extent over the next few years that by the time of the grouping its once deadly rival, the Taff Vale Railway, together with the Rhymney and London & North Western railways, worked bank holiday

Barry Town in Edwardian days. Despite being one of the more wealthy of the South Wales railways, Barry Railway coaching stock was of modest standard, was unheated (except for the saloons reserved for the directors and the manager), and until 1920 exclusively six or four wheeled. Yet surprisingly nearly all the stock was electrically lit, but being thus non-standard the GWR fitted oil lamps after 1923! (L&GRP)

Rebuilt Taff Vale Railway A class 0-6-2T No 390 working a football excursion, is halted by signals near Leckwith Junction in 1954. (H. Phillips)

excursions with their own coaching stock and locomotives. From this time on until the early 1960s Barry Island never looked back.

At one time or another nearly every class of Great Western engine, except of course Kings and 47xx class 2-8-0s, could be seen on excursions to the Island. Local depots would press into service every available engine they could find. Taff Vale A class 0-6-2Ts, vied with their brethren from the Rhymney in the shape of engines of the A and AP classes, together with, of course, Barry Railway engines, all of which were gradually replaced by the ubiquitous 56xx class as the years went by. 41xx class 2-6-2Ts from Ebbw Junction, and in later years the Rhymney valley, would also be seen. The smaller 45xx class 2-6-2Ts were certainly not unknown on these trains either. Pannier tanks were also often used, and excursions from the valleys behind Llantrisant or Tondu were frequently in the capable hands of 57xx class 0-6-0PTs. In the years after nationalisation the larger 94xx class of pannier tank was also a visitor. From the Sirhowy valley came London & North Western Railway 0-8-0s, together with the occasional London Midland & Scottish Ivatt class 2 2-6-2Ts, and in earlier years such workings could be headed by an L&NW Coal Tank from Tredegar. From further afield came Halls, Granges, and Castles, and in the early 1950s even a British Railways Britannia class 4-6-2 once worked an excursion to the resort. On these long-distance services 43xx class 2-6-0s predominated for many years however, anything larger having to be sent to Cardiff for turning before its return journey, until an alternative route through the docks which avoided the steep climb behind the Barry Railway's locomotive works used by the 43xx class 2-6-0s, eased this restriction.

Barry Island trains from either the Barry main line or the Cardiff direction, met at Cadoxton South Box, to the east of Cadoxton station. Immediately west of the station at Docks Line Junction, passenger trains took up the northernmost pair of the now quadruple running lines. Shortly after the southernmost pair of this quartet branched into a further pair and all four tracks began their descent to the low-level dock lines, while beyond them the high-level goods lines ran between fans of sidings above Barry's two docks. Beyond Barry Dock station,

British Railways Standard class 3MT 2-6-2T No 82002 entering Barry Town station on a return working to the valleys, a few moments before a thunderstorm broke in the summer of 1954. (H. Phillips)

overshadowed by the handsome offices of the Barry Railway, the long left-hand curve past the No 1 Dock high-level sidings, and the red-bricked locomotive works, took trains to Barry Town station. The high-level sidings adjacent to the No 1 Dock were used to stable empty excursion stock, which could be found stored as far back as Cadoxton if these were full.

The down platform at Barry Town station was an island, both faces of which could be used for excursion traffic, a convenient feature if a Barry to Bridgend train was waiting to depart from its usual position at the inner platform face, since an excursion to the Island could be diverted around the outer face. This would give any train spotters aboard a better view over the engine shed, which was adjacent to the station but at a lower level. At the western end of the station the lines to Barry Island diverged from the Vale of Glamorgan line on a very sharp curve and a falling gradient, then climbed again at 1 in 80 before swinging gently left into Barry Island station.

The layout at this station was improved in 1929 by the Great Western in order to cope with the burgeoning excursion traffic, but even its efforts were limited by the restrictions of the site, and at times of intensive working it was not an easy station to operate. The station still has a platform (No 1) that opens directly out on to the road on the seaward side, the beach being a short distance away beyond the funfair. This platform was extended into No 2 platform as a terminal road, but it was only possible for an engine to run around its train or haul it to the nearby carriage sidings from a crossover at the end of No 1 platform, thus reducing its usefulness. Platforms 3 and 4 were on an adjacent island platform, with carriage sidings beyond. At the eastern end of the station the line to Barry Pier descended past platform 2, on the up side, and the carriage sidings on the down, and entered the tunnel through the headland to terminate at Barry Pier station. Originally double tracked the line to the Pier station was singled in 1929.

The working of the excursion traffic at the Island station was fascinating. It would be signalled into one of the faces of the island platform and the engine uncoupled. Meanwhile the train engine of a previous excursion, which would usually be waiting in a short siding near the West Signal Box, would couple on to the rear of the train. When ready the empty stock would be dispatched back to Barry, take the up relief line past Barry Town station and park the stock beyond in the high-level sidings nearby, if any were free, or in similar sidings further eastwards if they were full. The engine would then return light to the shed to be prepared for its return journey, although it was not unknown for it to return to the Island for another load of empty stock. Tender engines would have to be turned of course before working their trains back from Barry in the evening.

When the excursions returned in the evening the procedure was reversed. Engines came off shed and picked up a rake of empty coaches from, say, behind Barry locomotive works, and hauled them to the Island. The train engine for this stock was already there having previously brought in another train set, and having uncoupled was waiting on an empty road or in the siding near Barry Island West Signal Box. At these times engines did not haul their own stock from stabling sidings to the Island. This practice could make for some interesting engine and stock combinations if a returning excursion to, say, Birmingham and rostered to a Hall, was to be preceded from the Island by a Merthyr working of non-corridor stock, hauled by a Taff Vale Class A engine. On peak days like these the normal timetable was thrown out of the proverbial window, and a special timetable for that day put into operation. This would indicate the revised timings to Barry

In this view of Porthcawl taken on 7 July 1962, 64xx class 0-6-0PT No 6431 is seen entering Porthcawl on an auto working from Pyle. The fine array of semaphore signals is noteworthy. (S. Rickard)

(since the loads could be much heavier than usual), train numbers, the following turn to be worked to the sidings after arrival at Barry Island, together with the return times and departure platform. Back-up trains in the Cardiff valleys were also available if needed and their paths allocated. Thus would thousands be returned homewards from a day out to visit the sea, the sands, and not least, the funfair.

Returning excursions departed at a rate of one every five minutes for a period that could extend for up to four hours. This traffic would use three principal routes beyond Barry, before reaching the main valleys and dispersing to their many final destinations, just as it had done, in reverse, earlier in the day. Excursions from Merthyr, Treherbert, Maerdy, and Aberdare would most likely have been 'all stations' to Pontypridd, thence from Treforest be routed to the Barry Railway main line and arrive by way of Wenvoe and Cadoxton. In fact it was not uncommon for these trains to work back immediately to the valleys and return later on a similar working. If congestion was especially severe on the Barry main line, excursions would be routed by way of Radyr and on to the Penarth lines, and arrive via Grangetown and Cogan. But since this interfered, south of Penarth Curve, with the regular services to Barry and Penarth, as well as any Barry Island excursions from Cardiff, Newport (and beyond), or the lower Rhymney valley, it was avoided if possible.

For this reason excursion traffic from the Rhymney valley north of Aber Junction, together with that from the Sirhowy, was routed to Penrhos Junction. From here it ran to Tyn-y-caeau Junction where it joined the Barry main line. Trains from the Taff-Bargoed valley joined the Rhymney valley line at

Jokes at the General

In common with others, in the times that it existed, the Great Western Railway was, let us say, less than enthusiastic about the Welsh language. This was frequently put to good account by the staff of the Booking Office at the (then) Cardiff General station when a new ticket clerk – from England of course – joined the staff there. As is mentioned elsewhere Cardiff General station had one of the most extensive ranges of tickets on the Great Western, covering every eventuality, or so it thought. However what was not allowed for was some wag, another railwayman of course, being asked to come to the appropriate window when a new clerk was on duty, and *demand*, not ask, for a ticket to Abertawe (which those beyond Offa's Dyke know as Swansea). At such times all the staff in the Booking Office would swear, of course, that they had never heard of the place. Many such a clerk was almost driven demented by such insistent 'passengers', their reactions varying from patient questioning and eventually finding out where Abertawe was, and then attempting to persuade the 'passenger' to purchase a ticket to Swansea (these were the clever ones), to adamant refusal to admit to the existence of such a station.

Ystrad Mynach South having left the Pontypool Road to Neath line at Penalltau Junction. The Sirhowy valley excursions probably had the most interesting route, as well as motive power. They would begin, perhaps, at Nantybwch or Brynmawr on the London & North Western Abergavenny to Merthyr line, travel by way of Tredegar to Pontllanfraith (High Level) where they would join the Pontypool Road to Neath line at Bird-in-Hand Junction, and thence by way of a spur to Ystrad Mynach North, join the Rhymney valley line. From here they would follow the same route to Barry Island as other excursions from the northern end of this valley.

From the valleys of Monmouthshire excursion trains would run by way of Newport. Those from Ebbw Vale or Nantyglo in the Western Valleys took the westward spur from Park Junction to Ebbw Junction where they joined the main line, while those from Blaenavon or Abersychan in the Eastern Valleys travelled by way of Pontypool (Crane Street) and Panteg & Griffithstown to Llantarnum Junction, reaching the main line east of Newport High Street station at Maindee South Junction.

The third route taken by excursion traffic was from the west, but only infrequently included anything from West Wales as they had a choice of seaside resorts closer to hand. Excursion traffic from the Llynfi, Garw and Ogmore valleys, by way of Tondu, therefore provided the bulk of this traffic from this direction, and excursions from these valleys kept the Vale of Glamorgan line quite busy on a summer Saturday. Such workings, however, terminated at Barry Town station, since the junction for Barry Island faces Cardiff and not Bridgend. Passengers either walked across the causeway or waited for a scheduled service to reach their destination. Finally one should not forget the excursions originating in the Ely valley from Gilfach Goch, Tonyrefail and Penygraig. From Llantrisant these trains ran along the main line to Cardiff and deviated at Leckwith Junction to Penarth Curve, and thus approached Barry from the Cardiff direction.

That such volumes of traffic were so successfully handled each summer weekend, for many decades, is a testimony to both the men and machines who worked to their limits to ensure that the service ran smoothly, and that all passengers had an enjoyable day out.

As popular as the seaside was, however, excursion trains were also run to other destinations, particularly on bank holidays. In Monmouthshire during the Whitsun weekend of 1935 such workings included a Whit-Sunday half-day excursion to Bournemouth, via Westbury, Salisbury and Poole, for the princely

Valley terminus at Senghenydd at the head of the Aber valley. The Rhymney Railway station stands just before the Universal colliery, the connection to which curves away on the right hand side of this undated photograph. (L&GRP)

A selection of Rhondda & Swansea Bay Railway notices at an ungated crossing at Jersey Marine on 14 August 1949. (L&GRP)

Cymmer Afan was the Rhondda & Swansea Bay Railway's station at Cymmer. Out of the photograph to the left was the Great Western Cymmer General station, the pannier tank is standing on the exchange sidings between the two stations. In the background can be seen the GWR viaduct that crossed the valley and connected with the South Wales Mineral Railway, near the end of which was Cymmer's third station, Cymmer Corrwg. Cymmer Afan was unique in that it housed a licensed bar, a feature that ensured the building's survival and continued use after all the other railway buildings had been demolished. (L&GRP)

sum of seven shillings (35p). The train departed from Newport High Street at 10.40am (having connected with special valleys' workings). Five minutes later a similar excursion departed for Southampton and Portsmouth, the slightly more expensive fare of seven shillings and sixpence (37½p) covering not only the longer journey, but also included, at Southampton, the option of a guided tour of the liner *Berengaria*. On Whit-Monday the West Country was not forgotten since Taunton, Exeter, Dawlish, Teignmouth, Newton Abbot, Torre, Torquay and Paignton could all be visited. However, an early start had to be made and the day was long. Newport was left at 2.10am, but one did have the, perhaps dubious, advantage of reaching Paignton as early as 6.15am. Return from here was at 11.00pm, Newport being reached at 1.15am the following morning. There were also special trains to Bristol (the Zoo has always been popular with South Walians, and such excursions were known to local railwaymen as the 'monkey specials'), Windsor (with a steamer trip to Marlow), as well as Hereford, Reading, Tenby, Pembroke and Fishguard.

Closer to home local sporting events that Whitsun were well covered. Glamorgan Cricket Club played the South African touring team at the Arms Park, and there was greyhound racing at Newport. There were no special trains to Ely (Main Line) which was the station for the nearby Ely Racecourse, since unusually there was no meeting that Whitsun, connoisseurs of the turf having to content themselves with a steeplechase at Caerleon, or catch the 7.16am excursion from Newport for a day out at the Wolverhampton course. For those not so inclined there were special trains to a Baptist rally at Pontsarn, a hospital fête at Merthyr and, for the politically minded, a Labour demonstration at Pontypridd.

Glyncorrwg station in the isolated Corrwg valley. The coaching stock is an ex-GWR suburban set used on the colliers' trains. (R. O. Tuck)

78

Accounts

The accounting system once in use on the Great Western Railway was such that the responsibilities that fell on the shoulders of stationmasters could be quite daunting, as at their small single platform station at Ebbw Vale. Until nationalisation the Ebbw Vale Steel Company (and its successor) used to pay in at his station the quarterly account for all outgoing traffic from the steelworks carried by the company. This account, which whilst varying, depending upon the level of traffic, was frequently in excess of a quarter of a million pounds.

These are only a small selection of the excursions that were on offer in the thirties, a time when bank holiday advertisements for such trains came not as leaflets, but as twenty-page booklets. Amongst them all, however, I have a particular favourite. This was the combined rail and theatre ticket, as it was termed, run from certain stations in the Western valleys of Monmouthshire to Abertillery. They were valid, by certain trains only, for any of the town's four cinemas. For no more than one shilling (5p), if one was unfortunate enough to live as far away as Brynmawr or Crumlin, one could, for example, during Easter week in 1931, enjoy films starring Constance Bennett, Mary Astor, and the incomparable Greta Garbo.

What are now termed commuter services were also run, those operated by the Barry Railway have already been referred to, but many other similar services were developed by other companies, particularly in or around Cardiff and Swansea, as well as between other towns in the area. No directly comparable services were developed in the valleys, except perhaps, the intensive workmen's services built up over the years to serve the collieries, steelworks, industrial estates and, during World War II, munitions factories.

The most intensive commuter services were in the Cardiff area, established in the early years of this century by the Taff Vale, Barry and Cardiff railways. They were maintained, largely as they stood in 1922, by the Great Western, and only drastically revised in 1953 when the Cardiff Valleys interval services were introduced. The Taff Vale services, using steam rail-motors and auto-trains, as well as conventional stock operated from Bute Road to Queen Street and beyond to Llandaff, interspersed with which were shorter runs to the two halts on the fringe of central Cardiff, Cathays and Maindy (North Road). Services from Clarence Road also featured highly, with businessmen's trains to Penarth and beyond operated by the Taff Vale, and to Barry operated by the Barry Railway. These services were run over Great Western metals as far as Penarth Curve South Junction, and both Clarence Road and Riverside stations (the latter merely the outlying platforms of Cardiff General station) were GWR property, yet that company did not operate the passenger service between them until after the grouping. As if this were not odd enough, the freight service on the branch was only ever operated by the Great Western. Such could be the complexities of train operation in South Wales, although in certain parts of the valleys even this arrangement would have appeared simple.

As Cardiff's northern suburbs flourished the Cardiff Railway provided an excellent means of reaching the central area. In 1938 some twenty-two up and twenty-three down trains operated Monday to Friday on its branch, the fortunes of which have varied widely over the years. Originally intended as an alternative route to bustling Pontypridd, when this scheme fell through it mouldered as an inconsequential branch beyond the suburbs that then existed. As Cardiff grew apace it became a flourishing commuter line, then nearly perished in the 1950s as the use of the private car spread wider. But it survived and today flourishes once again in the revival that Cardiff's local lines have undergone in recent years.

Outside the Cardiff area commuter services were virtually non-existent. The only comparable services were in Swansea and were operated on the London & North Western line between Swansea (Victoria) and Pontardulais. On this section in the early thirties some fifteen workings each way were run Monday to Friday, and in addition a further half a dozen through trains each way ran to and from the Central Wales line. With the exception of one to Cardiff, which was quite intensive, Newport had no such services at all. Last to be recalled of these services was the longest, that from Cardiff to Porthcawl. Although twenty-nine miles distant from Cardiff it boasted an up businessmen's train in the morning, and a return, in 1938, at 5.10pm, the journey time of which, including five stops, was fifty-seven minutes.

Within the valleys, however, one important class of working, comparable to the commuter services of Cardiff, were the workmen's trains, which were not shown on the public timetable. By far the majority of these trains were for colliers, which for obvious reasons before the introduction of pithead baths, used old rolling stock exclusively reserved for their use. But in addition similar services for the various steelworks were also run, and in later years for other industries that came to the area, such as the Northern Aluminium Company (now Alcan) at Rogerstone, and the factories on the Treforest Trading Estate. There were also, during the forties, important munitions factories at Pembrey, Tremains (near Bridgend), and Glascoed (near Pontypool), which employed many thousands, many of whom lived considerable distances away. For the workers at Tremains services would run as far as Treherbert, by way of Llantrisant and Pontypridd, while workers for Glascoed were brought in from as far afield as Rhymney, Ystrad Mynach and Brynmawr. Trains from the latter worked via Llanhilleth up the steeply graded mineral connection to the Pontypool Road to Neath line, and were the only regular passenger workings this connection ever saw.

By far the longest running services though were the colliery workings. In the days before the grouping it was not unknown for the colliery to provide the rolling stock and the railway company the engine, passenger brake van and train crew. This was certainly the case in the Rhymney valley, and this method of contract working applied to both the Brecon & Merthyr and Rhymney railways. In the Sirhowy valley, though, the London & North Western provided complete trains of old four- and six-wheeled stock for this purpose, in addition to which they also had an agreement with the Tredegar Iron & Coal Company allowing the latter to run its own workmen's trains, powered by one of its engines and using its own stock, to its collieries at Whitworth and Ty-Trist. Immediately before World War II the variety of such services was immense. They included trains from Dowlais (Central) to Bargoed and Bedwas, Pengam to Fochriw, Fleur-de-Lis to New Tredegar, and Newport to Machen in the Rhymney valley alone. In the Western Valleys could be found similar workings such as the shuttle services between Aberbeeg and Cwm of the 'Partridge Jones & John Paton' colliery trains, and the workmen's services between Abercarn and Brynmawr or Aberbeeg and Beaufort. These are but a few examples of this once intensive traffic found outside the public timetable which made up yet another part of the pattern of services designed for the inhabitants of the valley towns.

The village of New Tredegar in the Rhymney valley rises above 94xx class 0-6-0PT No 9488 as it waits to depart with a Newport train. The Spartan waiting room of this ex-B&M station is noteworthy. (R. E. Toop)

5
ENGINES LARGE AND SMALL

It is probably impossible to count or estimate the number of steam locomotives that for one hundred and twenty years or more toiled in the South Wales valleys. Those that are within the memory of today's generations were the successors to some eighty years of development, tailoring in certain cases the general design of the steam locomotive to the specific requirements of the South Wales valleys. Development, however, implies a conscious attitude to change, which was not always the case. In fact trial and error, combined, in the less prosperous companies, with harsh economic attitudes, would be a better description of what actually occurred.

To find logical developments in the design of South Wales locomotives one has to look at the policies of the major companies that operated in the valleys, including of course the Great Western whose locomotive activities in the area were a reflection of its continuous changes and improvements elsewhere. Of the South Wales railways only the Taff Vale, between 1856 and 1897, built its own locomotives, both the Rhymney and Barry railways contenting themselves with detailed specifications to locomotive builders. Home built or not, however, such designs were based on engines originally supplied by locomotive builders and modified by experience, and gave rise to a number of classes of engines.

On the Rhymney Railway from 1908, for example, there appeared the closely related R, P, A and AP classes. All these locomotives were 0-6-2Ts, the R and A classes being designed for mineral traffic, while the P and AP classes were for passenger duties. There was also the S class 0-6-0T designed for shunting. Although there were minor differences between the original boilers of the P, A and S classes, which were of the round-top type, they later shared the same design. After 1913 all new engines were built with Belpaire boilers (becoming the P1, A1 and S1 classes respectively), and some of the earlier engines were rebuilt with these boilers. The AP class, the last Rhymney Railway design, carried Belpaire boilers from the start. All these locomotives also had the same pattern of inside cylinders which were of 26in stroke and diameters of either 18in or 18½in.

All these locomotives were designed by Mr C. T. Hurry Riches, the Locomotive Superintendent of the Rhymney Railway from 1906 to 1922. He was the son of Mr T. Hurry Riches who held the same position with the neighbouring Taff Vale Railway between 1873 and 1911, where he was responsible for the introduction of standard classes as early as 1874 with the commencement of building of the K class 0-6-0, of which no fewer than eighty-five of this, and the almost identical L class, were built. The Hurry Riches, père et fils, were not the only related locomotive superintendents on South Wales railways. J. H. Hosgood and his brother W. J. Hosgood held this position on the Barry Railway (1888–1905) and the Port Talbot Railway (1896–1905) respectively.

Trial and error, which usually meant buying the standard product that the

While Rhymney Railway R class 0-6-2T No 35 could not be described as beautiful it had a certain powerful and rugged appearance, a feature it shared with all the later engines built for the Rhymney Railway which survived, basically unaltered by the Great Western, until their withdrawal. No 35 is seen here at Cardiff East Dock shed on 29 October 1955. (D. K Jones)

An example of the GWR practice of selling surplus locomotives to South Wales railway companies. The locomotive is Alexandra (Newport & South Wales) Docks and Railway No 28, formerly GWR No 1683, an 0-6-0ST of their 1661 class. It was purchased by the ADR in November 1906. The coaching stock is also second-hand and is in fact two of the three 'Barnum & Bailey' coaches formerly used in their circus train that had toured the country a few years earlier. They were purchased by the ADR in 1909. For a number of years following their purchase these coaches were used on the Pontypridd to Caerphilly service, however the location of this photograph is unknown. (Pontypridd Library)

locomotive builders had on offer – obviously cheaper than specifying modifications – went hand in hand with the purchase of second-hand engines. In the majority of cases, however, the smaller companies placed their reliance in the standard products bought off the shelf from the private locomotive builders, and over the years all the major ones and a few lesser known ones, such as the Brush Electrical Engineering Company, supplied them. When the purchase of second-hand engines was undertaken these came principally from major English railways, including the GWR, LNWR, LBSC, LSWR, North London and Mersey railways. They also came from second-hand suppliers, such as the Bute Supply company, from the contractors who built the line, and even local mines or steelworks. Such expedients were resorted to by a number of railway companies, including some quite large ones such as the Alexandra (Newport & South Wales) Docks and Railway and the Brecon & Merthyr Railway. Such policies rarely provided the purchasing company with appropriate motive power, but did provide them with a wide variety of engines, frequently in the form of non-standard one offs, often quite inappropriate for the type of traffic to be moved, but which must have been quite an entertainment for nineteenth-century enthusiasts.

Of the more improbable second-hand purchases, seven LNWR tender locomotives converted to tank engines, and originally dating mainly from the late 1840s no less, purchased by the A(N&SW)DR between 1875 and 1880, and the somewhat large-wheeled LSWR 4-4-2T of the Brecon & Merthyr, are two examples that spring quickly to mind. Only a little less improbable were the purchases by the Burry Port & Gwendraeth Valley Railway of two 0-4-4-0 Fairlies, although to be fair one of them, *Mountaineer*, had a reasonable lifespan, as did the three outside-framed 0-6-4Ts bought by the A(N&SW)DR from the Mersey Railway. Such then was the locomotive legacy handed over from fiercely independent local railways to the GWR in the early nineteen-twenties.

It might well be asked what the GWR was doing in the area during this period, and the answer must be – very little specifically tailored to South Wales' needs. Despite having owned collieries in the Rhondda and Afan valleys, the Great Western's share of the export coal trade was small compared with that of the local companies. Even those with which it was closely allied, the Rhondda & Swansea

The 'Lady' that went home in style

Long before the demise of steam many a South Wales engine was regarded with affection not only by enthusiasts, but also by railwaymen as well. Nowhere perhaps is this better illustrated than in the story of the last days of 2906 *Lady of Lynn*. She was one of Churchward's Saint class, built in May 1906 and withdrawn in August 1952, the last example of that famous passenger class to work from a South Wales shed. Officially condemned on 16 August it remained 'on shed' at Canton, in its usual resting place

alongside the southern wall of the straight shed until the 28th when the call came to return for the last time to Swindon. During this period however, the old lady was not forgotten or allowed to languish in the grime of her hard work. Under the orders of the shed foreman *Lady of Lynn* was polished until she sparkled, particular attention being given to the safety valve cover, which had not long previously been replaced (and in the full knowledge that she had not long to go; the old lady having been easily recognisable for many a

long day by the very unusual absence of this distinctive Great Western feature). Despite the fate that was in store for her, *Lady of Lynn* was going home clean and tidy, and she was not being towed up to Swindon to die either, she was going to leave South Wales as she had arrived, many years before, as a revenue earning engine! And she did, resplendent at the head of the 6.25am Cardiff to Moreton Cutting Goods, finally working light engine back from there to Swindon in the early evening at the end of that turn.

Rebuilt Taff Vale Railway 04 class 0-6-2T No 282 poses at Aberdare shed circa 1950. (S. Rickard)

Bay and the Port Talbot railways, by and large followed their own independent ways in matters of locomotive policy before 1908, and thereafter took what the Great Western had on offer from its range of standard engines, or their second-hand cast offs.

The Great Western owned no major ports in South Wales before 1922 and was therefore never, in South Wales terms, a major exporter of coal up to this date, although its interest in the Port Talbot Railway should not be overlooked. Its involvement in the Monmouthshire, Ely, Ogmore, Llynfi and certain smaller valleys were therefore largely confined to the English market for coal. Even here though, it held no monopoly since it had to compete with coastal shipping, a largely unremarked-upon traffic in the annals of the South Wales coal trade, but one that once moved substantial tonnages. The position in the Aberdare and Neath valleys was somewhat different, since over its metals was the only access these valleys had to the docks at Swansea.

Thus the Great Western concentrated on the long haul to inland English markets in the Midlands, for which it was well placed, and the South and South West, where until 1886 and the opening of the Severn Tunnel, it was at a considerable disadvantage. As a result, with two exceptions, it saw no need to develop locomotives specifically for the coal trade. The first exception was William Dean's Aberdare class, an outside-framed 2-6-0 introduced in 1900, and so named from the preponderance of that class allocated to the Great Western shed in Aberdare. The second was G. J. Churchward's 42xx class 2-8-0T introduced in 1910 and which was the tank engine version of the well known 28xx class 2-8-0. The majority of the class spent most of their lives in the area, and for a few it was the only home they knew.

It has been written, and I have heard it said, that in South Wales, following the grouping, the reputation of the Great Western Railway was not as high as elsewhere. Perhaps there is some truth in this. The pre-grouping companies were long established and had provided safer and more continuous employment in the days during which the valleys were developing and the economy was buoyant. The GWR though, through no fault of its own, had within only a few years to manage the newly combined system through times of desperate economic problems, and in order to survive was forced to take many painful measures. But even if there is some truth in what has been written and said, such a reputation is largely undeserved. Reference has already been made to some of the Great Western's efforts to sustain, and where possible stimulate, the trade of South Wales and to ensure that technically the area was to the fore, and perhaps it is in the area of locomotive power that this can be most clearly seen.

In 1922, 1938 and 1947 the Newport, Neath and Cardiff Valleys Divisions together operated respectively some 44%, 40% and 37% of the total of Great Western locomotives, but while the total number of GWR engines in South Wales fell from a peak of some 1,700 as the twenties and thirties progressed, eventually stabilising from about 1938 to 1947 at around 1,400, their composition changed dramatically. Between 1922 and 1947 some 808 newly built engines were allocated directly to South Wales, and up to the end of construction of steam locomotives of GWR design in 1956, no fewer than 1,000 such newly built engines had been allocated here. These new locomotives arrived in substantial numbers over three distinct periods. The first influx was between the years 1925 and 1930, when a total of 355 engines were added to stock, with 1928 and 1930 being the peak years with 72 and 74 engines respectively. This was a rate of building never surpassed in later years. In this period those new engines allocated to valleys sheds were principally of the 56xx and 57xx classes and represented the Great Western's programme of replacing old and worn-out pre-grouping locomotives with their own standard types. In addition a number of 42xx class engines were allocated to the main line sheds. Such was the Great Western's commitment that Collett even broke with the company's standardisation programme by designing an 0-6-2T (the 56xx class) in deference to the proven abilities and usefulness of this type in the South Wales valleys.

The second surge in new engine allocation to South Wales occurred between the years 1934 and 1939 when a further 239 engines came brand new to the area. This time however the majority of these new engines were of the 72xx class as well as further examples of the 57xx class. Interestingly, however, in this period was the appearance of 64xx and 74xx 0-6-0PTs, 41xx class 2-6-2Ts, 48xx class 0-4-2Ts (better known perhaps as the 14xx class following their renumbering), together with eight Castles and nineteen Granges. Valleys' sheds saw a reasonable number of the 57xx class and the majority of the 64xx class, which were introduced to run the auto-train services, replacing older engines of this type. However the main line sheds were the principal beneficiaries during these years.

South Wales saw one final period of rapid introduction of new locomotives. Between the years 1949 to 1952, 136 such engines were introduced during the post-war replacement period, when locomotives of GWR design were still being built. Hawksworth designs now predominated, although it was not until 1950 that No 6779, the last 57xx class engine to be sent new to South Wales was built.

It was allocated to Cardiff East Dock shed, which coincidentally, in 1956, had rendered to its care the last GWR-designed locomotives to be built by British Railways, when the 94xx class 0-6-0PTs 3401–9 were sent there.

In complete contrast to the GWR policy was that of the LMS, or more truthfully perhaps their lack of one. Long before the turn of the century the ambitions and influence of the London & North Western and the Midland railways had passed their peak. As a result South Wales thereafter never figured largely in their thinking, nor that of their successor the LMS, so much so that even as late as 1945 that company's locomotive representation in the area was still predominantly of LNWR or Midland Railway vintage. Only Paxton Street in Swansea, with some fourteen Stanier 8Fs, and a handful of Fowler 2-6-4Ts, together with Upper Bank in the nearby Swansea valley, which had a sprinkling of early 1930s 0-6-0Ts, developed from an earlier Midland design, could sport anything approaching modern locomotives.

While the Great Western's programme of new locomotive allocations to South Wales was in progress there was a reverse side to the coin. Many of the engines taken over in 1922, or shortly afterwards, were in poor condition, particularly those of the Barry Railway. The effects of World War I had taken their inevitable toll on locomotive maintenance, following which the pending take-over did little to encourage local management to invest in renewals or heavy repairs, although the Taff and Rhymney companies did invest in new locomotives at this time.

As a result withdrawal of South Wales engines was immediate and sweeping, although up to 1925 the rate of renewal was greater than that of withdrawal. But

While the locomotive stocks of the South Wales railways were, in their later years dominated by the tank locomotive, tender types were once quite common. This was particularly true of the Taff Vale Railway which bequeathed 41 such locomotives to the GWR at the grouping, all of which were K or L class 0-6-0s. Here in earlier years TVR No 46 of the K class is a pilot engine on the Blaenrhondda branch, at the very top of the Rhondda valley. The date of the photograph is unknown. No 46 was built in 1879 and renumbered in 1910. (Gordon Coles Collection)

From the Appendix to Section 9 of the Service Time Tables, *March 1950.*

COLLIERY LINES AND PRIVATE SIDINGS OVER WHICH W.R. ENGINES WORK OR EXCHANGE TRAFFIC.

Station (or Signal Box).	Name of Siding.	Point to which W.R. Engines work.
CARDIFF TO PONTY-PRIDD.		
Maindy Bridge ..	Cardiff Corporation Water-works Siding	Not to enter Siding.
" "	Wagon Works	As far as necessary.
" Fuel	Wagon Works	To Board.
" "	British Wire Ropes Siding ..	To Board on Loop Line.
" " " ..	" " " ..	To Board.
Roath Branch Junction..	Fram Works	" "
Pentyrch Crossing ..	Melingriffith Tin Plate Works	" "
Taffs Well Siding ..	Taffs Well Siding	Nos. 1 and 2 Roads 50 yards beyond gate Nos. 3 and 4 Roads, to board.
Maesmawr	Maesmawr	As far as necessary.
"	Trading Estate	56XX and 66XX to Northern connection only, Engine No. 2000 elsewhere.
PONTYPRIDD To BLAENRHONDDA.		
Pontypridd Junction ..	Penrhiw Colliery	Clear Crossings beyond Railway Boundary.
" " ..	Maritime Colliery & Coke Ovens	To Board on all roads.
Gyfeillon, Lower ..	Tymawr Colliery Outlet ..	As far as necessary on full roads.
" " ..	" " " ..	To boards on roads on Boiler Sidings.
" Upper ..	" " Inlet ..	As far as necessary.
" "	Gyfeillon Colliery Inlet ..	To Hand Points.
Eirw Branch Junction ..	Woodfield Colliery ..	To Board, Nos. 1, 2, 3, 4 and 5 Roads.
" " " ..	" " " ..	To Board on No. 6 Road.
" " " ..	Coedcae Colliery Outlet ..	To Board, both roads.
" " " ..	" " Inlet..	To Board.
" " " ..	Cymmer Gas Works ..	"
" " " ..	" Colliery ..	To boards, No. 2 Level Road and Gullet Road.
Llwyncelyn	Trehafod Colliery ..	To Boards, all roads.
Naval Colliery Junction	Naval Colliery Outlet ..	To post about 90 yards south of Weighbridge.
Pwllyrhebog	" " Inlet ..	To Boards.
Llwynypia Upper ..	Llwynypia Inlet ..	Gullet road, to board ; to clear of connections on other roads.
Gelli	Gelli Colliery	To boards on Nos. 3 to 8 Sidings.
"	Ystrad Gas Works Siding ..	To Unloading Shed.
Maendy Ystrad ..	Maendy Colliery, Ystrad ..	To post about 316 yards from gate, Nos. 1 and 2 Sidings.
" "	" "	To post 250 yards from gate, No. 3 Siding.
" "	" Eastern ..	To Board.
Ystrad	Ystrad Timber Yard ..	30 yards inside gate.
Cwmparc	Cwmparc Siding ..	As far as necessary in Sidings. Not to enter Wagon Repair Yard.
Abergorkie	Abergorkie Siding ..	To Board.
Ynisfeio	Factory	"
Ynisfeio	Ynisfeio	" South side River Bridge.
Treherbert South ..	Bute Merthyr Colly. Outlet ..	"
Treherbert ..	" " Inlet ..	
R. and S.B. Junction ..	Tydraw Colliery ..	To. Nos. 1, 2, 3 and 4 Sidings only.
Fernhill	Fernhill Colliery Outlet ..	To Weighing machine.
"	" " Inlet ..	To points leading to Screens.
"	Blaenrhondda Colliery ..	As far as necessary.
"	Washery	No. 1 Road as far as necessary.

Colliery Lines and Private Sidings over which W.R. Engines work or exchange traffic—
continued.

Station (or Signal Box).	Name of Siding.	Point to which W.R. Engines work.
PORTH TO MAERDY.		
Ynishir	Lady Lewis Colliery Outlet ..	Nos. 1, 2 3 Roads as far as necessary. No. 4 Road to board.
National	Ynishir Standard Inlet ..	Nos. 1 and 4 Roads, as far as necessary. Nos. 2 and 3 Roads, to Points.
,, ...	United National Colliery ..	To board on Empty Road. As far as necessary other roads.
Tylorstown	Cynllwynddu Colliery Outlet	To Board.
Pendyris Lower	,, ,, Inlet ..	To board on No. 3. As far as necessary on Nos. 1 and 2.
,, ,, ..	Generating Station Outlet ..	To second pair of Points in Main Line.
,, ,, ..	,, ,, Inlet ..	To first pair of Points after Catchpoints.
,, ,, ..	Pendyris, Lower Outlet ..	As far as necessary.
,, Upper ..	,, Upper Inlet ..	To Board.
Ferndale	Ferndale, Pitwood Siding ..	To Boards.
Ferndale, Lower ..	Ferndale, Lower ..	As far as necessary on Nos. 1 and 2. To crossings on Nos. 3 and 4.
,, Upper ..	1 and 5 Sidings Inlet ..	Clear of all Crossings.
Maerdy Junction ..	Ffaldau Colliery	To Board.
,, ...	Maerdy Colliery ..	As far as necessary. To Board No. 4, Outlet Sidings Nos. 1, 2, 3 and 4 Sidings.
PWLLYRHEBOG BRANCH.		
Blaenclydach	Blaenclydach Colliery ..	As far as necessary.
Brook Vale	Brook Vale Siding ..	One wagon length inside gate.
Clydach Vale	Clydach Colliery ..	To boards on Full Sidings.
PONTYPRIDD TO MERTHYR.		
Pont Shon Norton ..	Craig-yr-hesg Quarry ..	To Board.
Stormstown	Abercynon Colliery ..	To Boards.
Black Lion Crossing ..	Merthyr Vale Colliery ..	To Board.
Plymouth Sidings ..	Plymouth Colliery ..	Nos. 1, 2, 3 and 4 Sidings to post.
Abercanaid Crossing ..	,, ,, Abercanaid	To board.
Brandy Bridge	Gas Works Siding	As far as necessary, except Red and Blue Engines.
ABERCYNON TO ABERDARE AND BWLLFA.		
Pontcynon	Pontcynon Junction ..	As far as necessary.
Penrhiwceiber, Lower ..	Penrhiwceiber Siding Outlet ..	Nos. 1 to 7 as far as necesary. Nos. 8 and 9 to Board.
,, Upper ..	,, Inlet ..	To Boards on Nos. 1, 3 and 4 roads.
,, ,, ..	,, Gas Works ..	To the Weighing Machine.
Mountain Ash	Nixon's Navigation, Mountain Ash.	To Board.
,, ,, ..	Nixon's Deep Duffryn ..	To Board.
Abercwmboi	Abercwmboi, Lower ..	To Board for road with sharp curve. As far as necessary other roads. 56XX Class Engines not to enter 3, 4 and 5 Sidings.
,, ...	Middle Duffryn ..	To the bridge.
Cwmbach Junction ..	Park Siding	As far as necessary.
Aberaman	Aberaman Colliery ..	Half mile inside gate on main road. To Boards other roads.
Bwllfa, No. 2 Lower ..	Bwllfa No. 2 Outlet ..	To Board.
,, ,, Upper ..	,, ,, Inlet ..	,,
YNYSYBWL BRANCH.		
Windsor Passing Siding	Windsor Siding ..	To Boards, Nos. 1, 2 and 4 outwards roads ; as far as necessary other roads.

Both reports from the Appendix to Section 9 of the Service Time Tables, *March 1950.*

Colliery Lines and Private Sidings over which W.R. Engines work or exchange Traffic—
continued.

Station (or Signal Box).	Name of Siding.	Point to which W.R. Engines work.
CILFYNYDD BRANCH.		
Cilfynydd	Albion Colliery Inlet	To Post or Board.
	,, ,, Outlet ..	,, ,, ,,
COWBRIDGE BRANCH.		
Llanharry	Glamorgan Quarries	South end, to, but not over, safety points.
		North end, to Shoot.
,, ...	Glamorgan Hematite Iron Ore Co.	To the Screens.
,, ...	Llanharry Limework Co. ..	To the Screen on Screen Road.
		To Red post on Lime Kiln road.
LLANTRISANT BRANCH.		
Llantrisant	Newpark (Ministry of Food) ..	As far as necessary, except through the crossover road, which is prohibited.
Llantwit Fardre ..	Cwm Colliery	As far as necessary.
,, ,, ..	Nova Oil and Solvent Co. ..	To the gate.
LLANTRISANT—		
No. 1 BRANCH.		
Creigiau	Creigiau Quarry	As far as necessary.
PENARTH BRANCH.		
South Wales Portland Cement Siding.	South Wales Portland Cement Siding.	Inlet. Clear of safety points.
		Outlet : To first turntable by old iron Stone Road to Shearman's. Clear tail of Crossing.
Grangetown	Cardiff Gas Co.	To Board on old Gantry Roads.
		As far as necessary on new Gantry Roads.
Ely Paper Mills	Ely Paper Mills	To Warehouse on Pulp Road.
		To Office on Paper Road.
		To Board on old Van Road.
		Not to enter Sidings off Pulp Road.
PENARTH HARBOUR BRANCH.		
Grangetown Low Level	Gas Works Sidings	To Board.
Penarth Harbour Branch	Windsor Slipway	To Board.
,, ,, ,,	Shell Mex Ltd.	As far as necessary.
,, ,, ,,	Henry Pritchard & Co. ..	To Board.
,, ,, ,,	Principality Wagon Works ..	To gate.
,, ,, ,,	Currans Ramp Sidings ..	As far as necessary.
Penarth Harbour Branch	South Wales Public Wharf and Transport Co.	Prohibited.
,, ,, ,,	C. Kite & Co., Ltd.	To gate.
,, ,, ,,	Dixon's Rope Works	Prohibited.
,, ,, ,,	National Benzol Co. ..	To Board.
,, ,, ..	Vacuum Oil Co.	,,
,, ,, ,,	Anglo-American Oil Co. ..	As far as necessary.
,, ,, ,,	Taff Wagon Co.	To Board.
,, ,, ,,	Western Trinidad Lake Asphalt Co. Ltd.	,,
,, ,, ,,	Victoria Wharf	Prohibited.
PENARTH DOCK.		
Penarth Dock ..	Pontoon Siding	Prohibited.
ROATH BRANCH.		
Roath Branch ..	Cardiff Corporation Siding ..	To Corporation Iron Fence Gates.
,, ,, ..	C.W.S. Siding	Clear of Safety Points either end.
,, ,, ..	Marcroft Wagon Co. ..	To gate.
,, Goods Yard ..	International Alloys	To gate.
,, ,, ,, ..	General Plant Reconstruction Co. Siding	To gate.

Colliery Lines and Private Sidings over which W.R. Engines work or exchange traffic—
continued.

Station (or Signal Box).	Name of Siding.	Point to which W.R. Engines Work.
EAST BRANCH.		
Cardiff Queen Street Sth.	Welsh Cold Storage Co.	As far as necessary.
STONEFIELD TO RHYMNEY BRIDGE.		
Cardiff (Crwys)	Cairn Street Sidings	To gate.
,, ,,	Cathays Coal Yard	,, ,,
,, ,,	Crwys Coal and Timber Co.'s Siding.	,, ,,
,, ,,	Victoria Coal Co.'s Siding	To Wheel Stop.
Caerphilly (Wernddu)	Wernddu Brickworks	30 yards inside gate.
,, ,,	Tar Distillation Plant	To Boards.
,, ,,	Cefn-On Dolomite Co.	As far as necessary.
,, (Aber Jct.)	Welsh Metal Industries	Clear of points only.
Llanbradach	Llanbradach Colliery	As far as necessary.
,,	,, Coke Ovens	,, ,,
Pengam (Bargoed Pits)	Bargoed Colliery	,, ,,
Brithdir	Elliott Pit	,, ,,
Pontlottyn	Rhymney Merthyr Colliery	To Red post on either Siding. South end 80 yards from Catch Points. North End 30 yards from Catch Points.
Rhymney	Rhymney Iron Works	As far as necessary.
HEATH JUNCTION TO NANTGARW.		
Whitchurch	Phoenix Brickworks	As far as necessary.
	D. Morgan Rees & Sons	,, ,, ,,
	Hopkinsons, General Motors	As far as necessary, but not to exceed 4 m.p.h. over weighbridge.
,,	R.O.F.	To Board.
CAERPHILLY TO SENGHENYDD.		
Abertridwr	Windsor Colliery	To Boards.
Senghenydd	Universal Colliery	To gate.
CAERPHILLY TO TAFFS WELL.		
Taffs Well	Rockwood Colliery	To Weighbridge.
,, ,,	Garth Works	45 yards beyond points.
YSTRAD MYNACH TO DOWLAIS (CAEHARRIS) AND ZIGZAG BRANCH.		
Ystrad Mynach (Tredomen)	Tredomen Engineering Works	As far as first crossing inside gate.
Bedlinog	Bedlinog Colliery	Not over Weighing Machine. As far as necessary on other Sidings.
Cwm Bargoed	Fochriw Colliery	Over all Sidings.
Dowlais Cae Harris (Dowlais Junction)	Furnace Top Sidings	No. 4 to Board. Others as far as necessary.
,, ,, ,,	Dowlais Trading Estate (Steel Works Branch).	As far as necessary.
Dowlais Cae Harris	Hall's Factory	To Board, 560 yards beyond connection with Zig-Zag Line.
CYLLA BRANCH.		
Ystrad Mynach (Penrhiwfelin)	Penalltau Colliery	To Crossings from road leading to Colliery Weighing Machine and Screens.
BARRY AND COGAN JUNCTION.		
Barry Docks	Gas Works Sidings	Engines heavier than Barry " B " class not to enter these Sidings, and railway engines must not go beyond the buildings adjacent to the Sidings.
,, ,,	Syndicate Siding	No restriction on Engines not heavier than Barry " B " class.
,, ,,	Wagon Repairs Co.'s Siding, near No. 4 Tip (High Level)	" A " and " B " class engines to points only.

from 1926 onwards as the economic stormclouds gathered, withdrawals exceeded renewals, a situation that was to remain unaltered (except for a few years in the late 1930s and early 1940s) until the final demise of steam in the valleys. This imbalance between the new and the old, coupled with the inevitable transfers away as industrial activity declined, saw the total locomotive stock in South Wales fall continuously from the mid-1920s.

1926, 1928, 1932 and 1934 were particularly bad years, with the latter two seeing not only extensive withdrawals of pre-grouping engines, but also substantial scrapping of locally based GWR engines too. 1926 saw 84 withdrawals of which 82 were pre-grouping engines, while in 1928 the figures were 109 and 42 respectively. In 1932 numbers were much the same, but in 1934 out of a total of 94 withdrawals no fewer than 55 were of Great Western origin. A roll call of these engines gives a vivid snapshot of the South Wales situation regarding Great Western locomotives (as opposed to pre-grouping ones) at this time. Of perhaps some thirty to thirty-four classes represented in valleys and main line sheds, scrapping occurred in nine of them. The axe fell most heavily on the elderly 0-6-0PTs, thirty-three in all being scrapped, with the 1076 class losing sixteen, the 850 class eight, the 1813 class five, the 1501 class three, and with the remaining engine coming from the 1016 class. Twelve four-coupled tank engines also disappeared, six each from the 517 and Metropolitan classes. Seven Aberdares were also scrapped. The remaining three engines were 3901 class 2-6-2Ts, conversions of Dean Goods engines to suburban tanks and dating from the 1907 to 1910 period. Used on local passenger workings these were the last of the class to be withdrawn, two from Landore shed and the remaining one from

Cardiff Canton in high summer. Identifiable in this line-up of 14 August 1951, are three Castles, five Halls, a WD 2-8-0, and the shed pilot (1205 ex-A (N&SW)DR). (Seaton Phillips)

Let her go!

A spectacular sight in the Rhondda valley was afforded on the rare occasions that a locomotive worked unassisted up the Pwllyrhebog Incline. The technique was to draw back as far from the foot of the incline as possible and let her go! The sight, not to mention the sound, of one of the TVR 'H' class 0-6-0Ts hurling itself up that 1 in 13 was something to behold.

Neath. 1934 has, it will be recalled, been mentioned as one of, what might be termed, 'the better years' for the allocation of new locomotives to South Wales. While this is certainly true, the forty-five new engines came nowhere near replacing the numbers of those withdrawn.

As far as the pre-grouping locomotives were concerned, by the end of 1929 more than half the locomotives taken over from the A(N&SW)DR, TVR, B&M and P&M companies had been scrapped and by the end of 1934 of the fifteen South Wales companies more than half of the engines of thirteen of them had been scrapped, or sold. Of the valleys' companies only the BPGV engines escaped for any length of time. So much so, that of their admittedly small number of fifteen, only two had been scrapped by the end of 1951. Conversely no less than 136 TVR locomotives had gone within seven years of take-over. Despite all this, though, only two companies' engines, those of the Gwendraeth Valley and the Neath & Brecon railways, did not survive the 1930s. In fact 243 of the original 793 pre-grouping locomotives which passed into Great Western stock, some 31% in all, survived into British Railways ownership. A decade later, however, it was nearly all over. Only nine remained beyond 1957, all shunting engines. The last survivor was the Cardiff Railway 0-4-0ST No 5, better known as GWR No 1338, which after some seventeen years at Bridgwater Docks, between 1943 and 1960, was withdrawn from Swansea East Dock shed in September 1963. The last 'main line' pre-grouping engines to be withdrawn were Nos 36 and 38, Rhymney Railway R class 0-6-2Ts, which departed on their final journey to Swindon and oblivion in October 1957.

To talk of the locomotives of the valleys, or for that matter those of South Wales in general, is to talk of hard-working freight and shunting engines. None has ever been exalted as have the passenger classes, and when such eulogies to Castle, Star, Saint and King have been penned, the South Wales main line has featured last in the writer's mind by a long way. Notwithstanding this lack of attention, South Wales was home to some outstanding engines. They were worked hard, often overworked and misused in fact, but for all that many gave years of reliable service in the valleys that they served.

Above all, one type, the 0-6-2T, became well nigh synonymous with these valleys. First introduced into them by the Taff Vale Railway in 1885 it proved an immediate success, providing an engine that had the majority of its weight available for adhesion, combined with that extra bunker size made possible by the trailing axle, which gave it sufficient range, due to the extra coal and – more importantly – water it could carry, to make the docks from the furthest colliery at the top ends of the valleys. High speeds were not a criterion of these engines, even on passenger workings, so the necessity of a leading pony truck was avoided, allowing a short overall wheelbase, usually of the order of 20 to 22ft, which avoided the use of large-diameter turntables in valleys sheds where space was often at a premium.

*On 25 April 1953 No 215, an
ex-Taff Vale Railway 04 class
0-6-2T is seen at Barry.
(D. K. Jones)*

The majority of the pre-grouping 0-6-2Ts came from the TVR (209) and the RR (53) and represented some seventeen individual and frequently closely related classes of these companies' engines. As in many areas of life, within a group someone has to be different. In this case it was Cornelius Lundie of the Rhymney Railway, that grand old man who rigidly ruled the locomotive affairs of that company for no less than forty-five years. He it was who, when all about him were building side-tank engines of this wheel arrangement, built forty-six of a unique saddle-tank version between 1890 and 1900. In all, the pre-grouping companies owned 400 0-6-2Ts, some 50% of their entire stock of locomotives in 1922 in fact, to which the Great Western added a further 186 out of the 200 such engines it built between the years 1924 to 1928. It was these latter, the famous 56xx class, perhaps more than any other, that gave what in today's terms would be called the 'corporate image' to the valleys.

Equally at home on mineral or passenger duties it was a highly successful design, although it has been said that there was some initial teething trouble related to the valve gear, but this was corrected at a very early stage. In the valleys, with the exception of the Gwendraeth, they were ubiquitous, only one of the main sheds, Llantrisant, appears never to have had an allocation, a claim it shared with only a handful of sub-sheds which included Branches Fork, Dowlais Central and Pwllyrhebog. They never featured prominently at the Docks sheds of Swansea or Cardiff, which is to be expected, but neither, and this was possibly a reflection of the differences in practices and preferences between the local railways and the GWR, did they appear in large numbers in those valleys monopolised by the GWR before 1922, and then only at Aberdare after World War II.

Concentrated therefore in the Cardiff Valleys Division, whose total allocation from 1928 to 1938 does not appear to have dipped below about one hundred, and had only fallen to seventy-seven by about 1955, these handsome hybrids of valleys and Swindon practice, quickly established themselves as strong, reliable replacements for many a local type. The design was basically a blend of Swindon No 2 boiler on a modernised underframe, but of identical wheelbase, taken straight from the, then, most powerful valleys' 0-6-2T, the Rhymney Railway R class. At 200lb/sq in, the boiler was pressed to a higher figure than any South Wales pre-grouping type, and this, combined with 18in × 26in inside cylinders and the standard Great Western wheel diameter for freight engines of 4ft 7½in gave it, at 25,800lb, the highest tractive effort of any 0-6-2T to work in South Wales. The spacious cab was also an improvement on that provided before in the valleys, but by the mid-1930s all the class stationed in South Wales had had sliding steel shutters fitted to the cab side-openings. Need any more be said about Welsh weather?

Completely versatile in their abilities these sturdy tanks, which Swindon in a rare fit of generosity graced with copper-capped chimneys, could regularly be seen handling coal trains in excess of 900 tons down the valleys, a rake of sixty empty wagons up, normal passenger workings, or heavily loaded excursion trains. Thankfully for the traffic department their power was sufficient for them to handle the latter trains with ease, for frequently a sizeable proportion of the population of a mining town, from babies to grandmothers, would be crowded aboard for a day at the seaside, which usually meant Barry Island. On such a working it was a wonderful sight to see, and hear, them blast away from that

No 803 was Llanelly & Mynydd Mawr Railway Ravelston, and was built by Hudswell Clarke in 1911. From the mid-thirties, after a spell 'abroad' on the Cleobury Mortimer & Ditton Priors Light Railway it returned to Danygraig shed for much of the remainder of its life, where it acquired its warning bell for roadside work, before moving to Llanelly shed from where it was withdrawn in 1951. This photograph was taken in 1947 at Llanelly. (D. K. Jones)

station and cross the causeway to the mainland when returning on a Saturday evening to Treorchy or Mountain Ash or whatever town the population of which had descended on Barry Island for the day.

On their regular and more mundane duties, on say the 2.07pm Merthyr to Pontypridd, or the 11.18am Caerphilly to Rhymney Bridge, they had a fair turn of speed, if pushed. Such efforts, particularly when accelerating, were always accompanied by a surging motion, most noticeable in the first coach of the train. This was due to the combination of the balance weight distribution on the driving wheels, which, as on all two-cylinder locomotives could never completely cancel out the piston thrust, and the short coupled wheelbase of only 15ft 3in which was originally designed for negotiating curves of as little as 4½ chains radius. But perhaps their most arduous passenger turns were those from Nelson & Llancaiach to Dowlais (Cae Harris). Never enjoying a frequent passenger service, in 1932 only four such trains each way traversed the full length of the Taff Bargoed branch between Mondays and Fridays, this narrow defile would ring as, with a load of perhaps only two coaches, one of Cae Harris's allocation struggled to the bleak moorlands between Bedlinog and Dowlais up long, vicious grades much of which was at 1 in 49 or worse. So difficult was this branch that even these, the most powerful of the 0-6-2Ts, once worked iron-ore trains to the Dowlais steelworks in threes, two hauling and one banking, and I recall in the late 1950s when there was a regular pig-iron traffic from Cardiff East Moors steelworks to Dowlais Foundry, that it took two of the class to haul at most a dozen wagons to the exchange sidings below Zig-Zag Junction.

The 56xx class was one of the classic designs of locomotive used in the valleys and followed hard on the heels of a series of such pre-grouping classes. To describe them all is inappropriate here but two classes deserve mention as being among the best of the local types, although one only became so after thorough rebuilding by the Great Western.

The Taff Vale A class was introduced in 1914 and was conceived as the Taff Vale's premier passenger class. As built they had 5ft 3in driving wheels and large-diameter parallel boilers with Belpaire fireboxes. This combination ensured that they were topped with squat domes and chimneys, features that produced an impressive but rather ugly engine, the visual effect further marred by their restricted cab size. In this form the A class, which by 1921 numbered fifty-eight engines, was not an efficient design, poor steaming apparently being the reason. By late 1923 two of the class were at Swindon for rebuilding, one of them receiving a standard No 10 Swindon superheated taper boiler, together with an enlarged cab and bunker. This treatment proved to be highly successful and the complete class was rebuilt between 1926 and 1932, thirty-five at Swindon and twenty-three at the newly modernised works at Caerphilly. In this form they were an extremely reliable and handsome class of engines, both powerful and well liked, and with a good turn of speed. Never straying far from their original valleys they remained on passenger duties until 1953 when they were relegated to coal and shunting turns to finish off what was left of their lives. The largest group of exiles which did stray from their own valleys were fourteen at Barry, but these of course worked the passenger turns from there to Cardiff and the Rhondda. Only a handful wandered any distance, one getting as far as Danygraig, and another to nearby Swansea East Dock, while another pair performed banking duties from Pontypool Road shed.

The majority of 0-6-2Ts were designed however for mineral duties, and

LOCOMOTIVE COALS.

Lengthy experiments, both at home and abroad, go to prove that semi-bituminous varieties—14% to 22% volatile—are the most suitable and economical as a locomotive coal, where the draught is so strong that a slightly cohesive coal is preferred. This quality of fuel admits the use of firebars with wider air-spaces than can be used with "dryer" less binding coal, which would be liable to fall through the bars unconsumed, or only partly consumed.

To run strictly to scheduled time is the engine-driver's great aim in life, and to enable him to do so it is essential that he should be supplied with a fuel that will easily maintain at the proper pressure the head of steam required.

An ideal locomotive coal should possess the following qualities· The consumption should be small, and, per pound of coal burned, capable of converting the maximum quantity of water into steam· Its ignition should be rapid, and require but little, if any, lifting or breaking apart in the firebox. It must be low in ash, and what ash is left after combustion should be of a loose, flaky nature, absolutely free from iron pyrites, which, combined with other deleterious matter, and subjected to the intense heat evolved in the burning of the coal, may be converted into slag or clinker. From sulphur it should be as free as possible, and that the sulphur does not combine with iron is of the utmost importance. A fuel with very little smoke, soot or cinders is also highly desirable.

Of the many varieties of South Wales semi-bituminous and bituminous coals there are a number which conform with the foregoing requirements.

In tabulating the coals, due consideration has been given to their heating properties and physical characteristics, and especially to the fusing or non-fusing properties of their ash. The list contains about half a dozen coals which may be found to fuse slightly during combustion; and to know such coals, or to ensure that they be proportionately mixed with absolutely non-fusing kinds, so as to avoid any risk of clinkering, is essential. All the named fuels would give satisfactory results when used in the firebox of slow moving trains or shunting locomotives, but, as already indicated, there are a few varieties in the list which, if burnt unmixed with absolutely non-fusible ash coals, may clinker and cause endless trouble when burnt in a fast running express locomotive. On this point consumers are strongly recommended to an Analyst.

From The South Wales Coal Buyer's Handbook, *1824*

CARDIFF AND NEWPORT LOCOMOTIVE STEAM COALS.

Aberdare Graig.
Albion.
Bedwas Navigation.
Blaenclydach.
Britannic.
Cambrian.
Celtic.
Cilely.
Dowlais Cardiff.
Dowlais Merthyr.
Ebbw Vale Marine Waunllwyd.
Ebbw Vale Abercarn.
Graham's Navigation.
Great Western.
Griffin Nantyglo.
Hood's Merthyr.
Insole's Cymmer.
International.
Llanbradach.
Lewis Merthyr.
Mynydd.
Nantdyrus.
National Merthyr.
Naval
Newport Abercarn B.V.
North's Navigation.
Ocean.
Oriental Merthyr.
Penllwyngwynt.
Powell Duffryn Rhymney Valley.
Powell Duffryn Rhymney Merthyr.
Powell's Tillery.
Pyman's Merthyr.
Risca B.V.
Russells.
Sirhowy B.V.
Standard Merthyr.
Tirherbert.
Tirpentwys.
Tredegar.
Waun Wyllt.
Welsh Navigation.
Werfa Dare.
Western Valleys B.V.
Windsor.
Wyndham.

amongst them perhaps the best remembered is the Rhymney Railway R class. Originally dating from 1907 the final two were not added to stock until 1923, after the amalgamation, and in total the class comprised fifteen engines. Unlike the TV A class, rebuildings were few, only five engines being so treated between 1926 and 1949, a fine testimony to their sound design and the high standard of maintenance they received. Despite acquiring the usual Swindon adornments over the years, the unrebuilt engines, two of which survived to be the last of the class to be withdrawn, had a powerful rugged appearance, and for half a century were always equal to the tasks for which they were built.

Not all classes lasted as long however, either through poor design, or maintenance or the changing economic conditions. One that suffered because of this latter effect was the Barry Railway's F class 0-6-0ST. It deserves mention here since although its numbers were decimated in the 1930s, no fewer than twenty-two of the twenty-eight members of the class were sold to collieries. Ten of these remained in the valleys and had long lives, the last, still carrying its GWR number – 780 – surviving at Hafodyrynys colliery until June 1964.

Mention of the Barry Railway is a reminder that although wedded to the 0-6-2T type for much of their traffic needs, two local companies, one of which was the Barry and the other the Port Talbot Railway, desiring more powerful locomotives, turned to the eight-coupled type. The Barry's need for this extra power came from its practice of re-forming trains at Cadoxton sidings for the coal tippers, a journey of at most a mile and a half, and working forward much heavier loads. These engines were reputed to be able to move loaded coal trains of more than one hundred wagons on these short journeys. The requirements of the Port Talbot Railway were somewhat different, since it had some of the steepest 'main line' gradients of the valleys' system, with over three miles at 1 in 40 up the Duffryn valley through Bryn and on to the entrance of the Cwm Cerwin tunnel. Between these two companies sixteen such engines, four 0-8-0s, and twelve

All large sheds had 'shed pilots' – old engines eking out their last few years – but at Cardiff (Canton) between May 1951 and December 1955 ex-A(N&SW)DR 2-6-2T No 1205 was more interesting than most. It and a sister engine were built by Hawthorn Leslie in 1920 to work coal traffic from Pontypridd to Newport, their design being similar to a group of Mersey Railway 2-6-2Ts purchased some years before, and which had impressed the A(N&SW)DR by their performance. No 1205, which is seen here on 24 March 1954, would perhaps call for no further comment except that the year it was withdrawn, 1955, Hawthorn Leslie were building identical locomotives again for coalfield use, after a gap of 35 years, but this time for New South Wales. (D. K. Jones)

0-8-2Ts were operated. The first dated from 1889, when the Barry bought two second-hand tender engines from Sharp Stewart & Co. The last were three 0-8-2Ts bought by the PTR in 1902, one of which survived into British Railways ownership, not being withdrawn until February 1948. Not amongst the longest survivors were two PTR engines bought from the American Cooke Locomotive Co in 1899. Rebuilt in 1908 with a modified Swindon boiler (so much for the fiction that the PTR was independent of the GWR) the pair lasted until 1928/9. They were then a fascinating combination of GWR practice above the footplate and American below, where the only concession to English convention appears to have been the adoption of inside valve gear, even though the cylinders were outside. At first sight it may appear odd that these two companies chose such closely similar methods of overcoming their totally different operating problems, but it will be remembered that the locomotive superintendents of these two companies at this time were brothers.

While the introduction by the Barry and Port Talbot railways of eight-coupled locomotives proved that it was possible to use such types successfully in the area, as was later confirmed by the GWR itself, one such design turned out to be far from successful. The engines in question were H. P. M. Beames's 88-ton 0-8-4Ts, an LNWR design, but not introduced until after the grouping by the LMS in 1923. Naturally enough the LNWR had considered it needed something more powerful to raise to a reasonable tonnage level loads that had to be hauled up the valleys instead of down, as well as empties up the horrendous grades between Abergavenny and Brynmawr. Based on the G2 class 0-8-0 its ability to move loads up those banks was unquestioned, trials in 1923 establishing that they could re-start a train in excess of 200 tons on the 1 in 34 section of the climb through the Clydach gorge. But with that weight and with a four-wheel trailing truck their effect on the sharply curved tracks that occurred in some areas of the valleys can easily be imagined. In fact such was the propensity of these engines to derail or

No 5687 of Cathays shed rests between duties outside Duffryn Yard shed on 11 March 1959, probably having worked through from the Rhondda valley over the Rhondda & Swansea Bay line. (D. K. Jones)

damage the permanent way that towards the end of 1924 the GWR banned them altogether over the ex-Rhymney Railway lines into Cardiff, over which the LMS had running powers inherited from its predecessor. Obliged to persevere with them the LMS, while confining them in the main to the Abergavenny to Merthyr line, did allow them down to Newport on occasional passenger workings. As soon as reboilering became necessary from 1944 onwards the opportunity was taken to withdraw them quietly. In 1945 twelve were in South Wales, five at Abergavenny, three at Tredegar and four at Swansea (Paxton Street), but by 1951 the class was extinct.

Much more successful were the GWR eight-coupled tank engines, the 42xx class, introduced as that company's answer to the heavy short-haul traffic of the area. A compromise design produced when a tank-engine version of the 28xx class 2-8-0 main line freight engine was contemplated, this variant, built with a Standard No 4 boiler instead of the Standard No 1 of the 28xx class, together with, in its final form, 19in × 30in cylinders, proved an eminently suitable alternative. In view of the duties it was to perform it was built with tyres on the second and third pair of driving wheels thinner than those on the leading and trailing coupled axles, and perhaps more importantly, the trailing coupling rod bushes had spherical seatings at the forked end. Thus the design was able to traverse tight radius curves without the unfortunate effects upon the trackwork that the Beames 0-8-4T had.

The class had a long and very successful life in South Wales, and for over two decades the numbers in the area fluctuated very little, hovering around the 144 to 148 level. In complete contrast to the 56xx class they were almost exclusively allocated to the sheds of the Newport and Neath Divisions, only Barry shed in the Cardiff Valleys Division having any allocation. This practice dated from the panic in 1922 when the Swindon boiler inspector came to view the new additions to the Great Western stable, and stopped a large number of Barry Railway engines on the spot. To fill the gap a handful of 42xx class tanks were transferred there (together with some 2-6-2Ts) a situation that was to last until the mid 1950s. Their main stamping ground, however, was the Newport Division, with Newport itself usually having some thirty to forty, having settled at that figure from a peak of over fifty in the early twenties. As a consequence of this distribution pattern they were a common sight only in the Monmouthshire valleys, and to a lesser extent in those of the Neath and Llynfi. On the other hand they were the workhorses of the short-haul main line mineral workings from Llanelly to Severn Tunnel Junction. Because of their small bunker size their range was rather limited and, as is well known, in order to overcome this problem, which restricted their usefulness from the early 1930s, a number were rebuilt as 2-8-2Ts, the 72xx class, from 1934. In this form they roamed much further afield. Their range now included the West and South of England and they also worked the once very important iron-ore trains from Oxfordshire and Northamptonshire to the steelworks of South Wales.

The working of this latter traffic up the valley to Ebbw Vale, together with that of imported iron ore from Newport, was always arduous, taxing both crews and engines on the seventeen miles from Newport. Banking was normal. This traffic grew considerably in the 1950s, and as a result British Railways introduced its Standard 9F 2-10-0 to Newport to work these trains. One of British Railways' best known and most successful designs, their work on the iron-ore trains from Tyne Dock to Consett has been extensively recorded, but, strangely, not their

Abertridwr on the Rhymney Railway's Senghenydd branch on a peaceful summer afternoon. (L&GRP)

Maesycwmmer station in the Rhymney valley looking northwards, where the Brecon & Merthyr main line squeezed itself between the piers of the Hengoed viaduct, that spanned the valley at this point carrying the Pontypool to Neath line high above the valley floor. Parallel to the B&M on the opposite side of the valley at Hengoed, the Rhymney Railway performed the same feat as it too headed northwards. The rather bleak, no-frills architecture of many of the B&M stations is well illustrated in this photograph. (L&GRP)

The Rhymney Railway's Tirphil station with its distinctive layout of buildings which was dictated by the constraints of the site which was against the steep valley side with the road approach at a higher level on the left, circa 1920. (L&GRP)

Two of the 0-4-0T locomotives built at Dowlais works by the Guest Keen & Nettlefolds Company pose with officials during the visit of King George V and Queen Mary to the works on 27 June 1912. The engine on the right, coupled to the royal train, is No 40 King George V, *built in 1907. The engine on the left, despite the nameplate* Sandyford, *is in fact another member of the Dowlais fleet, the nameplates having been transferred to this engine on the day of the visit.*
(Dowlais Library)

similar duties from Newport to Ebbw Vale. Nos 92000–7 were first allocated to Ebbw Junction shed in 1954, and after trials in which two of them worked forty-four wagons up grades as steep as 1 in 59, more than doubling the previous maximum loads that could be worked, settled down to many years on these trains. For a period though, perhaps due to the well known prejudice at that time of ex-GWR drivers to the Standard types, they were used as bankers rather than train engines.

While the eight-coupled type sufficed for the majority of the higher power engine needs of the South Wales lines, two private companies had such unique requirements that they resorted to Beyer-Garratt-type locomotives to solve their problems. Vivian's Copper Works in Swansea had a steep and very sharply curved connection to the main line. Similarly the Guest Keen Iron & Steel Co in Cardiff had the same problem in the track layout either side of a dip that carried their line from the blast furnaces to the slag-tipping area on the foreshore, where the line ran beneath the incoming docks lines which were at road level.

Unique locomotive types such as this, designed to overcome specific operating problems, were unknown among the valleys' railway companies except in one instance. This was the Taff Vale Railway's H class 0-6-0T, introduced in 1884, for working the Pwllyrhebog incline to the Clydach Vale colliery, half a mile of which was at 1 in 13. Before 1884 it had been the practice to use old locomotives scheduled for scrapping on this incline, but the continual changing of the haulage equipment was a constant nuisance and expense. Hence the TVR decided

102

to build three specially designed engines solely for this work. They had steeply tapered boilers and inner firebox crowns, thus ensuring, since it was the practice to work with the boiler facing down the incline, that there would be no problems with uncovering the firebox crown. The wheel diameter was 5ft 3in, the Taff Vale's standard driving-wheel diameter for passenger engines, which was unusually large for an engine of this type. The working was counterbalanced however, an engine with its load working up the incline connected by a wire rope running around a drum at the top of the incline, to a similar engine and load descending, so large-diameter driving-wheels were no disadvantage. In addition it gave ample clearance for the haulage gear which was fitted beneath the engine. These three locomotives worked the incline until its closure in 1951, and they were unique as a class in the annals of engines absorbed by the GWR in that none was ever rebuilt.

Any reference to the steam locomotives that once worked in the valleys of South Wales, from the twenties onward, must include the Great Western 0-6-0PT types, and their saddle-tank predecessors. The sheer numbers of 57xx, 64xx, 94xx, 16xx and the earlier 1076, 1854, 2021 and 2721 class six-coupled tanks demand their mention. Again like the numerous 0-6-2T types they cannot all be described in detail here. But the success of the 64xx class is worth some attention. Derived from the 2021 class of pannier tank, which as saddle tanks had been introduced as far back as 1897, they were intended for auto-train working in the hilly areas where the gradients were beyond the capabilities of their larger-wheeled sisters, the 54xx class. The majority of the class were always shedded in the valleys, their numbers, between 1937 and 1955, varying between twenty-seven and thirty out of a total of only forty. They were concentrated mainly in the Newport and Pontypool areas in Monmouthshire, and Cardiff and the Taff valley sheds in Glamorgan. Lively and sparkling little engines with an excellent turn of speed on the two-coach auto-trains for which they were designed, they were the mainstay of the smaller branches and the more lightly loaded valleys 'main line' turns. In fact the South Wales main line itself was not unfamiliar territory to them, as twice daily in the fifties they scurried along from Cardiff General to St Fagans on Pontypridd-bound trains. Their small driving wheels certainly added to this air of speed that they conveyed, but such was their climbing power too that when

Amongst the more unusual engines to be found in South Wales – although only two saw service, and that was in industrial use – were the Beyer-Garratt type of articulated locomotives. Here Guest Keen & Baldwin 0-4-0 + 0-4-0 No 12 is seen at the East Moors steelworks in Cardiff. (L&GRP)

the LNWR tank engines began to be withdrawn from the Abergavenny to Merthyr services, extra 64xx class engines were drafted in to work these trains.

South Wales also featured prominently in the use of steam railmotors from 1903, when their early promise as a cheap alternative to the conventional train formation had not been tarnished by their inability to cope with extra trailers. The Alexandra Dock, Barry, Cardiff, Port Talbot, Rhymney, and above all the Taff Vale railways all had examples, although with the exception of the Taff Vale their numbers never multiplied beyond three in any one company. The Alexandra Dock Railway ran its two between Pontypridd and Caerphilly, while the Barry's pair were mainly confined to the Vale of Glamorgan line. The Cardiff Railway's couple worked from the Rhymney Railway's Parade station in Cardiff to Rhydyfelin, while the Port Talbot Railway were perforce required to run their single specimen up the steeply graded line to Bryn and beyond. But at least they had the sense to use a larger (six-coupled) engine unit than their contemporaries who universally used a four-coupled engine. On the Rhymney system they actually built two specially designed 0-4-0T locomotives, permanently coupled to their coaches, that were strong enough to take a six-wheel coach as an additional trailer. They were used between Machen, Caerphilly and Senghenydd, or from Rhymney to Ystrad Mynach.

The Taff Vale Railway was an exception. It operated no less than eighteen steam railmotors in all on a variety of services throughout its system. Exceptional too was its use of transverse boilers as opposed to everyone else's longitudinal. A Taff Vale steam railmotor was always recognisable by the smokebox door at the side of the engine unit, instead of in the usual position. All of the steam railmotors, of all companies, had disappeared by 1920, and many had been withdrawn some years earlier. They were defeated by heavier loads, two coaches being beyond the haulage capacity of their small boilers, and were replaced by the more versatile auto-engine workings, which survived until the demise of steam in the valleys.

One must not forget either that the Great Western was also in the steam-railmotor business at this time. Its units operated in South Wales for longer than any of the local companies. They operated in the Dare valley, and from Merthyr to Newport via Nine Mile Point, and from Pontypool Road to Oakdale by way of 'Hall's Tramroad'. Further west they operated out of Llanelly shed on the Garnant to Gwaun-cae-Gurwen service, and their workings from Neath shed included Swansea East Dock to Glyn Neath turns together with the service that lasted the longest in South Wales, that from Neath (Canal Side) to Court Sart, not withdrawn until 1935.

As important in the working of the railways in South Wales as the locomotives of the railway companies, were those owned by local industrial concerns, of which the coal and steel companies, or their nationalised successors, were the major employers. The steelworks systems were, of course, quite large and intricate, and so too were some of the colliery networks in the valleys. In the Cynon, Powell Duffryn had its own private rail systems linking its pits from Aberaman to Cwmbach and from Mountain Ash to Pontcynon, while in the Llynfi valley north of Maesteg, a complex private system linked North's Navigation collieries. The use of such engines for works shunting is as old as the railways themselves, and it is regrettable that their story has never been fully told. More than any other locomotives they were abused, overworked, often poorly maintained, and frequently operated over track that would make a railways inspector blanch.

104

No 2167 was Burry Port & Gwendraeth Valley Railway No 14 and was built by Hudswell Clarke in 1919. It was one of six similar engines provided by that company between 1912 and 1920. It is seen here at Llanelly on 26 April 1950. (D. K. Jones)

Some companies had fleets that were quite large. Guest Keen & Baldwins Ltd operated eighteen locomotives in the mid thirties at its steelworks at Port Talbot and Margam, while at Dowlais works in 1911, Guest Keen & Nettlefolds Ltd operated at least the same number. The British Copper Company at Swansea had ten engines in service in 1935, and Stewarts & Lloyd Ltd at Newport had a stable of four immediately after World War II. Among the colliery companies in the valleys, Powell Duffryn had at least ten in operation at various mines just before nationalisation, and at the same time the Ocean Coal Company had three at Cwmparc and one at Treorchy, and almost certainly had others. There were also a number of brave one offs, for example at the Abercarn Tinplate Company, Beynon Colliery at Blaina, and the Britannia Merthyr Coal Company colliery at Gilfach Goch. Locomotives owned by power companies also shunted their sidings at Upper Boat and Uskmouth.

Among their numbers every major engine builder from Andrew Barclay to the Vulcan Foundry was represented, together with a few of the minor ones. These included Parfitt & Jenkins of Cardiff, one-time supplier to the Cardiff Railway, from which one of its 0-6-0STs found its way to J. Vipond & Co at Talywain, and at an earlier date the Neath Abbey Iron Company of Briton Ferry, one of its 0-6-0STs working for the Coalbrookvale Colliery Company at the turn of the century.

Mention of Parfitt & Jenkins is a reminder of the second-hand trade in small tank locomotives from the railway companies themselves. The Great Western's efforts in this direction have already been referred to, but it is interesting to note that the Ocean Coal Company at Cwmparc, and Guest Keen Iron & Steel, Cardiff, both bought six-coupled side tanks of 1887 vintage built by the Great Eastern at Stratford.

These methods of obtaining locomotives were not of course unusual; however it was unusual for industrial concerns to build their own. But this was done at Dowlais from 1906 to 1920. Between these years two six-coupled, and seven four-coupled tank engines, one of which was of 3ft 0in gauge for working in the Bessemer steelmaking shop, were designed and built there. They were also unusual among industrial locomotives in their design, in that they all combined side tanks with inside cylinders. They were eminently suitable for their jobs however, some being transferred to the Guest Keen steelworks at Cardiff after 1930, No 7, built in 1907, surviving there until 1950. Such examples of longevity are not unique, however; in the seventies examples of Peckett and Avonside engines dating from before World War I could still be found in action. But by this time the most common sight was the Austerity type 0-6-0ST, built for the Ministry of Supply by a variety of manufacturers in World War II, these engines having been purchased second hand in large numbers by the National Coal Board.

Before we take our leave of South Wales engines, the main line itself should not be ignored. The Newport and Neath Divisions were never blessed with the latest main line engines as they were introduced. With only rare exceptions Canton and Landore had to be content with accepting passenger engines displaced from London or the West of England as they in their turn were replaced by new members of existing types, or new classes. Although not an exception to this rule the introduction of the British Railways Britannia class 4-6-2 was noteworthy. In 1952/3 Nos 70025–9, the Star series, were allocated to Cardiff Canton. From here they performed very well indeed on the top link duties for many years, working turn and turn about with Canton's stud of Castles, a typical roster being the 8.00am Cardiff to Paddington, 1.55pm Paddington to Swansea, and 8.30pm Swansea to Cardiff, a diagram of some four hundred miles. Their entry into service in South Wales coincided with the period when British Railways Standard classes had a poor reputation on GWR territory, although well liked elsewhere. Prejudice by ex-GWR drivers was claimed to be at the bottom of the problem, but the Canton crews took to them and produced fine work from them. The first to reach South Wales in November 1952, was 70026 *Polar Star*. I well remember seeing it arrive for the first time at Cardiff General, so it was particularly sad to see it when it returned for the last time to South Wales in April 1967 to Cashmore's yard in Newport, to be reduced to scrap in forty-eight hours.

Such then were the steam locomotives that for over one hundred and twenty years toiled in the valleys of South Wales. Their story deserves to be told in full one day, not in the briefest of outlines as has been given here, nor as an adjunct to the Great Western types, but in their own right as a distinctive part of the British steam locomotive story.

6
VALLEY SHEDS AND STATIONS

To house, maintain and operate the varied fleet of locomotives working either in the valleys or on the main line, South Wales boasted some sixty engine sheds in 1922, although this number fell dramatically during the next few years so that by 1939 only thirty-six remained. The size and type ranged enormously from Ebbw Junction, the second largest shed on the GWR, to a handful of single-road sheds with perhaps only a single locomotive allocated to each, such as Blaenrhondda, Pontlottyn or Glyncorrwg. Between these extremes the valleys could sport a variety of sheds varying from the standard straight-road GWR product to some highly individualistic designs such as Danygraig and the original Taff Vale shed at Treherbert. This latter shed was unique. It was a stone-built semi-roundhouse with ten roads, only seven of which were under cover. These roads radiated from one side only of the turntable due to the restricted width of the site, the rail approach to the nearby Lady Margaret colliery running immediately behind the roundhouse. Again due to this restriction the coal stage was situated some little way to the south east of the shed. At the grouping twenty-four engines were housed here. Excluding one K class 0-6-0 and the three H class Pwllyrhebog locomotives, they were all 0-6-2Ts of various Taff Vale classes. Sixteen years later, at the new Treherbert shed, the allocation was twenty-seven locomotives, all 0-6-2Ts, with the exception once more of the Pwllyrhebog 0-6-0Ts; but this time sixteen were of the Great Western 56xx class. The old Taff Vale shed had been replaced in 1931 on the other side of the main line by a GWR standard four-road straight shed, a type also used at Radyr and Pantyffynon. It was the last of this design of shed to be built in the valleys under the 1929 Loan Act scheme. The

---

Regulations for the guidance of Train Examiners, Greasers and Oilers

23 – Examiners are to report all vehicles arriving from other Companies' Lines, Private Sidings, Collieries, etc., in a damaged condition; and all instances of damaged vehicles going to other Companies' Lines, Private Sidings, Collieries, etc., must also be reported; but wagons received from other Railway Companies in a damaged condition, or with parts missing, must be allowed to go on if they are perfectly safe to travel, after the Examiner has called the attention of the delivering Company's men to their condition.

26 – The lubricating of Private Owners' wagons before leaving their Sidings must be properly attended to by the Owners.

28 – Examiners are not to allow Repairers of private owners' wagons to take wagons to pieces in unsafe positions, nor to leave them standing without axleguards, or a pair of wheels. Wheels must not be taken from under wagons unless the Repairers have a proper pair ready to put under.

32 – In the event of a vehicle with a bent axle being stopped, no attempt must be made to straighten the axle on the spot, but the wheels must be taken out and sent to a repairing shop where the axle can be made hot and then properly and safely straightened. If any axle straightened while cold, by men in the employ of wagon repairing firms or wagon owners, is put under a vehicle, the Examiner must not allow such vehicle to go into traffic, but must report the case immediately.

Great Western Railway – October 1931

Colliery outing day in the Rhondda. The locomotives are being prepared at Treherbert shed in the summer of 1960 to take miners and their families to Barry Island or Porthcawl. (D. K. Jones)

Great Western Society depot at Didcot was built to the same design in 1932, under the same Government scheme, and most resembles Pantyffynon, Radyr and Treherbert being mirror images inasmuch as the coal stage was to the right as one looked at the front of the shed. This design had actually been introduced into the valleys when Abercynon was rebuilt in 1929, but in this instance it was a two-road not a four-road shed that was built.

Treherbert was a large and busy shed, for as well as working mineral, goods and passenger traffic to and from Cardiff, its engines and men worked to Swansea, Merthyr, Barry and Bassaleg. In the early 1950s there were thirty-one turns in the goods link, and twenty-eight in the passenger (a number that would rise during the operation of the summer timetable). In addition there was a pilot link of three turns and a shed link. There was also a Pwllyrhebog link based at the sub-shed in the Clydach valley, at the top of the incline that housed the special H class engines that worked there. The freight link at that time included such workings as TP1 from Rhondda & Swansea Bay Junction to Fernhill colliery, and TP3, another colliery turn worked from R&SB Junction which also included banking up to the Rhondda tunnel. TP4 shunted at Trealaw, while TP4R performed similar duties at Treorchy and Cwmparc. In all about seventeen target

108

numbers were in use on Treherbert mineral and goods turns at this time. The longer mineral workings were covered by targets T16 to T19 which were coal trains from the Rhondda Fawr collieries to Radyr and Cadoxton sidings. Their pick-up points as they worked down the valley from above Treherbert were a litany of once famous names, and included Blaenrhondda, Fernhill, Tydraw, Bute-Merthyr, Abergorki, Cwmparc, Maendy, Gelli, Llwynypia, Naval, Dinas, Hafod, Gyfeillon, Tymawr, Maritime and Penrhiw before Pontypridd was passed and the train could now, hopefully, work non-stop to its destination.

If such workings were one of the early morning turns the driver and fireman would have been knocked up by a cleaner on 'call-boy' duty. This entailed walking to the house of the driver and fireman at some ungodly hour and rapping on their doors to waken them. There was one driver at Treherbert, however, who was frequently late after such a call and would invariably complain to the chargehand that the boy had not called to wake him up. Naturally this would always annoy the cleaner who was on call duty, even though the chargehand knew that the call had been made. Then one night someone had a bright idea. Two cleaners knocked on the driver's door, made sure he was awake and returned to the shed, but not before carefully lifting his garden gate off its hinges and taking it with them. True to form the driver was late and complained, and the boys were summoned to the chargehand's office once more to confirm that they had indeed called. The reply of the driver when asked to explain how, if the boys had not called, he could account for the presence of his garden gate, which they had carried into the office with them, is not known; which is probably just as well.

The remaining sheds in the Rhondda in 1922, at Trehafod and Coke Ovens, were not so fortunate as Treherbert. The former, a Barry Railway three-road shed on the south side of the river near the viaduct that linked their metals to those of the Taff Vale, did not survive the initial rationalisation of facilities carried out by the GWR, and was closed in 1925. Coke Ovens, built in the expansionist last decade of the nineteenth century as the Rhondda traffic kept on growing remorselessly, survived until the end of 1933 before the economic conditions

Coke Ovens shed, near Pontypridd, was opened by the Taff Vale Railway in 1896 to cope with the ever expanding coal traffic, an expansion that was to continue unabated until 1914. In this photograph, taken circa 1929, a selection of Taff Vale Railway locomotives is on view. (L&GRP)

forced its closure. This brick-built four-road shed was, in common with many valley sheds, on a restricted site, being wedged this time between the main line and the back of a row of houses in Hopkinstown with the resounding name of Telelkebir Street. Perhaps the ultimate restrictions on shed sites though occurred at Ferndale where the shed, sited a little to the north of the station, was perched perilously above the river. It shared this distinction with another Taff Vale shed, that at Aberdare, where the problem was ingeniously overcome by building two sheds about 150 yards apart.

But Ferndale was luckier than Trehafod or Coke Ovens, it survived the depression and lasted until the end of steam, finally closing in 1964. The thirties did leave their mark though, for the shed was reduced from four roads to two and the turntable, which was situated at the northern end of the site was removed. After nationalisation it became a sub-shed to Treherbert. There was no room for the conventional coal stage with an incline leading to it, so coaling was done the hard way, from a wagon alongside the engine. The two roads on which the wagon and locomotive stood, the latter also being one of the shed roads, were protected from the weather by a corrugated steel awning. To run the shed in the 1950s required ten staff: three chargemen, the same number to work the coal stage, a boiler washer, a shedman and also a fitter and his mate. The shed offices were in a single-storey building separated from the main shed by a siding and contained offices for the chargemen and clerks, a fitting shop, messroom and enginemen's room. The shed stores were attached to the main building and ran behind the stops of the shed roads.

Ferndale's locomotive allocation was only about a dozen, its stable of Taff Vale engines giving way to 56xx class 0-6-2Ts and in later years the large 94xx class 0-6-0PTs. The panniers were useful on banking duties from Porth, usually on turn FP1, the line from there to Ferndale and beyond being heavily graded, much of it at 1 in 55 or worse. With its small size only two links, passenger and goods, were required. The destination of its mineral workings were, naturally enough,

A shunting hazard not covered by the rules

Propelling wagons is always a tricky business and operating practices take account of this. However, such rules are written for railwaymen, not members of the public in general, or housewives in particular, which perhaps they should be . . .

In the 1950s at Dowlais, pig iron from the East Moors steelworks at Cardiff was received via the Rhymney Railway/Great Western joint line in a yard on the site of the original works, adjacent to and just below Cae Harris station. Wagons were then picked up by the Dowlais Works shunter to be propelled to storage bunkers at the Ivor Works about half a mile away. The connection from the yard climbed to the level of Cae Harris station, ran im-

mediately in front of it and a hundred yards or so beyond crossed Dowlais High Street on the level and continued into the upper part of the Ivor Works. The length between the station and the road crossing was the problem. Immediately beyond Cae Harris the line curved to the right and for the rest of the way to the road ran between closely spaced high stone walls that were the back walls of short gardens leading from two rows of terraced cottages either side of the line. By this time rail traffic into the works was sparse and irregular. As a result it had become the practice of the housewives to stretch washing lines between the backs of the cottages, across the line. Thus one bright Monday morning having

taken a run up the bank to Cae Harris, half a dozen wagons with a shunting engine propelling, disappeared between the two walls. A few moments later, as the line straightened, both driver and fireman noticed something white flapping from either side of the leading wagon. Stopping near the road, as was mandatory, the fireman walked forward and to his horror saw two, now torn and oily sheets draped over the buffers of the leading wagon. Recovering quickly, he decided that discretion was the better part of valour, bundled them up and threw them into the nearest garden. A few moments later those wagons are reputed to have made one of the fastest crossings of Dowlais High Street on record.

Not all South Wales engine sheds were large and imposing, and contained comprehensive servicing facilities. In this photograph one of the three Taff Vale Railway H class 0-6-0Ts rests inside the Pwllyrhebog shed at the top of the famous rope-worked incline on 29 October 1949. (L&GRP)

the same as those at Treherbert. The afternoon F12 turn, for example, was typical. It ran from Ferndale colliery, picked up additional wagons at the National colliery at Wattstown, then from Porth it continued main line to Radyr, or perhaps Roath Sidings. With one exception the passenger services call for little comment, Ferndale engines working to and from Porth, with the occasional sally further afield. The exception was during the period when the munitions factories at Cardiff and Tremains were operating. The manning levels of these factories were such that extra services, scheduled to fit the shift patterns operating, were run from many parts of the valleys. Ferndale engines for Tremains ran via Pontypridd and Llantrisant before gaining the main line to Bridgend, while for the Cardiff service an early morning shuttle to Porth left Ferndale at 4.18am to connect with a Treherbert train working through to Cardiff, the stock of the Ferndale train returning empty meanwhile, ready for the first advertised working at about 6 o'clock.

Treherbert and Ferndale sheds were at the top of their respective valleys but the practice of siting sheds in such locations was not universal among the valley railway companies, and all of them sited their main locomotive depots at or near their dock outlets. The principal sheds of these companies could therefore be found at Cathays, Radyr and Penarth Dock (all TVR), Cardiff Docks (RR – the predecessor to the GWR-built Cardiff East Dock), Bassaleg (B&M), Barry, Danygraig (R&SB), Duffryn Yard (PTR), Burry Port (BPGV) and Bolt Street (Monmouthshire Railway). But the Taff Vale, Rhymney, and to a lesser extent the Brecon & Merthyr, found it convenient, as well as more economical, to begin their daily mineral services with full loads down the valleys rather than have to resort to numerous light-engine movements before the traffic of the day could begin from the collieries furthest from the docks. Thus they also built sheds at Aberdare, Merthyr, Dowlais (in conjunction with the GWR) and Rhymney. Outside these companies, however, examples of sheds built in such positions were uncommon, and there were different reasons for choosing such a site. Glyn Neath

111

was built to supply banking engines for the climb to Hirwaun. The LNWR sheds at Tredegar and Blaenavon were built there principally because that company had no suitable dock outlet in the eastern part of the coalfield, and Abergavenny was some distance away at the foot of a long, tortuous and steeply graded incline. Finally Aberdare, at the head of the Cynon valley, owed its position to its nearness to junctions with the Dare valley and Merthyr branches, as well as being situated at the largest town on the route between Pontypool and Neath. Of the larger local companies only the Barry had no shed of any consequence within the valleys. It never succeeded in penetrating far into the coalfield on its own metals, as a result it only maintained a small establishment at Trehafod in the lower Rhondda, its principal purpose being to provide banking assistance for the climb to Tonteg. Thus the Barry's day would begin, particularly on a Monday, with a procession of light engine and van movements. On a Sunday nearly every engine on the Barry system, which was 132 in 1922 and still in excess of 80 at nationalisation, would be on shed, stabled in long lines at the rear of the depot, ready for the following morning. Parking them in the correct order for going off shed was always a headache for the shed staff.

The best remembered Great Western locomotives in the South Wales valleys were the 56xx class 0-6-2Ts, sturdy, compact, reliable, and equally at home on freight or passenger duties. Here No 5613 stands at the unusual coal stage at its home shed of Ferndale on 1 March 1963. (D. K. Jones)

Merthyr shed on 26 August 1949. Two GWR panniers stand at the coal stage while alongside a third takes water. A down working from Merthyr (High Street) can be seen approaching headed by another pannier tank. (L&GRP)

The Great Western however chose sites at or near main line junctions close to their valleys interests; Ebbw Junction, Llantrisant, Bridgend, Neath and Llanelly were examples of this practice, with smaller sheds maintained at important junctions within the valleys as at Aberbeeg, Tondu and Pantyffynnon. Falling into neither of these categories was its large shed at Pontypool Road, the site of which was dictated by the needs of the line to Aberdare and Neath, while the positions of Cardiff (Canton) and Landore were dictated more by the locomotive needs of the through traffic along the main line, particularly passenger, rather than considerations relating to the locally arising mineral and goods workings.

Typical of the smaller Great Western sheds in the area was Llantrisant, set at the junction of the main line with the Ely valley branch, and its extension to Penygraig and the collieries in the Clydach Vale high above the Rhondda Fawr. Their passenger work included not only the Ely valley services but also those to Pontypridd, Cowbridge (and Aberthaw prior to its closure), as well as workmen's services to Tremains and excursions to Porthcawl, Barry and Ninian Park Halt when Cardiff City Football Club were playing at home. Outside the Ely valley and the Cowbridge branch on freight and mineral turns, their engines travelled as far afield as Pengam sidings on the eastern side of Cardiff, and Llandeilo Junction on the outskirts of Llanelly. To work these services the engine allocation, which was exclusively tank after the three Aberdare class 2-6-0s stabled there in 1922 moved away, varied between thirty-three, in that year, and eighteen in the mid 1950s. Of the eighteen shedded there in 1955, five of them, 3612/4/44 and 4620/74, all 57xx class 0-6-0PTs, together with 42xx class 2-8-0T 4268, were among the dozen steam locomotives on shed on the evening of 5 July 1964, shortly before closure.

During the early 1950s the passenger duties were in the capable hands of two of the diminutive 14xx class 0-4-2Ts, 1421 and 1471, which had taken over these services from the aged Metro tanks. 1471 had arrived by 1938 and was not moved away until June 1958 after the Penygraig service had been withdrawn, when it was sent to Ebbw Junction. After a brief spell here it found its way to Exeter where it finished its final years. 1421 had a much shorter life at Llantrisant,

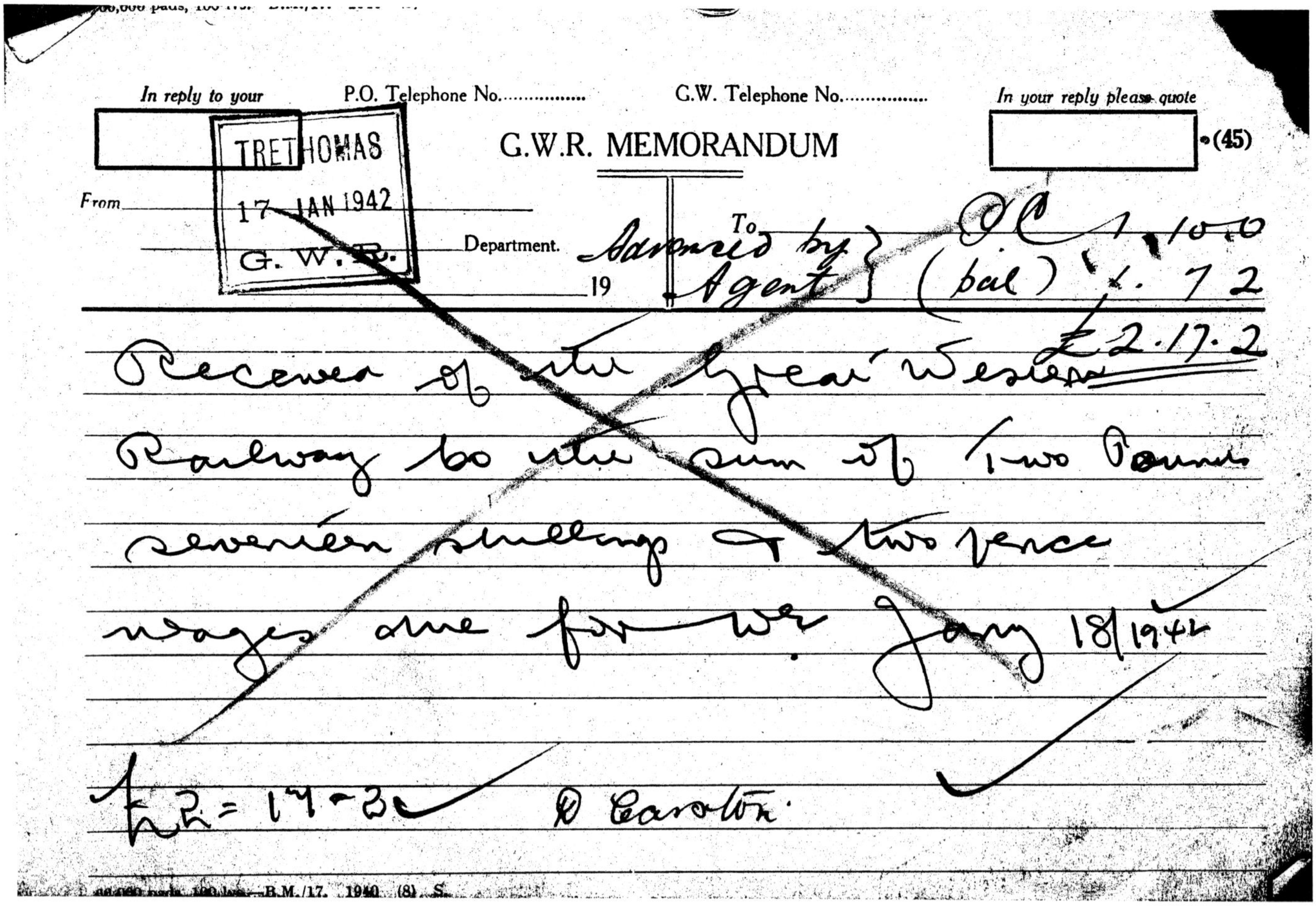

G.W.R. MEMORANDUM

In reply to your   P.O. Telephone No..............   G.W. Telephone No..............   *In your reply please quote*

TRETHOMAS
17 JAN 1942
G.W.R.

*From*_____   Department._____   19___

To   Advised by)   O/C   1.10.0
Agent)   (bal)   1. 7. 2

£2.17.2

Received of the Great Western Railway the sum of Two Pounds seventeen shillings & two pence wages due for we Jany 18/1942

£2 = 17 = 3   D Caroton.

(45)

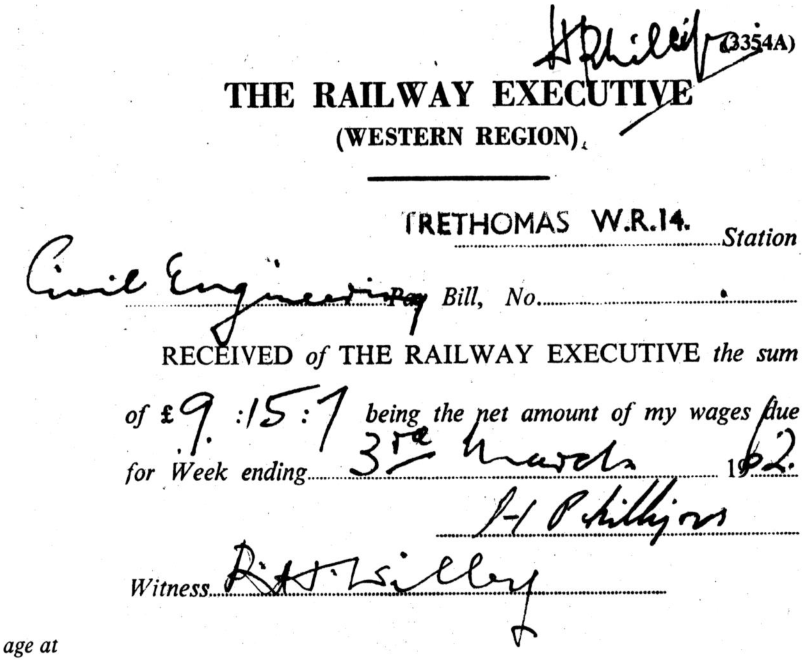

H Phillips (3354A)

THE RAILWAY EXECUTIVE
(WESTERN REGION)

TRETHOMAS W.R.14. .... *Station*

Civil Engineering Pay Bill, No..................

RECEIVED *of* THE RAILWAY EXECUTIVE *the sum*

of £ 9 :15 :7 *being the net amount of my wages due*

for Week ending............3rd March.........19 62.

H Phillips

Witness......R H Willey

Memorabilia of a bygone age at Trethomas.

An item from the station accounts at Trethomas.

TRETHOMAS W.R.14

14ᵗʰ September 19 64

P325B
(Revd. 41179/60)

Firm...... *British Railways*

POSTAGE STAMPS				NATIONAL INSURANCE STAMPS			
No. Req'd	£	s.	d.	No. Req'd	£	s.	d.
	½d.			7/8			
	1d.			9/2			
	1½d.			10/3			
10	2d.		1	8	11/5			
10	2½d.		2	1	11/6			
25	3d.		6	3	12/7			
	4½d.			14/2			
				16/-			
				19/2			
TOTAL c/fwd. to col. 2		10	0				

DETAILS OF CASH TENDERED							
Cheques							
Notes £5......							
,, £1							
,, 10/-		10	0				
Silver				TOTAL			
Bronze				b/fwd. from Col. I		10	0
TOTAL		10	0	GRAND TOTAL		10	0

NOTE.—The list must be handed in at the Post Office. If the purchaser of the stamps wishes to keep a copy he is advised to prepare a duplicate by the use of carbon paper. The copy will be date stamped and initialled by the counter officer if required.

Post Office Date Stamp

MACHEN
A
14 SP
64
NEWPORT. MON

Initials of Counter Officer......

51-6617 B & S 3/62

A reward for services rendered
At Penygraig in the early thirties the young son of the signalman frequently spent large parts of the day with his father at the box. One of his 'duties' whilst there was to meet the trains working through to Clydach Vale colliery and collect 2d (1p) from the driver. With this he would visit a local woman who sold bottles of home brewed beer and return to the station to meet the train on its return from the colliery. His well deserved reward for this service was to ride on the footplate of the bank engine up to Dinas Isaf and back.

The Great Western shed at Llantrisant, home of the locomotives that worked the Ely valley and Taff Vale branches to Cowbridge and Treforest, as well as main line destinations. The turntable was on the right hand side behind the coal line. The line running alongside the shed and rising steeply behind it gave access to the valleys' lines near Mwyndy Junction. (L&GRP)

The Great Western shed at Llantrisant, home of the locomotives that worked the Ely valley and Taff Vale branches to Cowbridge and Treforest, as well as main line destinations. The turntable was on the right hand side behind the coal line. The line running alongside the shed and rising steeply behind it gave access to the valleys' lines near Mwyndy Junction. (L&GRP)

arriving at the end of 1949 after Metro tank 3586 was withdrawn; it moved on in November 1952, also to Ebbw Junction in the first instance, following the termination of the Pontypridd to Llantrisant service in March 1952. The pair would start the day together shortly before 7am. The engine for the Pontypridd train, which for this working only was extended to Tonypandy, arrived first and coupled to the auto coach left overnight in the up bay at Llantrisant station. A few minutes later the engine working the first train to Penygraig would arrive and pick up its auto coach from an adjacent siding before moving into the bay ahead of the Tonypandy train. There they would wait in the early morning with perhaps Charlie Davies and Hadyn Shadbolt, driver and fireman on the Penygraig train, together with guard Tom Ballinger, and driver George Wilkes, fireman Doug Pearce, accompanied by Bill Crowley as guard on the Tonypandy. Promptly at 6.55am the Penygraig auto departed, followed around the curve to Mwyndy Junction five minutes later by the Tonypandy. Peace would reign once more in the bay until they returned to continue their shuttling to and fro along both these branches, or a quick run to Cowbridge.

The mineral and goods workings to the valleys, to Cowbridge and the majority of such workings along the main line, were identified by target numbers, the Cowbridge branch train Z8 having already been referred to in Chapter 2. Into the valleys at 6.20am went Z1 to Clydach Vale. Rostered to one of Llantrisant's band of panniers and with a load normally of forty empty mineral wagons, it was banked from Llantrisant. Returning with a full load the train was again banked from Clydach Vale as far as Dinas Isaf where the train halted, the brakes were pinned down, and the bank engine returned 'wrong line' to Penygraig. This working returned at 11.00am if there was sufficient coal to be moved later in the morning from the Cambrian colliery, and in the afternoon two more trips were made under the Target Z6. Workings to Gilfach Goch were covered by Z4 which left Llantrisant Yard at 8.20am, and returned with a full load which it worked through to Peterston sidings. Here the wagons were dropped off, a Barry engine

116

and crew working the train forward to Cadoxton, while the Llantrisant engine returned with a load of empties. There were ordinary goods workings to Cardiff at 5.00pm and 10.30pm, Z11 and Z12, the former frequently returning as engine and van if no traffic was offering, whereas the later turn was booked with a return load for Llantrisant Yard.

Llantrisant's 42xx class 2-8-0Ts, of which there were three at this time, 4208/61 and 5241, were only rostered to one of the valleys' services. This was the Z10 afternoon working to Coed-Ely colliery which on return worked right through to Pengam sidings. Apart from this the 42xx class turns were the 6.35pm to Llanelly and the 11.10pm to Landore. Unlike the trains for the valleys which were made up and worked from the series of northward curving sidings that ran alongside and slightly above the level of the shed, these long-distance workings were made up in the sidings that ran parallel to the main line to the west of Llantrisant station. Both were long workings, the 6.35pm usually stopping at Pencoed, Tremains, Port Talbot and perhaps Briton Ferry, while the later turn which was heavier would frequently require a banker over Stormy Down west of Bridgend. For many years both of these workings were 'double home' turns, the driver and fireman having to lodge overnight away from home, and were not liked by Llantrisant men.

The brick-built shed which was opened in 1900, replacing an earlier building nearer the station, had three roads and a northlight roof. It was situated on the eastern side of the sharp curve leading to Mwyndy Junction from Ely Valley Junction on the main line. The coaling stage, of traditional Great Western design, was on the inside of the curve, and beyond it was the turntable. Between here and the shed building ran a single road that climbed to the Ely valley branch,

Interlude at Llantrisant station as the train crews of the Penygraig and Pontypridd auto-workings pose for the camera. On the footplate of 14xx class 0-4-2T No 1471 are drivers George Wilkes and Alf Longstreet with fireman Hadyn Shadbolt, while on the platform are fireman Wyndham Lane, driver Charlie Davies, fireman Jack Bevan and on the right passenger guard Tom Ballinger. (Hadyn Shadbolt Collection)

joining it a little to the south of Mwyndy Junction Signal Box, which gave the shed direct access to and from the branch without the need to run through the yard. Immediately to the west lay a group of down sidings, which curved around the front of the shed, before the branch itself, which was double tracked at this point, was reached. Beyond the branch lay a second fan of up sidings. The shed offices were inside the building and situated along its west wall. The foreman's and chargehands' office was passed first as one entered the shed, while beyond it lay the booking-on office, stores, fitting shop, cleaners' cabin, and finally, tucked in the back corner of the shed, the enginemen's cabin.

During the 1940s and early 1950s some twenty-five drivers and firemen were employed here together with a shed staff of a further twenty-six. These included a foreman, three chargehands, a booking-on clerk, storeman, boiler washer, shedman, six fitters and their mates, three or four cleaners and two on the coal stage. Among such a group some memorable characters existed who are remembered to this day. Cleaners of this period recall Frank Saunders, one of the chargehands. Having finished cleaning the engines allocated to them the young cleaners would knock on his office door and invite him to inspect their work. This he would solemnly do, thoroughly inspecting the engine, including the motion which was of course inside the frames. But before he set foot from his office he would don not only a white coat, but remove his hat and replace it with a white cap. Any sign of grease or dirt on either after his inspection meant that the job had to be done again.

But it is the drivers who are remembered most, frequently with respect, but occasionally with somewhat less regard. One morning a cleaner knocked up a driver three minutes early for his 4.00am call. Nothing was said until the end of the cleaner's shift when the first intimation he had that anything was wrong was when he was given a reprimand by the chargehand, following a complaint from the driver. Many drivers welcomed new firemen into the cab, but others jealously guarded their domain. One in fact would go so far as to inform his new mate that under no circumstances was he to cross to the driver's side of the footplate, and if he considered that the fireman was using lumps of coal that were too large he would kick the shovel from his hands, accompanying the action with some caustic

To differentiate between LMS and GWR engine movements at Blaina, the following bell code was used between shunter and signalman.

			Beats on Bell.	How Given.
a	Can G.W. Train, with full Load, leave for Down Main Line			
		One lot of Wagons to be dropped on ...	5	4 pause 1.
a	,,	Two lots do. ...	6	4 pause 2.
a	,,	Three or more do. ...	7	4 pause 3.
a	,,	with 20 Wagons or less, leave for Down Main Line, Train already complete	3	Consecutively.
a	,,	One lot of Wagons to be dropped on ...	4	3 pause 1.
a	,,	Two lots of do. ...	5	3 pause 2.
a	,,	Three or more do. ...	6	3 pause 3.
a	Can L.M.S. Train leave Yard		5	5 consecutively.
a	Can Works Engine run out to make two or more shunts ...		5	2 pause 2 pause 1.
a	,, ,, to make one shunt		6	5 pause 1.
a	Can G.W. or L.M.S. Engines run out to make two or more shunts		4	2 pause 2.
a	,, ,, Engine run out to make one shunt		6	1 pause 5.
b	Cannot allow Main Line to be obstructed		6	2 pause 4.
c	Shunting complete—Bringing key back		3	2 pause 1.

118

remark. But others like Charlie Davies, George Wilkes or Alf Longstreet would help a new man, advising and encouraging him, and they were not above using the shovel themselves if the occasion demanded. Men such as these could be found in every shed across South Wales. Proud of their calling, and considerate to those who would follow them in what they considered to be the most satisfying of jobs.

Some of the workings from Llantrisant, and other sheds, that made the job of driving or firing so satisfying have already been mentioned, for after all it was these men who had to operate the timetables, working their engines, to quote the enginemen's manual, '. . . in the most efficient and economical manner consistent with the work to be performed . . .'. But there were a myriad of duties other than these that they, and others no less dedicated, would perform when necessary to ensure that the railway would operate under even the most adverse conditions. Winter always brought its special problems, and if snow or ice was expected an additional set of enginemen would be called out to run back and forth between Llantrisant, Penygraig and Clydach Vale, or elsewhere within the shed's orbit, to keep the lines open. If this occurred at night, which it frequently did, all the signal boxes would be kept open and the points operated frequently to prevent freezing. At Llantrisant shed it fell to the relief fireman to see that all the 'devils', that is the coal-fired burners kept next to all water columns, were kept alight. Not only did he have to see to those in the vicinity of the shed, but also those in the adjacent yards, at Llantrisant station, and the isolated column at Mwyndy Junction. In all each inspection was a round trip of over a mile, and by definition made under the most appalling conditions.

For the reasons described earlier the main concentrations of locomotive sheds came to be at, or near, Cardiff or Swansea. In total over the years that steam reigned supreme in South Wales, although never at one time, Cardiff had fourteen sheds situated locally (including Radyr and Penarth Dock). Nine were in existence in 1922, but only four survived into the postwar period: Canton, Cathays, Cardiff East Dock and Radyr. The numbers for Swansea were eleven, six and three respectively, the postwar survivors being Landore, Danygraig and Swansea East Dock. The overall total of eleven is however somewhat artificial, since eight of that number refer to various sheds situated in the docks at Swansea originally owned by the Swansea Harbour Trust and the contracting firm of Powsland & Mason, some of which had very short lives.

For many years Cardiff Canton was an enthusiast's dream. It was the principal shed for passenger engines in South Wales, with an allocation in excess of one hundred, and always busy. But above all it sported a footbridge that spanned both main line and shed throat. The unusually designed shed, with six straight roads with an offset roundhouse at the rear, dated from 1882. (The north wall is still in existence as the corresponding wall of the present-day diesel depot.) There was a disused coal stage of 1912 vintage at the eastern end which has also survived and is incorporated into the diesel depot as a water tower. The new coal stage dated from 1931, and was on the south side of the shed, being built into the embankment on which the carriage shed was situated. All in all it was a strange mixture of structures. As a complete contrast there was Cardiff East Dock. Opened in 1931 it was an eight-road version of the standard type built under the 1929 Loan Act, and occupied a site near the Rhymney Railway's Dock shed, replacing it and the Cardiff Railway shed at Tyndall Street. It was the final home of many of the area's remaining Rhymney and Cardiff Railway engines in the

119

Cardiff Cathays was the largest shed on the Taff Vale Railway, with ten roads, and an allocation in 1922 of 97 locomotives. The photograph shows a line-up alongside the coal stage which, although not of standard GWR design, was built by them when improvements were made to the shed in 1929, and judging by the rather pristine condition of the structure it would appear that the photograph was taken not long afterwards. The line-up of 0-6-2T locomotives includes members of the GWR 56xx class, a rebuilt TVR A class, a pair of Barry Railway B class, and a RR A1 class, the only locomotive here of South Wales origin that had at this time escaped modernisation by Swindon. (L&GRP)

years up to 1957. But true to the unwritten laws that governed engine movements in the valleys, few Taff Vale engines were shedded here, even though they may have been working in the docks. Their shed was Cathays and to Cathays they remained faithful. Closed in 1958 the shed reopened four years later to house Canton's engines during its conversion. I never saw the shed during this period, and looking back I am glad. The sights of those days of once honoured and proud machines eking out an existence on borrowed time was bad enough without the sight of their relegation to an equally fast fading dockland.

On the outskirts of Cardiff, at the gateway of the Taff valley, was Radyr shed, set in the vee of the junction of the Taff Vale main line and the mineral line to Penarth Dock, and bounded on its southern side by a loop of the river. The shed, like Cardiff East Dock, was also built in 1931 replacing one of 1865 vintage, or possibly even earlier. It accommodated not only the engines that shunted the nearby yards, sections of which rejoiced in such names as 'The Ragged', 'The Bog', 'No 15' and 'New Section', but also provided motive power for the Penarth and Roath lines, together with that for one working (Y6) along the Llantrisant No 1 branch. Engines from the shed also worked to all the valleys served by the TVR together with turns into the Rhymney valley, as far as Llanbradach colliery, which entailed working up the 'big hill' from Taff's Well to Penrhos Junction and beyond. But the longest journeys regularly performed by its engines were the coal trains to Salisbury. These were exclusively 72xx class 2-8-2T hauled, and during the 1950s 7202 and 7205 were allocated to the shed for this duty. The Radyr engine worked right through, but the crew were relieved by Bristol men at Dr Days Bridge Junction, usually returning home 'on the cushions'.

The duties of this shed were normally confined to mineral and goods traffic only, except at weekends when engines might be pressed into service on football excursions to Ninian Park Halt, or perhaps Barry Island. However, there was one workmen's passenger, target number Y3 and known as 'The Collier', operated by Radyr men, but curiously in the Rhymney valley. At one time this was the regular turn of one of the shed's trio of Barry Railway B1 class 0-6-2Ts. The crew would book on at 4.00am in the morning and work light to Caerphilly. Here they would

120

pick up a rake of four workmen's coaches from sidings near the locomotive works. These were run empty to Llanbradach colliery from where they returned with miners coming off shift, first to Caerphilly and then up the Senghenydd branch, calling at Abertridwr on the way. It refilled at Senghenydd and returned once more to Caerphilly where the stock was returned to the sidings. The engine then ran light to Aber Yard to shunt. The crew were relieved from here at 11.00am again returning home 'on the cushions', the journey being by way of Cardiff (Queen Street) where a change had to be made to reach Radyr where the men would book off at midday.

Swansea was always the mecca for the dock saddle tank, be it at Danygraig or Swansea East Dock sheds. Standing on the footplate, at the driver's invitation, of the Llanelly & Mynydd Mawr 0-6-0ST No 359 *Hilda* with coal above your ankles, and no matter where you stood some part of your lower anatomy being scorched by the close proximity of the firebox, some of the difficulties of the unsung duties of enginemen could be appreciated. In *Hilda*'s cab there was no room to pick up the proverbial cat let alone swing it.

During the 1950s South Wales, despite its losses, was still an area of bustle and activity. It was the Indian summer of steam. Peace and quiet descended only on a Saturday afternoon or a Sunday. At these times even the largest sheds were crowded. Sixty to seventy engines would be on shed at Canton or Ebbw Junction, with only slightly fewer at Severn Tunnel Junction or Llanelly. Pill and Barry sheds would be overflowing. But the lasting memory I have of one such Saturday afternoon is the little shed at Burry Port, lost in the wasteland of the long defunct dock, with three BPGV six-coupled tanks dozing in the hot afternoon sun.

As was normal throughout the country, running repairs could be carried out at most sheds, and to meet the requirements of heavier repairs the larger local companies had their own workshops, as did the GWR, for example at Ebbw Junction. The pre-grouping companies' workshops were at West Yard (TVR), Caerphilly (RR), Tyndall Street (Cardiff Railway), Machen (B&M) and Dany-

Photo-opportunity at Rhondda & Swansea Bay Junction in the 1950s. Driver D. Evans and fireman D. Jones pose with guard W. H. Howells, foreman T. Jones and shunter G. Lankshear. No 384 is a rebuilt Taff Vale Railway A class 0-6-2T locomotive. (Derek Jones)

On 28 July 1957 a wonderful collection of Great Western engines stand outside Duffryn Yard shed. Identifiable are 56xx class 0-6-2T No 6686 (with the fireman making some unknown adjustments) and No 6629, 94xx class 0-6-0PT No 9444, 57xx class 0-6-0PT No 6749 (foreground) and No 9799 (behind 6629), together with four other unidentifiable members of the same class inside the shed or in the background. The wooden-bodied coal wagon on the coal stage is also noteworthy. (Author's Collection)

graig (R&SB). Rationalisation, which meant concentrating all heavy repairs on one site, was obviously necessary following the Great Western take-over. As is well known Caerphilly was chosen as the site to be expanded, and existing facilities modernised. A new erecting shop, modelled on Swindon, with a central traverser giving on to repair bays on either side, was opened in 1926. Adjacent Rhymney Railway buildings were converted into boiler repair shops etc, and up to sixty engines could be dealt with, although nearer half this number was the normal level of activity. The building, instantly identifiable as of Swindon design, still stands today, in private hands, as one of the main factories in what is now the Harold Wilson Industrial Estate, as the works site is now known. Later the carriage repair facilities were also modernised when in 1939 a six-road carriage-repair shed was opened at the opposite end of the site to the erecting shop. Once again a distinctive Swindon design was built, the work executed in red brick, as was the erecting shop, as opposed to local stone with which the Rhymney Railway buildings were constructed. During this period of its life members of the majority of pre-grouping, Great Western, and British Railways Standard classes were dealt with, and the reputation the works achieved was as high as Swindon itself.

When writing of the running of the valleys' railways, one cannot ignore the work undertaken at the hundreds of stations that once existed there. The importance that the local station once had in the affairs of the community has been mentioned earlier, but here it is appropriate to touch upon some of the perhaps lesser known or now largely forgotten aspects of station working and duties, and the life of the railwaymen who worked on them.

While Tonypandy and Trealaw station remains open today, it is difficult to realise that it once occupied what was, in the heyday of the valleys railways, a strategic position in the Rhondda Fawr, being situated conveniently for the central part of the valley together with Clydach Vale. It was a position recognised by the railway authorities who built a large, well-equipped goods station nearby. Up and down platforms were provided flanking the three running lines that passed through the station. Like many a station in the valleys its site was restricted, being hemmed in by the river and the town of Trealaw on either side, together with the junctions to the Pwllyrhebog branch and the Naval colliery to north and south respectively. These restrictions accounted for the site of Trealaw goods station being beyond the road bridge and on the down side, opposite Pwllyrhebog Junction which diverged on the up, and therefore separated from the station. The narrowness of the valley at this point dictated that the road levels on either side, and the link across the river, were well above track level, which resulted in the booking office being set at road level at the Tonypandy end of the bridge that crossed both rail and river at this point.

In 1938 the goods station was well served by five up workings, including an early morning turn from Severn Tunnel Junction which, except on Mondays, arrived at 6.45am en route for Treherbert, for which it left, after detaching wagons, some ten minutes later. The remainder originated at either Radyr, Stormstown Junction or Coke Ovens, and all had called before midday, their balance workings arriving during the afternoon or early evening. A morning and afternoon 'pilot', that is a shunting engine, was also provided. The former, operating under target number TP4, left Treherbert shed at 6.32am and arrived at 7.00am. It was booked to shunt until noon and then return at 12.20pm with any wagons needing to be forwarded to Treherbert. The afternoon turn, TP6, left Treherbert at 1.40pm and worked a pick-up goods down the valley to Trealaw and arrived at 3.00pm. Its principal duty here was to marshal wagons for the return workings to Radyr and Stormstown (T24 and T20) before working a coal train back up the valley at 7.00pm.

Meanwhile over at the station, as well as dealing with some twenty-four up and the corresponding number of down trains between the hours of 6.00am and 11.00pm, which was an average of one every twenty minutes throughout the day, a not inconsiderable traffic in parcels, mails and perishables was handled. As was normal practice this traffic was usually dealt with in the early morning. First to arrive was the 3.40am parcels from Cardiff (General), which would steam in at about 5.15am, some ten minutes only being allowed for unloading. The train worked on up the valley to Treherbert, returning from there at 7.20am and running non-stop back to Cardiff. Half an hour later at 5.58am the mail train would arrive, and as was once the norm with such workings, hurry on its way a few short minutes later. The method of clearing the platform of the loads from these workings was unique among the valleys' stations. As mentioned earlier the

The ghost train

Y2 was the 2.10am Radyr to Merthyr freight working. Unremarkable perhaps except that at Plymouth Street Goods Depot in Merthyr it would be met, at about 6.00am, by Police with guard dogs. They were on hand to oversee the unloading of the bullion van that was regularly worked up the valley by this train. What the contents were I do not know, as the driver who used to work regularly on this train never felt inclined to leave his footplate to find out! To all at Radyr shed this working was known as the 'Ghost Train'.

platforms were below road level, and so a hydraulic lift was installed. The water to operate it, which was about 100 gallons for every lift, was purchased from the local water authority and discharged to waste into the nearby river, there being no way that water from the Rhondda Fawr could be used for this purpose. Some idea of how vital this lift was can perhaps be gauged from the memory of Roy Shadbolt who was a porter here over forty years ago. In the early hours of one morning, after severe weather had delayed their delivery, no less than 1,200 boxes of fish arrived by special train. All these boxes had to be moved up to road level as quickly as possible so that they would be ready for delivery around the district before the fishmongers' shops opened. That night all the station staff, including those from the booking office, worked on to move this enormous load. Milk would also reach road level this way, one local milkman, W. D. Jones, receiving twenty churns daily to satisfy his requirements.

In charge of all this activity was, of course, the stationmaster, upon whose shoulders rested the responsibility of running the station competently, and presenting to the travelling public the image of a clean, efficient and above all reliable system. The condition of the station was taken by the public, and the railway management, as a reflection of how well he performed these duties. One stationmaster in particular, whose name was Lloyd, would begin each day with an inspection of the station as soon as he came on duty. Inspection was thorough, and since he was a man of above average height he would even go so far as to run a finger along the top of every office or waiting room door, any dirt found there requiring that the room be cleaned again. Another task, on which he insisted, was that after the passage of a coal train all the platform seats were wiped clean of any coal dust.

Unlike Tonypandy and Trealaw station, Penygraig has long since closed and the position it once commanded in the local community is now only a memory. The station, which was built on a slight curve, was the terminus of the passenger

The restricted space available in the valleys is well illustrated by this photograph of the GWR shed at Aberbeeg in June 1939. Of standard Churchward straight-road design it was opened in 1919 and closed in 1964. No turntable was provided and the coal stage was situated in front of the shed and is just out of the photograph on the left hand side, although the extension of the embankment to the buffer stops can be seen. The tracks in the foreground are those of the Western valleys main line. (L&GRP)

workings from Llantrisant, although the branch continued for a further two miles to serve the collieries of the Clydach Vale. The platforms were slightly staggered and there was a goods yard immediately beyond on the down side of the branch. Run-round was by way of two pairs of trailing crossovers at the extreme ends of the platforms, while access to the yard was obtained from a long loop that separated the impressive stone-built goods shed from the running lines. All movements, including to and from the adjacent colliery sidings, were controlled from the signal box situated at the Clydach Vale end of the up platform.

For many years the yard was serviced each weekday by the 5.00am goods from Cardiff, a Canton turn, working as target number H4. After shunting at Llantrisant and Tonyrefail it arrived at Penygraig at 7.50am, and in the late 1930s the loading of this train was such that the timetable called for it to be banked from Llantrisant. Among the load could be fish worked up from Milford Haven to Llantrisant overnight, where perhaps a wagon for Penygraig would be dropped off before the main line express goods continued on to Cardiff, where incidentally further wagons would be detached for the valleys. Tea would also arrive in bulk, and was kept in a special store in the yard known as the 'Lyons' shed. As elsewhere seasonal fluctuations could affect the volume and type of such traffic. Shortly before Christmas it was once common for two large Siphon wagons to arrive from West Wales filled from floor to roof with fresh chickens, geese and turkeys for delivery to the local Co-operative Society's butchers' shops. For many years these and all other deliveries were made by horse and cart, a large stable built by the Great Western being situated in the goods yard, the hauliers delivering to Clydach Vale, Williamstown, Tonypandy, and Trealaw as well as Penygraig itself. During the autumn these stables had a few extra occupants. For generations onion sellers from Brittany, known locally as 'Shonny' onion men (I believe 'Shonny' is a corruption of Johnny), would come to South Wales and walk the streets of the towns and villages selling them from door to door. Those that

On a cold and overcast day near the end of steam in the valleys, a nearly empty Abercynon shed awaits its fate on 15 December 1963. The end finally came in November 1964. (D. K. Jones)

125

Pontypool Road shed in June 1939 with a wonderful line-up of Great Western Moguls, old and new pannier tanks, an ROD 2-8-0 and a Dean Goods 0-6-0 on display. The shed was set in the triangle formed by the lines to Newport and Neath on the eastern and northern sides and the Eastern valleys line to Blaenavon on the west. At this time it held over eighty locomotives. (L&GRP)

came to Penygraig lived for the brief period of their stay in the loft above the stables. Here they could be found of an evening stringing their onions, which had been delivered ahead of their arrival, into the characteristic 'ropes' that they carried either around their necks or across the handlebars of their bicycles.

As well as deliveries by horse and cart of large consignments, small loads and parcels would be delivered by hand cart by the station staff, usually the lad porter. Such was the personal service to the community that the railways once undertook. The variety of such loads was of course immense and if there were perishables to be delivered to local shops they had to be there before opening time, for as often as not the shopkeeper would refuse delivery and claim from the railway for lateness. Such work could have its rewards, however. At Ynyshir station, in the Rhondda Fach, for instance, it would fall on occasion to the lad porter to deliver a carefully packed basket, immediately upon its arrival at the station, to one of the most important local residents, such service being rewarded by a tip of 1d or perhaps 2d (0.5p or 1p). One day this eminent resident had startled a new lad porter as he left the station, for when asked for his ticket he had smiled patronisingly and replied, 'Don't you know me?', and when on receiving a blank shake of the head had produced a Great Western Director's Pass from his waistcoat pocket! In awed silence Sir William James Thomas passed on his way. The contents of the basket were hurried along the terraced streets, and what was delivered to the servants' entrance at the rear of *Brynawel*, his house at the northern end of the mining village? One large fresh salmon!

It is perhaps appropriate here to reflect that valley stations such as these frequently occupied narrow, cramped sites which on occasions resulted in the goods yards being separated from the station by some little distance as at Pontypridd, Trealaw and Abertillery. However, given only half a chance, as at Mountain Ash, where a convenient loop in the River Cynon produced a little extra width, it is little short of miraculous what could be done. The Taff Vale and the Great Western not only built their stations here within yards of each other, on opposite banks of the river across which a connection once linked them, but they also had their goods yards adjacent. In the case of the Taff Vale station (Oxford Street) it was actually behind the up platform, and on the Great Western side of the river room was found for the town's gas works. This entire layout was situated between Nixon's Navigation and Deep Duffryn collieries, which were less than half a mile apart.

126

7
CAKE TRAINS AND WET FISH

I weave through the crowds in the station concourse and slip into the goods subway and clock on at five minutes to two. It is too dark down here to read the list of timetable additions and alterations that I have been handed, so even though they seem thicker than usual, I innocently make my way to the lift and ascend to the daylight. The scene that greets me can be summed up in one word – bedlam!

The time is August Bank Holiday Saturday 1956, the place is the down main platform of Cardiff General station. The island platform is jammed solid. Never before or since have I seen so many people crammed on to it. The experiences of the West Country, of crowds, overloaded trains waiting for paths, and the chaos that once reigned west of Exeter up to the late 1950s are well documented. I can vouch that South Wales could suffer as much chaos as Devon and Cornwall at such a time.

Before I have moved a yard from the lift I am besieged on all sides. 'When is the train to Tenby? Has the Birmingham arrived yet? When does the Swansea leave?' (It is standing at platform 4, and should have left by now.) Desperately I leaf through the special train notice in my hand, but can make little sense of it before being rescued by an inspector. I shall always remember his aside to me a few moments later. 'Don't take any notice of those, nothing's in the right order or running to time.' As I scuttled to the porters' cabin at the London end of the platform I looked at a station clock. It was only five minutes past two; my thoughts at that moment can be imagined.

What an afternoon! With the timetable in tatters the platform staff were only saved by the station announcer, from whom we could pick out the correct train information on our list, but heaven help you if in the noise you missed one. As we all got our bearings and did our best to pass on what information we had, I remember the inspector who had helped me at the start of the shift hurrying along the platform with a look like thunder. I was straightway instructed to go to the down end of platform 3 and find out what had happened to the relay apparatus that was connected to Cardiff West Signal Box, which when a down train was ready to depart was activated, and rang a bell in the box. Apparently it was ringing in a random manner causing great confusion to the signalmen. Fearing an electrical fault, which would have meant even more problems on that

---

The GWR thought of everything

Cardiff General station is said to have once carried the second largest stock of *printed* tickets on the Great Western. As would therefore be expected nearly every eventuality was covered, including cheap rate tickets for excursions, workmen, commercial travellers, etc, etc. But perhaps the most surprising amongst these was the 'Shipwrecked Mariner' ticket, issued from Cardiff to any rail connected port in the United Kingdom to enable such, often destitute, unfortunates to sign on to a new ship.

hot afternoon, the answer was thankfully simple. An observant small boy, bored by a prolonged wait, had noticed the apparatus being used, and thought it would be a good idea if he could do it too, little realising the problems it would cause. Once returned to his parents things returned to what passed for normality that day.

The chaos of that particular day was never repeated although Cardiff General was a very busy station at this period. Between 6.00am and 10.00pm on a normal weekday its nine platforms, which were based on four islands, saw on average the arrival or departure of a passenger train every three to four minutes, and altogether some three hundred passenger workings were dealt with in a twenty-four-hour period. The main line platforms 1 to 4 were through roads, and 5 a westward, or down, facing bay, saw more than 120 of these workings. The remaining 170 or more local valley, commuter or coastal services were accommodated at platforms 6 to 9.

On the main line side the two busiest periods of the day were between 8.00am and 11.05am, which included the departure of four expresses to London; and between 4.00pm and 7.00pm which among other workings saw the arrival and departure in both directions of no less than seven to and from the capital.

In contrast to these prestigious trains these two periods also saw the majority of the local workings between Cardiff and Newport. It is perhaps hard to recall today, but interspersed between the long-distance workings, which invariably stopped at both Cardiff and Newport, was a main line commuter service. Throughout the full day some fourteen would ply back and forth hauled by a

Platform 3 at Cardiff (General) station in the 1950s. On a bright sunlit afternoon BR Standard Britannia No 70028 Royal Star *waits for the whistle at the head of a down working. The bay platform on the right was platform 5, which in addition to parcels traffic at this time, was the departure platform for the workings to Porthcawl.*
(David Rees)

This photograph taken on 27 July 1922 shows the main line platforms at Cardiff (General) station before their rebuilding, which was carried out in the mid nineteen-thirties. A down cattle working is at the platform road while in the distance the baggage bridge that spanned the station at this time can be seen (L&GRP)

variety of motive power ranging from a large Prairie tank or a 94xx class 0-6-0PT, to perhaps one of Ebbw Junction's pair of 14xx class 0-4-2Ts.

Between 8.00am and 8.35am platforms 1 and 2 were particularly busy. Following the departure of the 8.00am to Paddington from platform 2, the Cardiff to Bristol left platform 1 five minutes later. No 2 then saw the departure of the Fishguard to London at 8.15am, followed by the Newcastle train at 8.30am, while No 1 handled the 8.35am to Birmingham. Things quietened down a little after this, with departures settling down to about one every ten to fifteen minutes for the remainder of the morning. The most noteworthy of these later departures was that of the London-bound 'Red Dragon' at 10.00am. A similar peak occurred on the down main platforms, but between 10.00am and 10.28am. A working to Milford Haven from Bristol was the first, on the hour, followed by the arrival a couple of minutes later of a local from Newport. At 10.15am a stopping train, the 9.10am Bristol to Cardiff arrived, and finally the 8.30am from Cheltenham pulled in at 10.28am.

The busy afternoon period saw fourteen up and an equal number of down workings dealt with, but it contained no peaks similar to those of the morning. The most interesting working was the 5.30pm Cardiff to Porthcawl. This ran from No 5 bay platform and was frequently hauled by a large 2-6-2T. This train and its corresponding up working, which arrived at 3.20pm, were the last of the through trains which for many years provided a frequent service between Cardiff and Porthcawl, and which some thirty years before could sport a Bulldog class 4-4-0 at their head.

The local platforms, while they may have lacked the variety of workings and motive power of the main line side, certainly made up for this in the density of traffic they handled. Beginning before 5.00am and ending some time after 11.00pm an intense passenger service was handled. Nominally local trains, of non-corridor stock, or perhaps auto-train workings, some of their destinations hardly warranted the term local. Traffic from Merthyr, Aberdare, Treherbert and Rhymney had travelled some twenty-two to twenty-three miles before reaching here, and had another twelve to go if they were working through to Barry. Certain trains also worked the Vale of Glamorgan line, some as far as Bridgend, but they

Platform 9 at Cardiff (General) station on 2 May 1959. 64xx class 0-6-0PT No 6438 is ready to depart on the 12.50pm auto-train to Pontypridd via St Fagans. (Seaton Phillips)

Cardiff (Riverside) station on 22 July 1922. Before the rebuilding of Cardiff (General) station in the mid nineteen-thirties the GWR maintained the fiction of two stations on this site. The local platforms, which were built in 1894 for the use of the Barry and Taff Vale railways passenger traffic to Clarence Road station in the, then, business centre of Cardiff, being referred to as Cardiff (Riverside). The GWR did not operate any passenger services on the branch to Clarence Road until after the grouping. (L&GRP)

Cardiff Station (GWR) – 1907

The main station deals with 59 up and 60 down Great Western passenger trains, besides 25 up and 25 down Taff Vale Railway trains, the total service on an ordinary week-day thus being 165, whilst 108 Taff Vale and Barry Railway passenger trains run from Riverside station each week-day.

Railway Magazine – March 1907

started at Cardiff General or perhaps Clarence Road, a short distance away near the docks, in what for many years had been the business centre of the city.

As one would expect the most intense working periods were between 8.00am and 9.00am, and between 5.00pm and 6.00pm, fifteen and seventeen trains being dealt with respectively in each period. It will be recalled that by the mid 1950s the Cardiff Valleys interval service was operating, a recasting of the timetable of the local valleys and coastal services that had been introduced in 1953. Hourly departures throughout most of the day from Merthyr, Treherbert and Rhymney had been introduced with through workings to Barry and Penarth, resulting in a faster and more efficient service. The time-honoured basis of the timetables, developed by the individual railway companies, which had once operated in and out of the valleys, and whose trains frequently commenced or terminated at either Queen Street or Cardiff Riverside, and were orientated around Pontypridd, Barry and Caerphilly, at last being set aside.

Only one of the services was not integrated into this pattern. This was the twice daily return service between Pontypridd and Cardiff (Clarence Road) via St Fagans, an auto-train working nicknamed 'The St Fagans Pullman'. At this period a regular 64xx class 0-6-0PT turn, it made its daily dashes from Pontypridd at 7.46am and 1.40pm, which arrived at Cardiff General at 8.23am and 2.18pm respectively. The return workings left here at 12.50pm and 5.38pm reaching their destination, by what can only be described as the most roundabout of routes, at 1.26pm and 6.11pm. A last doffing of the hat one might say to the spirited competition that once flourished between those two deadly rivals, the Taff Vale and Barry railways.

Cardiff General was certainly a busy station and working there one learned much, although not always related to the working of the railways as I found out when I was taught a little country 'lore' in what many would consider the most unlikely of places. It happened one evening. The down 'Red Dragon' had arrived and I was detailed to go to the guard's van at the head of the train and remove a ewe and a ram which were to be delivered to a farm just outside Cardiff. I opened the door and sure enough there they were, both sitting down and tethered to a stanchion. I untied the rope holding the ram and gave it a gentle tug. Nothing happened. I pulled harder. The ram remained where he was. I pulled again, only to receive a glare as his annoyance began to show. To cut a long story short for ten minutes or more I pulled on the rope or tried pushing the beast, then I took hold of his horns and pulled again, only to be shaken off for my pains. I just could not move him. The next thing I knew the platform inspector was asking me, in rather colourful language, why was I holding up the train. I explained the situation. With a look of utter disdain, and a reply which I cannot repeat here, he brushed past me and untethered the ewe, which followed him out of the guard's van. Before I could move, that blinking ram stood up and followed her out.

Despite remarks made about British Railways timekeeping every effort was made by the platform staff to ensure that a train was ready on time. All passengers and goods on, and all doors closed. But one train above all was given the five-star treatment. That was the down 'Mail', arriving at 12.40am and departing at 1.00am sharp. Among the staff it was recognised as a 'hanging offence' if it were delayed due to sloppy platform working. The mail for Cardiff and the valleys was stacked in the first three vans, usually Siphons, at the head of the train. Each one, 65ft long with no interior partitions, was full of mail bags for its entire length, stacked to the roof and occupying the full width. Behind, ready to be moved up to the

BR Standard Britannia class 4-6-2 No 70015 Apollo *stands at platform 3 at Cardiff (General) station on a down working in the mid 1950s. The beautiful condition of this engine was typical of the turnout of top link engines from Cardiff Canton (86C) at this time. The Britannias were not popular on the western region, yet paradoxically, perhaps displaying that independence of spirit characteristic of South Wales, Canton achieved excellent results with them.* (David Rees)

doors were fifteen or twenty platform trolleys which had been moved there earlier in the night. As the train, usually Castle-hauled, although whether a London or a South Wales engine I cannot now recall, came to a halt, those trolleys nearest the van doors were pushed forward. The doors were then opened and every available porter, including foremen, and if time was slipping inspectors as well, fell upon the contents. Each sack had to be examined for the vans not only contained mail for Cardiff and the valleys but also Bridgend, Neath, Swansea and points west, together with any left over from the stop at Newport, which had to be sent back of course. As each trolley was filled, no particular number of sacks being loaded, individuals judging its weight, and more particularly its balance, by experience, it was pushed back to the edge of the adjacent bay platform and an empty one put in its place. This process was repeated until all mailbags for Cardiff and the valleys had been unloaded. If time was running short they went straight out on to the platform to be moved after the train had gone. Once it had blasted away into the summer darkness all that remained to be done was to haul each trolley to the goods lift, which, as is the way of things, was situated near the other end of the platform, accompany it down to the subway and haul it to the

132

front entrance to the station, the approach road of which at this hour was full of Post Office vans backed up ready to receive them. The trolley would be left, and an empty one picked up and returned to the Newport, or up end of the platform. All that remained then was to return to the down end of the platform pick up another trolley and repeat the process. This job was left to the platform porters working on the down side of the station, and I recall making up to four journeys each way on most night shifts. In 1956 mechanical platform tractors were unheard of at Cardiff.

It will be recalled that the trolleys were loaded solely by judgement of the height and apparent stability of the load. These were not always the best criteria as I found one night to my cost. Clearing one of the last trolleys, and moving it slowly since the overhang of the mailbags looked none too healthy, the inevitable happened. The mailbags toppled over not only on to the platform but also on to the track, and to my horror at that moment a pannier came running light engine along the platform road. What the footplate crew made of the sight of a wildly gesticulating figure hurtling along the platform towards them I can only guess. For myself I was more concerned as to the penalty for the destruction of Her Majesty's mails. Thank goodness the engine crew were alert. The brakes were applied, hard, and the pannier slid to a halt with one mailbag between its front wheels. Mercifully that sack had fallen completely between the rails for many of the others were straddling them. It was some little time before I could understand why the pannier's crew found it all so funny!

Other calamities that I recall could not be laid at my door I am glad to say. One night the goods lift failed just before midnight and it had still not been repaired by the time I left at six o'clock the following morning. In that time the contents of only two trains had been cleared, one the mail and the other the newspaper, and that was by carrying two mailbags or two bundles of newspapers at a time out to the waiting vehicles at the front of the station. The contents of all the others, to a greater or lesser extent, remained where they had been placed when unloaded. Mind you, the mattresses from the Hereford goods were put to good use! The scene by the early morning was indescribable. The platform was

Pyle Junction looking towards Bridgend from the eastern end of the Porthcawl platforms on 4 May 1949. The main line can be seen running past the far side of Pyle Junction signal box, on the left of the photograph, while ahead and to the right is the line to Tondu. (L&GRP)

full from end to end with crates, bicycles, carpets, a load of wheelbarrows and more boxes of all sizes than could be counted.

Another late-night incident could have had more serious consequences. A long loose-coupled train of empties headed by a 28xx class 2-8-0 had worked past the station on the down through road, which was worked by permissive block regulations, and been brought to a halt at the entrance to Canton engine shed, its wagons running back a short distance until all the couplings were taut, the guard's van eventually coming to a halt abreast of No 5 bay platform, where I was unloading a parcels van. Sometime later I became aware of an engine attacking the bank up to the station from the London end, and remember thinking the driver was going to be annoyed at having to stop just below the top of the steep climb. It soon became obvious that he was going to have to brake sharply, a thought almost immediately dismissed as it became equally as obvious that he was not going to stop at all. This thought had also struck most of the staff on the night shift for as I stepped from the van they were strung along this and the far platform watching in disbelief as a British Railways Standard class 4 4-6-0 running light engine came blasting over the top of the bank and on to the level section through the station. At that moment the driver saw the goods train in front of him, steam went off and the brakes came on, and we all waited for the inevitable. Shortly before impact the guard of the goods train became aware of what was going on and came out of the door of the ex-Great Western van, the veranda of which was facing backwards. His only words before he was jack-

Newport (High Street) station on 22 July 1922, before rebuilding. The signal box on the up main platform is 'Newport Middle Box', while the signal gantry further along the platform is a gem. (L&GRP)

knifed over the end of his van were 'What the b . . . .!' followed by the ringing crash of colliding buffers. Luckily for all concerned the taut couplings were able to close up and absorb the shock of the impact as the wagons were pushed together. I shall draw a veil over the ensuing altercations. The guard, once he had recovered the breath that had been knocked out of him, was to say the least, vociferous. Thankfully no one was injured and the only damage I recall was to one buffer of the locomotive. It was an incident that certainly enlivened the early morning.

Platforms 1 and 2, the up main platforms, were under the watchful eye of the stationmaster, or his assistant. His station inspections usually began here and were at their most strict. Woe betide the foreman if the windows of the various waiting rooms and offices were not clean or the platform swept. So you can imagine his reaction on the afternoon someone accidentally ran a platform trolley over a bag of coffee beans, and the aroma of ground coffee drifted along on the breeze.

Certain smells bring certain memories, and when I smell a freshly baking cake I am always reminded of the early morning cake train; fifteen or so fitted vans, usually behind a Hall or occasionally a Grange. As it stood at platform 3 the aroma that drifted from it as the doors were flung open and the trolleys pushed up to them was mouth watering. The reason for this was that each van was full of freshly baked, and still slightly warm cakes, ready for delivery to local shops. Chocolate cakes, fruit cakes, Swiss rolls and sponges, they and much else besides

Trundling westwards on a down coal working GWR 42xx class 2-8-0T No 4203 passes the goods yard at Pyle on 25 August 1948. (L&GRP)

135

were all there deliciously tempting. Unlike the mail train, unloading of the 'cake' was never frenetic. Each box or tray had to be, and was, handled with great care. There was no overloading of trolleys either. For a long time after the train's departure, so warm and penetrating was the smell, that if you let your mind wander for a moment you could easily think that it was still standing there.

In complete contrast was the 'wet fish'. It crept in at some variable hour between two and four in the morning and was shunted out of the way into platform 9, the island platform set a little apart from the main station that served the branch to Clarence Road. You had no need to open the van doors to catch this smell. The fish was packed in ice in wooden crates bound with rusty steel banding. The floor of the van was usually awash as fish scales and other debris frequently blocked the drain holes in the floor. The trick was to move the boxes and not let them come into contact with your clothing. If that happened, best friends suddenly found reasons to work three platforms away, and upwind. To my mind this was the worst job of the night shift. But an incident one night was, in retrospect, quite amusing, if perhaps a little unsettling at the time. I was manhandling a crate onto a trolley, barehanded as we had no protective gloves in those days, when it slipped and fell off the trolley onto the platform. The rest of the men on the shift who were working in other vans were around me in a moment, and examining my hands, face and anywhere they thought I could have been hit by the fish box. At the same time they were throwing questions at me. 'Are you all right? Not hurt? Not cut?' Surprised at first at their concern, and then a little irritated at the manhandling, for there was nothing wrong with me, I asked them why they were so worried. After all they had never shown any concern over my welfare before. There was silence for a long moment, then a solemn voice said that a couple of years before someone on his gang had cut his hand on the steel band on one of these crates. 'So what?' I asked. There was another silence before the same voice replied, 'He died.' I never did find out whether or not my leg was being pulled.

It took me a little while to recover from that incident, almost as long in fact as was my recovery from another that can best be described as macabre. Asked to check two Siphon H vans at the rear of a parcels working, I opened up the first one, which had emblazoned on its side the advertising sign of a nationally known manufacturer of sausages. As I stepped into the dark interior of the van I could see very little, and as a result walked into and nearly fell over what I thought was a crate. I found the interior light switch and switched it on. I had stumbled into the only article in the Siphon. It was not a crate however, it was a coffin. It was a long time before I ate that brand of sausages again.

Two final memories both relate to locomotives. The last up working of the day was the 12.05am Cardiff to Liverpool, known to all as the 'Northern', and except for this one occasion exclusively Castle hauled. One night in late August the 'Northern' stood as usual on platform 2, and from where I stood opposite on platform 3 I barely gave it a second glance, such was the familiarity of such a sight thirty years ago. Then something odd about the appearance of the cab caught my attention. For a few moments I could not define what it was until I realised that it had no side window, and was therefore a Star and not a Castle. Sure enough it was 4056 *Princess Margaret* at the head of the train. As it pulled away, with no hint as to its age (it was withdrawn a few weeks later), it was the last time I was to see a Star in action.

The other locomotive was also a veteran, but at the other end of the scale. It

Newport (High Street). Castle class No 4090 Dorchester Castle *waits impatiently on an up working in the 1950s.* (David Rees)

was 391, one of the last TVR A class 0-6-2Ts, and in a shockingly run-down condition. Like 4056 it, too, was withdrawn only weeks later. It was in the early hours when I became aware of an engine coming up the steep bank to the station from the east, which although only short is quite steep; commencing at 1 in 88 and finishing with a vicious length at 1 in 47. There was obviously something wrong, for regularly interspersed with the exhaust, which was more of a wheeze than the sharp bark one was used to, were distinct clanking noises. In the darkness beyond the station this combined wheeze and clank became slowly louder but progressively slower. It was obvious that it would be touch and go if she made it over the top. A pall of smoke and steam eventually came within the wash of the station lights, and slowly, painfully slowly, the 'Taffy' came into view. I have never heard a steam locomotive labour so much, and she only just made it to the top. As it reached the brow there was an exhaust beat, and immediately before the end of the interminable pause before the next the whole engine juddered and came within a hairsbreadth of stalling. Then came one last laboured, asthmatic, beat drawn from what reserves only the driver knew and could tap and she was at last over the top and on to the level through the station. The train was barely in motion by now and the 'Taffy's' troubles were not yet over as she still had to drag her long load of empty coal wagons over the brow.

137

One by one they slowly came, the clang of the wagons drowned by the engine as it struggled on, and after an age, and at a speed of no more than three or four miles an hour, eventually crossed from the down through road to Penarth curve on her way to the yard at Radyr. Long after the guard's van had disappeared the distressed sounds of her continuing heroic struggle could still be heard slowly fading in the darkness to the west.

Such are my memories and experiences of the working of the railways in South Wales in the summer of 1956. A snapshot, fixed in my mind, of one of the final summers of steam working in the area, when practices that had been built up over a century or more were as yet unchallenged. But, as we now know, irrevocable changes were close at hand and the days that such scenes as I now remember would be repeated were severely numbered.

On 3 May 1949 Great Western 42xx class 2-8-0T No 4257 heads a down freight along the main line at Laleston, (to the west of Bridgend). (L&GRP)

8
SOUTH WALES PORTS

The focal points of the railways of South Wales were the docks strung along the Glamorganshire and Monmouthshire coast from Newport to Burry Port. Their purpose was to ship first iron, and then more importantly coal, that had been brought to them from the narrow valleys running back from the coastal plain to the sea. In this task they were all, with few exceptions, remarkably successful. Not surprisingly the Great Western, seeing the advantages of dock ownership, entered the fray by way of purchase of local companies in the nineteenth century, thus ensuring for itself the dubious honour of being the owner of the only South Wales dock, Porthcawl, to close at a time when the coal export trade was nearly at its peak. The reputation of the GWR as a successful South Wales dock operator stems from the post-grouping period, when to its credit against overwhelming economic odds, and with a world war thrown in for good measure, it ran an extremely forceful enterprise. Not always profitable it is true, but no one could have done that in the early thirties.

It is almost impossible to estimate the tonnage of coal shipped through the South Wales docks over the century or more that the export trade existed. From the countless numbers of coal trains that wound their way to the coast at Cardiff alone, the latter's docks are credited with shipping a total in excess of 500 million tons. The methods by which the railways coped with bringing this traffic to the docks have already been described, but to complete the story we must turn to the dock side of the enterprise. Of the South Wales ports all except Swansea were owned by railway companies, although arguably one could exclude Cardiff from this statement. In its later years it was owned by the Cardiff Railway (actually the Bute Trustees in another guise), but since the company only ever served one colliery and tapped the traffic of no other railway, it could not be said to be a railway-owned dock in the sense that Barry and Port Talbot were. However, railway owned or not, the facilities and organisation that grew up to handle the coal traffic, which year upon year until the outbreak of World War I had never ceased to grow, were both efficient and reliable, and did not differ significantly from dock to dock.

Coal trains from the valleys would usually arrive at reception and storage sidings in the vicinity of the dock. Newport had a complex of such sidings near Alexandra Dock Junction on the South Wales main line. There were five in all. Four of them, Monmouthshire Bank, Eastern Valley, Low Level, and West Mendalgief all converged on East Mendalgief Junction to the north west of the docks, while Maesglas sidings were situated a short distance away to the west on the far side of the main line. All except one (Low Level) were elevated on embankments which eased their access to the tip roads in the docks. In all some 114 roads were provided when these sidings were at their fullest extent, a remarkable number when Newport's coal export tonnage is compared to other docks to the west. At Cardiff there was a similar concentration of sidings beyond

This historic view, taken circa 1910, shows the town dock and wharves on the River Usk at Newport. It was from wharves such as these that the earliest coal shipments were dispatched. The jetty in the foreground, together with its associated rail connections was the private loading and shipping facility of Lysaghts Orb Ironworks. (British Steel Corporation)

the east end of the Roath and Queen Alexandra Docks, at the end of the Taff Vale Railway's Roath Dock branch. They numbered six in all, Reception, Marshalling, Roath Dock Storage, Swansea Street, Low Level, and finally Beach Sidings. Here too there was access from the Newport direction allowing coal to be brought to Cardiff docks not only from the Monmouthshire but also the Llynfi, Ogmore and Ely valleys. Two additional sets were also situated to the north west of the docks. One was at Crockherbtown on the Taff Vale main line just north of Queen Street station, and quite near the city centre, while the other was at Crwys Road on the Rhymney line about one mile from the same station on the way to Caerphilly. Penarth Dock had its own set of sidings at Llandough, while Barry boasted a large spread of sidings at Cadoxton, together with others on the high level near the docks, and at Porthkerry one reserved for coal traffic off the Vale of Glamorgan line. It must be said however, that those at Barry were smaller than those at either Cardiff or Newport which speaks volumes for the efficient turnround they could achieve.

In the west, Port Talbot coal traffic was received either at the Docks Sidings adjacent to the new dock, or others nearby at Margam Junction or Duffryn Yard, and at one time traffic off the Rhondda & Swansea Bay line was exchanged at Burrows Junction Exchange sidings alongside the River Afan immediately to the west of the docks. The reception arrangements at Swansea were complicated by the number of railway companies having accesss at one time or another. This resulted in London & North Western and Midland Railway traffic being dealt with separately to the west and north of the docks, whereas to the east a series of sidings from the region of Jersey Marine South Junction to Eastern Depot, a

140

distance of some three and a half miles, were in operation to serve traffic arising from the Neath, Cynon and Dulais valleys together with that from the Rhondda & Swansea Bay line. Finally at Llanelly and Burry Port similar reception sidings could be found.

Once having been received at the docks the responsibility for their movements fell upon the siding inspector or shunter. It was their responsibility to organise the working to and from the coal tippers and also to inform the area controller of the 'state of play' so to speak, so that the flow of wagons to and from the docks could be smoothly maintained. The duties of the Marshalling Sidings inspector at Cardiff included arrangements for the disposal of incoming coal trains in all six sets of sidings from Roath Basin Junction to Beach sidings referred to earlier, together with the Pengam coal sidings adjacent to the main line. He informed Queen Street control at 6.00am, 2.00pm, and 10.00pm of the coal standing in these sidings, and every three hours of the number of empty wagons and those filled with pitwood, ready for dispatch. It was also his duty to arrange the working of the dock engines between the Dock Storage sidings and the Queen Alexandra, Roath Dock and Roath Basin, and arrange with the East Dock inspector the working of traffic between Pengam sidings and Tyndall Street for both East and West docks. He in turn was informed by way of the individual dock foremen and the appropriate storage siding inspector of the actual tipping requirements at 10.30am and 5.30pm daily. This information included all the coal that would be required up to the time of the next advice. If in the meantime alterations were necessary he was contacted immediately. In the reverse direction Queen Street control informed him of trains leaving the collieries throughout the day and also

South Wales sunset. The coaster Erik Boye loads coal from one of the low level coal tippers on the south side of the Queen Alexandra Dock, Cardiff, in 1960. A scene common for more than a century, this small coaster was amongst the last to load coal at Cardiff. (W. J. Bryer)

The 20-ton coal wagon

Port Talbot is another port of recent development, for practically all the docks have been built within the last thirty years. Its growth may be measured by the fact that in 1900 it dealt with half a million tons of traffic, and in 1923 with three and a quarter million tons.

It was at Port Talbot that the first 20-ton coal wagons were tipped in August, 1924, an event which marked the beginning of a new era in coal transport and shipping operations in South Wales.

The 20-ton wagon was an innovation for which the Great Western Railway must take the credit. The scheme for the introduction of these high-capacity wagons was actually in operation within less than six months of the date of the General Manager addressing a communication to South Wales coal traders telling them of the advantages to be gained by their adoption, in place of the old 10- or 12-ton wagons.

At that time there were about 110,000 private owners' coal wagons in South Wales, mostly of 10-ton capacity, and as the 20-ton wagon can be built at approximately a saving of 50 per cent on the cost of two 10-ton wagons, the economy in first cost, maintenance and renewals was obvious. The high-capacity wagon has other advantages, for a train of fifty 10-ton wagons measures 1,009 feet, and its capacity is, of course, 500 tons. Two such trains (1,000 tons) would have a length of 2,018 feet, but fifty of the new 20-ton wagons (conveying 1,000 tons) only occupy 1,225 feet of siding space.

You will see that there are all-round advantages to the use of 20-ton wagons, and in order to encourage their use the Great Western Railway grant a rebate off the railway rate and a reduction in the tipping and weighing charges at the docks.

The introduction of the 20-ton wagon has necessitated a heavy expenditure in the construction of new hoists and other shipping appliances and the adaptation of others, in order to take the larger and heavier wagons.

Here we see a large number of coal hoists of the same types as at other ports, but at Port Talbot there is another type of coal-shipping contrivance which we have not yet seen – the belt conveyor.

With this appliance the loaded coal wagons are brought down to a point at ground level about 40 yards from the ship's side. The pins holding the end doors of the wagons are then knocked out, the wagon tilted, and its contents poured into a shallow pit, the floor of which is formed by a sloping chute.

The coal slides down this chute on to an endless travelling band about three feet wide. This band travels along an inclined plane to the necessary height to reach the ship's side, where the coal is discharged on to another chute and thence into the ship's hold. With a sufficient and uniform supply of loaded wagons there is practically a continuous stream of coal passing along the belt and down the chute. When all conditions are favourable these belt conveyors can load coal into vessels even more quickly than coal hoists. In fact, so efficient is this form of apparatus for shipping coal that it has been decided to provide a belt conveyor for dealing with 20-ton wagons at Newport Docks.

(*W. G. Chapman, Twixt Rail & Sea – GWR 1927*)

of the collieries' requirements for empty wagons and pitwood. Similar duties were performed by the shunters at Crockherbtown and Crwys Road. They would arrange the disposal of all down coal traffic at their respective yards, and keep a record of all coal wagons standing in the sidings, with the dates of arrival. They too, at 6.00am daily, had to inform Queen Street control and the East Dock chief dock foreman of all wagons standing in their yards. They also arranged with the latter the loading of engines to the docks and informed control when such a train was dispatched.

The system in operation at Barry was slightly different. Barry Docks had its own controller who oversaw, through his inspectors and foremen, the disposal of all incoming trains and the marshalling of all outgoing. Reporting however was split. Information from the inspectors at Cadoxton storage sidings was reported to Queen Street control, whereas that from the foreman at Porthkerry sidings, which worked the traffic from the Llynfi and Ogmore valleys via the Vale of Glamorgan line, was reported to Tondu control. Specifically it was the duty of the Barry Dock controller to inform Queen Street of the departure and loading of the Cadoxton pilots and 'main line' trains. At 6.00am, 9.00am, 1.00pm,

6.00pm, and 11.00pm Queen Street was informed of the number of empty wagons on hand, and at 8.00am, 11.00am and 5.00pm they were given particulars of coal required at the tippers for shipment, especially any needed urgently. Every three hours an estimate had to be given of the number of empty wagons expected to be available for removal, while when appropriate, details were supplied of the Rogerstone traffic to the Monmouthshire valleys.

Activity at the docks was relentless with constant movements between sidings and tip roads through the complicated layouts that linked them. So complex was this activity, which of course could not be regularised and timetabled, that elaborate whistle codes were devised so that driver could inform signalman of his destination for the latter to set the road. At Cardiff, throughout the dock area together with the Crockherbtown and Crwys Road reception sidings, some eighty-one were once in use, while Barry managed to suffice with sixty-five for its dock operations. Obviously certain peaks occurred at particularly complex layouts or at traffic bottlenecks. At Cardiff the trackwork was particularly intricate in the Tyndall Street area near the East Dock where twenty-two were needed to cover the movements that could be made there, which not only included movements to and from the main line but also those to the nearby East Moors steelworks. Dock Storage South was only slightly less frantic with eighteen whistle signals. These ranged from one long blast, requesting permission to move from the up

Coal was not the only commodity handled at South Wales docks. Here a pair of Newport (Pill) 67xx 0-6-0PTs Nos 6726 and 6729 work iron ore wagons on the quayside of the South dock. (Welsh Industrial & Maritime Museum)

line from the Beach sidings to the Roath Branch line, to what some would describe as the cacophonous three long and two 'crows' needed to proceed to Pengam sidings (near the main line) from the No 1 up road. The greatest concentration however was at Cadoxton South. Here twenty-six whistle codes were in operation, the most intricate being the one 'crow', three long and one 'crow', requesting permission to move from the outer fan of down sidings (Nos 12–18) to No 2 Dock via the Cogan branch tracks through Cadoxton station.

On the down side of such sidings, which were almost always a series of loops, the train crew would hand over their load to the engines that would work the wagons forward to the tip roads. The engine would then either go on shed or move across to the up side to pick up a return load of empties, these having been worked back from the tips by dock engines. As described earlier it was most likely that each trainload would be destined for only part of the cargo of one ship. It could have arrived ahead of the vessel as part of the build-up needed to ensure that coaling could commence immediately it berthed, or be one of the follow-up loads arriving as the first wagons were emptied in order to keep up the continuous flow necessary to fill its holds. A trainload would be perhaps 500 tons, whereas the vessel would possibly require a cargo of say, 12,000 tons, thus requiring twenty-four trainloads to fill it. If a single coal tipper was working, at a maximum rate of perhaps 600 tons per hour, which was achievable by the fastest appliances,

All coal from the Ely, Llynfi, Garw and Ogmore valleys destined for shipment at Cardiff docks was worked to Pengam sidings to the east of the city, and then worked forward to the dock reception sidings by a pilot engine. On such a duty on 21 April 1955 Rhymney Railway P class 0-6-2T No 83 heads such a transfer working out of Pengam sidings to the docks. (S. Rickard)

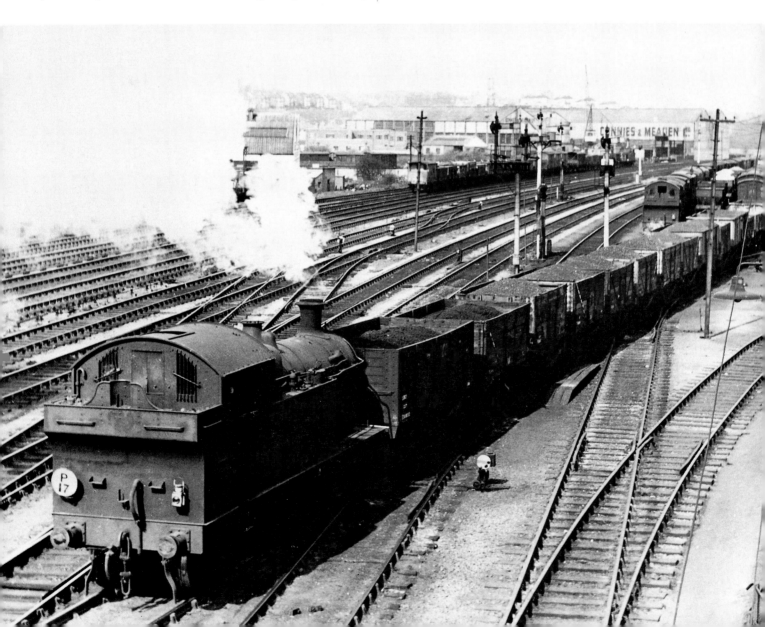

PENARTH DOCK.
PENARTH DOCK HOIST ROADS.

From the Appendix to Section 9 of the Service Time Tables, *March 1950.*

The attention of Trainmen and others, whose duties require them to perform shunting and coupling operations on the Hoist Roads at Penarth Dock, is directed to the narrow spaces between some of the Hoist Roads and the adjoining walls supporting the full roads. They are warned to keep a special look out when engaged in any of the undermentioned roads where the clearance between a siding and an adjoining wall or siding is less than 6 feet.

Guards, Shunters and others are forbidden to operate brakes or couplings while vehicles are moving in the undermentioned sidings, nor must Trains be drawn out of such sidings until the Guard has satisfied himself, and informed the Driver, that no person is engaged upon a line where a narrow space exists.

The roads referred to are :—

Siding known as	Situated between	Spaces between Siding and Wall vary		Narrowest part.
		From	To	
		ft. in.	ft. in.	
No. 4 Hoist, Empty road	2 and 4 Hoists, full roads	3 6	4 9	Left-hand side, 850 ft. from points.
No. 5 Hoist, Empty road	4 and 5 Hoists, full roads	3 0	7 10	Right-hand side, 650 ft. from points.
No. 5 Hoist, Empty road	5 and 6 Hoists, full roads	3 4	5 2	Left-hand side, 250 ft. from points.
No. 8 Hoist, Empty road	7 and 8 Hoists, full roads	2 11	3 10	Left-hand side, 250 ft. from points, and Right-hand side, 400 ft. from points.
No. 9 Hoist, Empty road	8 and 9 Hoists, full roads	3 0	7 8	Right-hand side, between 350 ft. and 450 ft. from points.
No. 10 Hoist, Empty road	9 and 10 Hoists, full roads	3 0	4 0	Right-hand side, 236 ft. from points.
No. 11 Hoist, Empty road	10 and 11 Hoists, full roads	2 7	3 8	Right-hand side, 229 ft. from points.
No. 12 Hoist, Empty road	11 and 12 Hoists, full roads	3 3	4 4	Left-hand side, 400 ft. from points.
No. 13 Hoist, Empty road	12 and 13 Hoists, full roads	2 10	4 7	Right-hand side, 280 ft. from points.

Note.—The narrowest spaces herein mentioned are from the outside rail to the wall, and inasmuch as wagons overlap the rails by 2 ft., the free space between the wagons and the walls must be calculated as 2 ft. less than the actual space between the rail and the wall indicated above.

it would take some twenty hours of continuous working to load such a vessel. If possible coal tippers would work in multiples thus reducing the loading time, but obviously requiring a much faster delivery and turnround of wagons.

Variations of this practice abounded. If the cargo required mixing the loads of wagons containing different grades of coal, perhaps from different collieries, they had to be shunted before being brought to the tip road to ensure that the correct proportions of the differing coal grades would be mixed as tipping progressed. An example of this would have been an order for 'Powell Duffryn Admiralty List' coal a cargo of which would be made up of one half Aberdare and one half Rhymney valley grades from different mines owned by the Powell Duffryn Company in these two valleys. The shunting procedures to enable the wagons to arrive at their appointed tippers, and possibly in a specific order, were therefore extremely complicated and would proceed day and night.

Obviously the reception sidings at which train loads arrived could not contain all the wagons awaiting tipping or returning. So between these and the tip roads were situated storage sidings. At Barry for instance, such a set of sidings once existed along the north side of the No 2 Dock, and similar large sets existed near the Roath Dock at Cardiff. These are just two of the many that of necessity grew

145

Stonefield Junction, Cardiff docks, 1960. The double track leading to the right foreground leads to the sets of marshalling sidings at the eastern end of the docks, while those to the left lead to the north sides of the Roath and Queen Alexandra docks. Just out of view to the left is East Dock shed, and at this date a line of withdrawn panniers can be seen on the shed sidings. The embankment beyond once held sidings running to high level coal tippers on the eastern side of the East dock, while in the left background one of the last remaining high-level coal tippers on the west side of this dock is visible. (W. J. Bryer)

up in parallel with the reception sidings at the largest of the South Wales docks. There would be a continuous movement of wagons between these two sets of sidings, and also it was not unknown for loaded trains to be brought directly to the storage sidings instead of being left at the reception roads. The 'main line' engine of course worked its train to this point before leaving it for the docks shunter.

So either directly from the reception roads, or by way of the storage sidings a rake of wagons would be hauled forward to the dockside tipping appliances. These came in three varieties, and since two of them could exist in high-level and low-level forms, five separate types of tipping appliance could be found at one time in the docks of South Wales. These appliances could be of the fixed type, that is they were immovable dockside structures which meant that as ships became larger it would be necessary for them to be moved along the quay in order to fill both fore and aft holds. Alternatively they could be movable, which meant that not only could they move along the quayside and be stopped alongside the hatches of the vessels to be loaded, but also up to four could be used simultaneously. Both these types of appliances could be designed to be fed from a high or a low level, the loaded coal wagons being offered to them either from an embankment or from the quayside. The final type, of which only three were introduced at Port Talbot, and then only late in the days of the coal trade, was the conveyor, one end of which could be raised to a suitable height for discharge into a ship's hold.

The methods of operating these tippers, particularly the high-level ones, was

146

very efficient. Once the line of wagons had been placed on the incoming road the shunting locomotive could be dispensed with to work elsewhere, only needing to return when ordered with a fresh rake of wagons and to remove the empty ones from the previous visit. On the high level at Barry for example, the loaded wagons were backed into curved sidings with a gradient of 1 in 233 falling towards the coal tipper. In South Wales the wagons were built with a hanging door at one end only, unlike those of the north of England where the coal was discharged through the bottom of the wagons. Loaded wagons were dispatched from the collieries with the doors facing uphill, in order to prevent them opening on steep inclines, and so in most of the South Wales docks they had to be turned before being tipped. This was borne in mind when Barry Docks were laid out so that wagons from their main line when shunted into these sidings had the doors facing the correct way for tipping. Coal traffic by the Vale of Glamorgan line required turning of course, as did rogue wagons facing the wrong way off the main line, and to allow for this each appliance had a wagon turntable immediately before the weighbridge which was situated in front of the tipper.

The wagons were run forward one at a time on to the weighbridge and after weighing were drawn to the coal tips by hydraulic capstans. They came to rest here in a cradle standing on a tip-up table that was hinged at the front and could be tilted by a hydraulic ram situated beneath, and which could be moved vertically up or down to the correct height for loading. The height to which a wagon could be raised above the quayside (not the embankment) could vary from approximately 37–45ft depending upon the tipper. Once in the cradle a chain,

To the east of Cardiff docks was a complex series of sidings to hold wagons awaiting discharge or returning to colliery. In this 1960 scene at 'Storage Sidings' as this particular set were known, the coal trade is not as evident as it once was, but on the left side full and empty coal wagons standing alongside wagonloads of pit props can be seen, although more general traffic is also evident. (W. J. Bryer)

147

fixed at one end, was hooked on to the rear of the wagon and the catch securing the hanging door released. The cradle was then raised or lowered, depending upon the size of the vessel being loaded, and the tip-up table tilted discharging the coal into an inclined steel chute that extended over the ship's hatchway. South Wales steam coal was susceptible to breakage if dropped from a great height, which from the wagon to the bottom of a hold could easily be 50ft or more, and dropping coal from such a height could also damage the bottoms of the coal ships themselves. To minimise this what was termed an 'anti-breakage box' (in reality a hopper with a remotely operated bottom opening door), was suspended at the end of the chute from a crane jib attached to the tipper, at the commencement of loading. The coal fell into this 'box' which was then lowered to the bottom of the ship's hold and emptied. By repeating this technique a cone of coal was built up until it reached the bottom of the chute. The 'box' was then swung away and the following loads of coal allowed to slide on to the cone and into the hold where it was trimmed. This was done by hand, gangs of coal trimmers shovelling the coal evenly throughout the hold from the foot of the cone so that the vessel would remain level. Frequently the coal would be screened to remove any small coal as it slid down the chute, and would fall on to the ship's deck from where by way of a skip it was periodically transferred to a rail wagon standing on the quayside line near the tipper. If screening was not necessary hinged plates could cover the screens and the coal pass directly into the hold.

After the wagon had been emptied the tip-up table was returned to the horizontal position and the cradle brought back to its starting place. The chain was then unhooked from the empty wagon, which was pushed off the cradle to run on to a line with a falling gradient of 1 in 80 to a second weighbridge where the tare weight was obtained. It was then pushed on to a further falling gradient, this time at 1 in 70, which shortly levelled out, and came to rest at the end of the line of the previously emptied wagons to which it was then coupled by a shunter. From here the rake of empties was drawn out of the tip sidings up a 1 in 45 gradient and taken to departure sidings for sorting prior to return to the collieries. A few of the tippers had two roads for full wagons instead of the usual one. This provided not only additional storage, but was also intended for wagons filled at different pits, so that vessels could be loaded with mixed coals in whatever proportions were needed. Such sidings of course were also of benefit in reducing the amount of shunting necessary to mix wagons for such orders.

On the south side of Barry's No 1 Dock and on the mole that projected into it from the western side, low-level tippers were employed, and wagons had to be lifted from the quayside to the required height for tipping. For these appliances

BELL SIGNALS FOR DOWN TRAINS BETWEEN TYNDALL STREET JUNCTION AND STONEFIELD JUNCTION SIGNAL BOXES.

The following Bell Codes are in operation. Drivers must give the prescribed Whistles at Tyndall Street Junction to notify the Signalman of the destination of trains.

	Bells.
To Queen Alexandra Dock via North-East Box	2–2–1
To South side Roath Dock via North-East Box	2–1–2
To East Side Roath Basin via North-East Box	1–2–2
To Dowlais Works, East Moors	1–2–2–1
To Machine Road North Side Roath Dock	3–2
To connecting Line Sidings, North Side Roath Dock	3–2–1
To East Side Roath Basin via Roath Dock Swing Bridge	5
To Stonefield No. 1, not over Roath Dock Swing Bridge	2–2
To West Side Roath Basin	1–1
To Loco. Sheds	1–2

From the Appendix to Section 9 of the Service Time Tables, *March 1950.*

148

they were pushed into sidings having a falling gradient of 1 in 200, and one at a time were pulled forward by a hydraulic capstan on to a further falling gradient of 1 in 140 to a weighbridge. They then ran to a turntable, were turned through ninety degrees so that the hanging door was facing the vessel to be loaded, and drawn on to the tipping cradle at the hoist. Each hoist had a steel frame nearly 60ft in height which supported the chute for conveying the coal into the ship's hold and guided the cradle during its ascent or descent from the quayside. The height to which a wagon could be lifted was the same as for the high-level tippers. After being emptied and returned to the level of the quay the wagon was run to a second turntable, turned again through ninety degrees and pushed to another weighbridge for taring. From here it was drawn, this time on to a 1 in 70 falling gradient, to a level section of line where empty wagons accumulated, was re-coupled and later removed by a shunting engine along with other such wagons.

Although they varied somewhat in size and methods of operation from dock to dock, this, in outline, was how the coal tippers operated throughout South Wales. The rate of coaling, for example, could vary from 250 tons to 600 tons per hour depending upon the size of the tipper and the speed with which it could be operated. At Penarth the low-level tippers on the north side of the basin were designed to lift a loaded wagon of 25 tons gross weight 45ft above the quay, to

Flanked by Great Western panniers Swansea Harbour Trust 0-4-0ST No 1143, built by Peckett, with one of the Avonside built GWR 1101 class 0-4-0Ts behind, stands outside Danygraig shed on 6 July 1958. (S. Rickard)

tip the contents, return the wagon to the level of the quay, and run it off the cradle in less than thirty seconds. Loaded ten-ton wagons (approximately 16 tons gross) could travel up or down at a rate of 180ft per minute – this, a design of 1899 vintage. This speed of operation was fully matched by the railways. Coal was frequently worked to Penarth, and was standing on the tip roads within two hours of leaving the mine. It was not unknown for wagons to make a journey to the dock and back to the colliery and be loaded again for a second journey that day. It was also recorded that on one occasion 2,250 wagons were worked to the dock, shipped, and returned in twenty-four hours. At an average of fifty wagons per train that added up to forty-five loaded trains arriving and the same number of empty trains departing in this period. Records such as this were matched too by the turnround time of vessels being loaded. It was Penarth's boast that it could load vessels of up to 2,500 tons at such a rate that they could arrive, load and sail in no more than about three hours.

These methods of train handling and coal shipping, which in their day were amongst the most efficient in the world, only reached this position after almost a century of continuous expansion and improvement. The evolution of the large South Wales dock specifically built for coal exporting began with the piecemeal opening between 1855 and 1859 of the Bute East Dock in Cardiff. It was certainly true that coal shipping was already underway on a limited scale from existing docks such as those at Newport (Town Dock), Porthcawl, Swansea (North Dock), Llanelly, and of course the nearby Bute West Dock, but each of these had been conceived and opened before the export coal business reached a predominant position in the trade of South Wales. The Bute East Dock was the first to be built in response to the new, and rapidly growing, overseas markets which had been opened after 1840 following the pioneering efforts of John Nixon, a mining engineer. In that year he arranged that for three years he would sell the output of one of the new mines near Aberdare owned by Thomas Powell for a commission of 6d (2.5p) per ton on all coal exported. Realising the steam-raising potential of this coal he chartered a sailing vessel and shipped a cargo to Nantes, the first South Wales steam coal to be shipped outside the United Kingdom. Here he distributed the cargo free to suitable customers. The risk paid off, and the export of Welsh steam coal had begun, and later amongst its regular customers could be found the French Navy and French railways.

Following Nixon's success steam colliery development in the Aberdare valley moved quickly, and by 1853 fourteen mines yielded some 2,500 to 3,000 tons per day. Steam coal was proved in the upper Rhondda in 1855, and by 1859 sixteen collieries were producing. In 1840 Cardiff exported 43,651 tons, by 1853 this had risen to 834,221 tons and by the time the East Dock was in full operation in 1859, 1,506,651 tons, and the boom was only just beginning. From the 1860s steam-driven iron ships became the norm, and with this change in shipbuilding practice came larger vessels that could reliably sail greater distances. Trade across the Atlantic and to the Far East grew rapidly and Welsh steam coal was soon in ever increasing demand. After the opening of the Suez Canal in 1869 large coaling, or bunkering, stations were provided at strategic ports on the voyage to India, as well as other major ocean routes. Between South Wales and these coaling stations an enormous trade grew up in bunker coal, for the demand now became almost insatiable. From the earliest days of steam-powered Naval vessels, Aberdare 'dry' steam coal had been used. However in 1864 a Government committee (at the insistence, it appears, of Members of Parliament representing constituencies in

150

Restrictions on Engines Working on Dock Lines.

From the Appendix to Section 9 of the Service Time Tables, *March 1950.*

Engines are prohibited from working over the Dock Lines as set out below :—

	Points.	Engines allowed to work.	Engines prohibited.
(A)	(1) Top of West Dock, West side roadside to dockside	Nil	All types.
	(2) Mountstuart Dry Dock beyond stopboard at Crescent Road	,,	,,
	(3) Line into Gainey's Yard	,,	,,
	(4) " The Circle " South side of Roath Dock ..	,,	,,
	(5) Curve from quayside road East side, East Dock to " A " Warehouse top of East Dock	,,	,,
	(6) Mill Road on roadside of Channel Mills to top of East Dock	,,	,,
(B)	(1) Collingdon Road and West side, West Dock ..	0-6-0T. type	
	(2) Low Level sidings, West side, East Dock	67XX	
	(3) Low Level sidings, East side, East Dock	2021 class	
	(4) Curves leading to top of East Dock, East side (" A " Warehouse)	54XX	
	(5) East Moors and East Tyndall Street	64XX	
	(6) The Old Way and Gulley to Dockside roads, North side, Roath Dock	74XX	All other types
	(7) Traders' sidings at North end of Lewis Road up to stopboards	1701 class	
		2301 class	
	(8) Spillers Mills and Jetty area	22XX	
	(9) Empire Wharf Shed Road	57XX	
	(10) Denny, Mott's Middle shunt	27XX	
	(11) Channel sidings to Roath Basin Bridge	8750 class	
	(12) Feed roads South side Roath Dock, except Nos. 1 and 2 belt conveyors		
(C)	(1) Running lines between Cork Wharf and top of dock West side of East Dock	All engines in list " B " and in addition—	
	(2) Running lines East side, East Dock	0-6-2T.	
	(3) Feed road from slip roads to landside of King's Wharf Cold Stores	56XX	
	(4) All lines between No. 6 Weighing Machine and roadway, North side Roath Dock	66XX Ex T.V.O.4	
	(5) South East Junction to slips, Empire and King's Wharf roads	Ex T.V.A. Ex Rhymney A.P.	All other types.
	(6) Line leading to No. 1 Power House	14XX	
	(7) Short foreshore roads, South side Q.A. Dock ..	2-6-2T.	
	(8) Lewis Road from N.E. Junction	45XX	
	(9) Beach Sidings	55XX	
	(10) Coal feed roads, S. side, Q.A. Dock	44XX	
	(11) G.K. & B. Coke Ovens	Austerity 2-8-0	
		Austerity 2-10-0	
		L.M.R. 2-6-0	
		L.M.R. 2F	

the coalfields of the North of England) recommended that future Naval contracts should specify a mixture of two-thirds Welsh and one third Newcastle coals. The experiment was not a success and after complaints from Naval officers the Admiralty reverted to the exclusive use of Welsh steam coal from 1872. This was the highest accolade that could be bestowed, following which demand exploded.

But this is running ahead of events and we must return to see how the development of shipping facilities coped with this trade. In the year that the Bute East Dock was finally completed, 1859, two more docks were opened, South Dock in Swansea and the Tidal Harbour on the Ely river. Two years later the small harbour at Briton Ferry opened, and in 1865 relief to the growing congestion at Cardiff was found in the opening of Penarth Dock (it was extended in 1884). In 1867 the old harbour at Porthcawl was enlarged with the opening of the inner harbour, following which there was a pause of seven years, the longest gap in dock construction until the eight-year period between 1899 and 1907. The years 1874 and 1875 saw, respectively, the opening of the Roath Basin in Cardiff and the North Dock at Newport. The action now moved to the western end of the coalfield. Swansea's third dock, the Prince of Wales, opened in 1881 and was extended seventeen years later, while in 1883 Llanelly North Dock shipped its first coal. The battle between the Bute Trustees together with the Taff Vale Railway, and the Barry Railway, was now reaching its climax, the outcome of which was the Roath and Barry No 1 docks of 1887 and 1889 respectively.

   Still dock facilities continued to fall short of those needed, and between 1893 and 1909 there was a further large expansion. Newport South Dock was the first of the next series of docks to be opened (it was extended in 1907 and yet again

Although a postwar photograph, taken well past the peak of the South Wales export coal trade, this scene at Cadoxton on the Barry Railway sums up the raison d'être of the valleys' railways. (Welsh Industrial & Maritime Museum)

On the edge of Newport docks was situated Pill engine shed, home to the dock shunters, and this photograph illustrates a cross section of its allocation in June 1939. Built by the Alexandra Dock Railway it was in later years a sub-shed to Ebbw Junction. (L&GRP)

in 1914), Barry completed its No 2 Dock in 1898, and the same year saw the new dock at Port Talbot opened. Cardiff finally reached its zenith in 1907 with the formal opening by King Edward VII of the Queen Alexandra Dock, and the completion of the King's Dock at Swansea two years later at last saw the end of dock construction for the South Wales coal trade. One final dock was built however; this was Swansea's Queen's Dock, but it was not opened until 1920, by which time South Wales had no need for further coal-shipping facilities, and its major purpose was as a crude-oil terminal for the nearby Anglo Persian Oil Company's refinery at Llandarcy.

Thus in every decade from 1841 to 1910 at least two docks were opened, and in two of those six decades no less than four were completed. This was an average of one new dock opening every thirty months in these two decades, which were 1851 to 1860 and 1881 to 1890. Some idea of the scale of this expansion in facilities, as if just the total of individual docks was not enough, can be gauged from the areas of the docks constructed. In the ten years from 1851 to 1860 a total of 94 acres of water were created, whereas in the decade 1881 to 1890, just under 150 acres were enclosed by the four new docks built in this decade. Yet whereas after 1890 the rate of dock building slackened the acreage enclosed expanded even more rapidly. In the next decade the three docks opened aggregated 157 acres. The next two added a further 147 acres, and finally with the completion of the Queen's Dock, this one single facility added no less than a further 150 acres to the total.

Not all the cargoes were export coal, however, imports also featured but by comparison the quantities handled were never great, a factor which led to the decline of the South Wales docks with the loss of the export coal trade, although during the days that steam still reigned supreme only one, Penarth, was actually closed. But import traffic there was, and much of it related closely to the traditional South Wales industries, of very long standing. Foremost amongst that destined for local usage was the ubiquitous pit prop. Wooden props were always preferred, and the continuous demand, having outstripped home

153

production generations ago, gave rise to a lively trade with Scandinavia. The sight of coal wagons returning to their colliery with pit props was almost as common as that of the loaded coal trains themselves. Similarly it was a familiar sight at the docks to see large stockpiles of pit props awaiting call off to the mines. These stockpiles grew to enormous size at certain times of the year as orders were delivered before the Baltic ports froze in the winter. Of such long standing was this trade, and so regular were the calls by Scandinavian vessels, that churches were established within the docks for their sailors. These churches, although simply built corrugated-iron structures, were a distinctive landmark near the entrance of both Swansea and Cardiff docks.

Another long-standing import was iron ore, particularly from Spain, in which some of the South Wales steelworks had a financial interest. This traffic continues to this day but only through the British Steel Corporation harbour at Port Talbot, and the only rail haul is now along the main line to Llanwern to the east of Newport. At Cardiff the ore was used by the nearby steelworks, but before 1930 there was also a brisk traffic to Dowlais via Caerphilly, Ystrad Mynach, Penalltan Junction, Nelson & Llancaiach and the fearsomely graded and isolated Taff-Bargoed line to the treeless windswept heights at Dowlais. This was perhaps one of the most difficult workings in the annals of South Wales freight trains. Even such powerful engines as the Great Western 56xx class or the Rhymney Railway R class 0-6-2Ts, both Group D engines in the GWR power classification, were restricted to an unassisted load of eleven full ore wagons, while the Rhymney Railway A and A1 classes were limited to only nine. Little wonder that double heading and banking were frequently resorted to. Another regular working of imported iron ore was from Newport to Ebbw Vale, which has already been referred to in connection with the British Railways class 9F 2-10-0s which worked this traffic in the 1950s and early 1960s. But, for years before that, standard Great Western classes laboured valiantly on this traffic, which was frequently banked north of Aberbeeg. The maximum unassisted load was twenty-eight wagons up the valley from Aberbeeg to Ebbw Vale, or twelve of the Ebbw Vale Company's 21-ton hopper wagons. Trains of thirty-two such hoppers were worked to Ebbw Vale North however, working instructions calling for an engine of power class E in front (a 42xx class 2-8-0T or a 72xx class 2-8-2T), with a power class A engine (a 57xx 0-6-0PT) banking at the rear to Aberbeeg, with an additional class A engine, also in the rear, from Aberbeeg northwards. Typical of such a working was the 10.15am from West Mendalgief, one of the three daily workings that in 1938 once ran from here. Having taken water at Risca it would arrive at Aberbeeg at 11.52pm, it was allowed 5 minutes to attach the banker and then no less than 45 minutes for the five and a half miles to Ebbw Vale North, up gradients no better than 1 in 85, and at their worst as steep as 1 in 52.

By comparison the remaining import traffic was relatively small but did include important rail workings of timber (other than pitwood), woodpulp, flour, grain, frozen meat and live cattle. At both Cardiff and Swansea fish was once landed in appreciable quantities generating its own rail-borne traffic for what was principally local consumption. But perhaps the most surprising of imports was at Penarth. Here, according to a proud boast in a 1908 publication of the Dock Company, it imported gas coal for use by the Cardiff and other gas companies.

To work all this traffic in the dock area generations of small but powerful shunting engines were used, as counterparts to their larger and better known brethren that plied between pit and port. Those of most recent memory are of

The diminutive White Hart halt on the Brecon & Merthyr line between Machen and Caerphilly. This halt was situated on the down line; the up line is to the right and below the photographer, and contained a corresponding halt of the same name. The up and down lines, on what was known as the Machen Loop, were separated for part of the way towards Caerphilly in order to ease the gradients for eastbound (down and loaded) coal trains. The B&M main line can be seen above and to the left. (L&GRP)

From 1871 the Rhymney Railway terminus at Cardiff was at the Parade station a few yards from Crockherbtown Junction with the Taff Vale Railway immediately north of Queen Street station. This view shows the station on 23 July 1922 looking northwards towards Llanishen. The signals behind the fencing are Taff Vale somersaults, and their Crockherbtown Lower Junction signal box can be seen behind the awning on the up platform. The station was demolished in 1928 following the rebuilding of Queen Street station and the diversion of Rhymney valley trains into that station. (L&GRP)

Rhiwderin station on the Brecon & Merthyr Railway. Probably the most handsome station on this line, its buildings were far superior to anything else that company could offer. Converted to a private house they stand today, as does, coincidentally, the signal box on the down platform, which can be found at the Caerphilly Railway Society's site within the former Rhymney Railway's Caerphilly locomotive works. (L&GRP)

Great Western origin that had gradually replaced the older pre-grouping engines. The greatest number of any one class were the 67xx series of the Great Western's largest pannier-tank class, the 57xx, which numbered 863 in total throughout the whole GWR system. The 67xx series, which eventually numbered eighty in all, were built with steam brakes only, unlike the remainder of the class which were vacuum fitted. They were very much South Wales engines. Of the first fifty built, thirty-three had been allocated to docks sheds here in 1938, while in 1953 no less than seventy-four out of the eighty were similarly stabled. In fact seventeen of them spent their entire working lives at only one shed, 6703/5/6/8 and 9 were always at Cardiff East Dock, 6710/26-32/5/56 and 59 at Newport Pill, and 6733 at Barry. The engine allocated for the longest period to a single shed was 6728. This engine went new to Newport Pill in April 1930 and was withdrawn from there in May 1960, just over thirty years later. A lifetime's work spent plying between sidings and tippers, or as that trade declined, on other dock duties. Before the introduction of these engines the Great Western made great use in this area of engines of the predecessor of the 57xx engines, the 2721 class, and to a lesser extent their forerunners the 1854 and 1813 classes of six-coupled pannier tanks, all or most of which had by this time been rebuilt from their original saddle-tank form. This at least ensured a continuous variety as the years passed by in the locomotives that could be seen engaged in this work.

The requirements at Llanelly and Burry Port, where shunting had to be performed in areas of very tight curves, and in addition, in the case of the Burry Port & Gwendraeth line, some exceptionally tight clearances, demanded that smaller engines be used. In this case they were met by the introduction of the 850 class 0-6-0PT to Llanelly and Burry Port sheds, the class actually being established at the former shed well before the grouping, and extended to Burry Port afterwards. These diminutive panniers (the class had started life as far back as 1874 as saddle tanks) could perform prodigious feats of haulage, and are also remembered for their great longevity. The last to be withdrawn from South Wales was 2008 in September 1953 when it left Barry shed for Birkenhead, the last outpost of the class. In fact this engine survived to be the last to be withdrawn in March 1958, and if I can interpose a personal note here, this and 2012 of Llanelly were the only members of the class I ever saw. My view of 2008 at Barry in the early months of 1953 working light engine up the short, steep incline at the rear of the locomotive works connecting the low-level docks lines and the shed, with the crew huddled against the elements in the open-backed cab which many of this class retained throughout their lives, remains one of my most memorable. 2008 was the only pannier with an open-backed cab that I was ever to see.

A slightly larger pannier than the 850 class, and one that had a wider field of application was the 2021 class. Just before World War II eight of these engines could be found at Llanelly, five at Newport Pill, two at Swansea East Dock, and one lone example at Duffryn Yard. Rather surprisingly their successors, the 16xx class which was introduced as late as 1949, did not find such wide application. While they replaced the older panniers and a few of the remaining BPGV engines in the Llanelly area (there were eleven there in 1953), where their restricted clearances made their use particularly relevant, only a further five could be found elsewhere throughout the South Wales dock system at that time. Two each were at Barry and Danygraig, and one was at Swansea East Dock.

Unique amongst the shunters provided by the Great Western were the six locomotives of the 1101 class introduced in 1926. These were not a Great Western

Swansea East dock shed in June 1935. Sharing the sunshine with two GWR 56xx class 0-6-2Ts

is one of the Swansea dock shunters which originally belonged to either the Swansea Harbour Trust or the agents, Powsland & Mason (L&GRP)

design, but a standard Avonside Engine Company product, and were intended to replace some of the older four-coupled saddle tanks inherited at Swansea from the Swansea Harbour Trust and Powsland & Mason. These powerful four-coupled engines – their tractive effort was only exceeded in Great Western shunting engines by the 57xx class – spent their working lives at Danygraig shed, although one would occasionally work from the nearby East Dock shed.

The predecessors to the Great Western engines in the arduous and unsung work of haulage from siding to tip road, or around the multitude of quaysides, were much more varied, only the Port Talbot and Barry railways achieving anything like standardisation. The Port Talbot Railway, before its affairs were taken over by the Great Western in 1908, numbered nine 0-6-0ST shunting engines among its locomotive stock, all but one surviving until the grouping. Although supplied by two manufacturers, three from Robert Stephenson & Co and six from Hudswell Clarke, they were of similar design and were sturdy machines. The eight survivors beyond 1922 were withdrawn between 1928 and 1934. One (PTR No 26, GWR No 813) was sold into colliery service in 1934 and, happily, is now preserved on the Severn Valley Railway.

By far the most orderly of the dock-owning pre-grouping companies was the Barry Railway. It introduced standard classes from its inception, of which three, the A, E and F were specifically designed for shunting duties, and in which they were joined some time after 1922 by the B class when the Great Western relegated them to such duties. The largest of these, numbering twenty-eight engines in total, was the F class 0-6-0ST. Well designed and strong, these engines were obviously regarded favourably by the Great Western who had had experience of them in 1917 when they borrowed six for duties on their tracks in South Wales. Eleven were rebuilt as pannier tanks between 1924 and 1932, during which time they began to be allocated away from their home at Barry. In the early 1930s only nine remained there, and of the remainder eight were at Cardiff East Dock, six at Cathays and three at Canton. They were also known to have worked from

157

From the Appendix to Section 9 of the Service Time Tables, *March 1950.*

Special Whistle Codes—continued.

Stations and Junctions.	Whistles.	Stations and Junctions.	Whistles.
BARRY JUNCTION—continued		**BARRY STATION**—continued.	
Up Passenger Line through Crossover to Carriage Shed Siding	2 short & 1 crow	Mineral Line Up and Down High Level and Low Level ..	5 long
Up Passenger Line to Motor Shed and vice versa ..	2 crows	Light Engines for East Dock ..	1 crow when passing Signal Box
Up Passenger Line through Crossover to Down Island Line	1 crow, 1 long and 3 short	Setting back on the Up Passenger Line	2 crows & 2 long
Carriage Shed to Up Island Line and vice versa	2 crows & 1 long	Down Passenger Line to Up Platform Bay	2 short & 1 crow
To and from Low Level ..	5 long	Up Passenger Line to Up Platform Bay and vice versa ..	1 crow & 3 short
To draw up to Catch Points Up Mineral Line (Vale of Glamorgan)	2 long & 2 short	Crossover Station Yard to Up Platform Bay and vice versa ..	3 short
From Up Island Line to Up Mineral Line	3 long & 3 short	Station Yard to Up Platform Bay and vice versa through new Crossover east of Barry Signal Box	3 short & 1 crow
Up Passenger Line through Crossover to Down Mineral Line	2 short 2 long	Down Main to Down Mineral Line	1 long & 3 short
Trains leaving Barry Sidings to proceed Main Line	2 short, 1 crow	Down Main to Turntable Line..	1 long & 4 short
		Trains requiring to shunt or cross from Up High Level Mineral Line to Down Mineral Line against Signal Box ..	3 long & 1 crow
BARRY SIDINGS.			
Up Main to Up Mineral Line ..	1 long, 4 long		
Down Mineral Line to Down Main	4 long, 1 long	**BARRY DOCK.**	
Down Main to Up Mineral Line	1 crow, 4 long	Up Passenger Line to Up Mineral No. 2 Dock and Storage Sidings	1 long & 1 crow
Up Mineral Line to Down Main	4 long, 1 crow		
Down Main to Down Mineral Line	2 long, 4 long	Down Passenger Line to High Level	3 long
Down Main to Sidings	1 long, 2 crows	Passenger Lines to and from Holton Sidings	1 long & 2 crows
Sidings to Down Main	2 crows, 1 long		
Down Main to No. 6 Sidings and vice versa	6 long	Up and Down Stop Signals Nos. 19 and 8	3 short
Down Sidings to Dead End ..	5 long, 1 crow	East Dock, Storage and Down Mineral Line to Down Passenger Line (calling-on Arm No. 9)	3 long & 1 crow
No. 6 Siding to Dead End ..	6 long, 1 crow		
BARRY STATION.		**LOW LEVEL JUNCTION.**	
Down Main to Island Loop and vice versa	1 long & 2 crows	High Level Lines Up and Down	4 long
Island Loop to Up Passenger Line and vice versa	4 long & 1 crow	High Level Lines to No. 2 Dock, and vice versa	3 long & 1 crow
Up Passenger Line to Down Mineral Line	1 long & 2 short	High Level Lines to Storage Sidings, and vice versa ..	3 long & 2 short
Up Mineral Line to No. 4 Bottom Siding and vice versa ..	4 short & 1 crow	High Level Lines to Low Level Through Line, and vice versa	3 long & 3 short
Up Mineral Line to Up Main Line	2 short & 1 long	Main Line to Jetties, and vice versa	2 long
Down Mineral Line to No. 4 Bottom Siding West End and vice versa	1 crow & 4 short	Main Line to. No. 1 Gladstone Siding	1 long & 2 short
Island Loop to No. 4 Siding or High Level and vice versa ..	4 short	Nos. 2 to 9 Sidings, Gladstone to Main Line	2 long & 2 short
Turntable Line to Up Passenger Line and vice versa	1 crow & 1 long	Crossover in Low Level Through Lines	2 short & 1 long
Turntable Line to Up Mineral Line and vice versa ..	1 crow & 2 long	Crossover in Low Level Line ..	1 crow & 2 short
Turntable to Down Mineral Line and vice versa ..	1 crow & 2 short	Gladstone Sidings to Jetty Line, and vice versa	2 long & 3 short
Turntable Line to No. 4 Bottom Siding and vice versa ..	2 short & 2 crows	To Cadoxton Goods Yard ..	2 crows & 1 long
		To and from Dead End Bay ..	2 crows
Stores Siding to Station Yard and vice versa	2 crows & 1 long	High Level to Loop or Bay Line, and vice versa	1 crow & 3 long

Special Whistle Codes

Stations and Junctions.	Whistles.	Stations and Junctions.	Whistles.
LOW LEVEL JUNCTION—continued		**GRAVING DOCK JUNCTION—continued.**	
Storage Sidings to Loop or Bay Line, and vice versa	1 crow & 2 long	To and from Nos. 1 and 2 Coppers Road	2 long, 1 crow
East (No. 2) Dock to Loop or Bay Line, and vice versa ..	1 crow & 1 long	To Main Line beyond Cadoxton	5 short, 1 long
Drivers of Up Goods and Mineral Trains must give the destination whistle when approaching Low Level Junction Signal Box.		To Cogan Branch beyond Cadoxton	3 short, 1 long
		CAISSON.	
CADOXTON SOUTH.		To and from Roller Bridge ..	3 short
To and from Down Sidings and Quarry Sidings	3 crows	To and from Jetties	1 crow, 2 short
Down Branch to Up Main Line, and vice versa	2 short	To and from Graving Dock Box	2 long, 1 short
Down Branch to Up Branch ..	3 short & 1 long	To and from No. 2 Dock ..	4 long
Branch Line to Bay Line, and vice versa	3 long	**DOCK ROAD.**	
Down Sidings 12 to 18 and Bay Sidings to High Level via Branch Line	1 crow & 4 long	To and from Cadoxton through Lines	1 long
Down Sidings 12 to 18 and Bay Sidings to Storage Sidings via Branch Line.	1 crow, 3 long and 2 short	To and from Graving Dock Signal Box	2 long
Down Sidings 12 to 18 and Bay Sidings to East Dock via Branch Line.	1 crow, 3 long and 1 crow	To Main Line beyond Cadoxton	5 short, 1 long
Down Sidings to Down Branch Sidings and vice versa ..	6 long	To Cogan Branch beyond Cadoxton	3 long, 2 short
Down Sidings 12 to 18 and Bay Sidings to Down Branch Passenger Line	3 long & 2 crows	**CADOXTON NORTH.**	
		Up Sidings Nos. 1—7 to Up Main Line	1 long & 1 crow
Down Sidings 12 to 18 and Bay Sidings along lead towards old outlet to Down Main ..	4 crows	Up Sidings Nos. 8—19 to Up Main Line	2 long & 1 crow
Cogan Branch to High Level (through Bay)	1 crow, 3 long	Up Sidings Nos. 1—7 to Down Sidings and vice versa ..	4 long & 1 crow
Cogan Branch to Storage Sidings	1 crow, 2 long	Up Sidings Nos. 8—19 to Down Sidings and vice versa ..	5 long & 1 crow
Cogan Branch to East Dock ..	1 crow, 1 long	Up Sidings Nos. 1—7 to Nos. 8—19 and vice versa ..	3 long & 1 crow
Cogan Branch to Low Level ..	1 crow, 5 long	Engine requiring to shunt to or from Up Siding Nos. 1—7 ..	4 long
To and from Dead End Bay Lines	2 crows		
To and from Down Branch Sidings	1 crow, 6 long	Engine requiring to shunt to or from Up Sidings Nos. 8—19	5 long
Up Main to No. 1 Down Siding	2 short & 1 crow		
No. 1 Down Siding to Up Main	1 crow & 2 short	**WENVOE.**	
Up Sidings to Down Sidings ..	2 short & 2 crows	Up Main to Down Relief and Down Relief to Up Main ..	2 short & 1 long
Down Sidings to Up Sidings ..	2 crows & 2 short	Goods Yard to Relief Line, and vice versa	1 crow
Down Sidings to High Level ..	4 long	Quarry Road to Down Relief ..	2 crows, 2 long
Down Sidings to Storage Sidings	3 long & 2 short		
Down Sidings to East Dock ..	3 long & 1 crow	**DROPE JUNCTION.**	
Down Sidings to Low Level ..	3 long & 3 short	To and from Up Sidings ..	1 long & 2 crows
Down Sidings to Gladstone Sidings	1 long & 2 short	To and from Down Sidings ..	1 long & 1 crow
Down Sidings to Jetties ..	2 long	To unlock points on Branch ..	6 short
		TYNYCAEAU SOUTH.	
GRAVING DOCK JUNCTION.		To and from No. 1 Down Relief Line	1 crow & 1 long
To and from Dock No. 1 ..	1 long	To and from No. 2 Down Relief Line	2 crows & 1 long
To and from Dock No. 2 ..	5 long		
To and from Jetties	2 long	To and from No. 3 Down Relief Line	3 crows & 1 long
To and from Caisson	1 crow, 4 long		
To and from Graving Dock ..	1 long & 1 crow		
To and from Up Siding ..	1 long & 2 short	To and from No. 4 Down Sidings	1 crow

Neath, Duffryn Yard and Newport Pill sheds. Notwithstanding this popularity however, the economic depression of the 1930s saw the class decimated, but as has been mentioned earlier the majority had long lives following their sale either to local or distant collieries. Of the other Barry classes the E should not be overlooked. In complete contrast to the F class whose dock duties were to haul the incessant coal traffic to the tips, they were a class of small 0-6-0Ts designed by Hudswell Clarke for light duties in the docks. They are of interest as they were the only engines allowed access to the breakwater at the entrance to Barry harbour. The siding that led to this passed through a small rough-hewn tunnel and crossed the Barry Pier branch at right angles immediately outside the double-tracked tunnel that led it to the Pier station. What was unique about this breakwater line, which only saw infrequent use, was that in order to save the expense of complex interlocking it was laid above the level of the Pier branch and a removable section was inserted across the top of this whenever access was needed to the breakwater.

No other dock railway achieved such a high degree of standardisation, although the Cardiff Railway, which despite its name and pretensions remained a dock railway, did achieve a modest level of uniformity in its locomotive stock. Best remembered are the four sturdy 0-6-0STs from Hudswell Clarke built in 1920, which on the basis of tractive effort alone were more powerful than their 57xx class companions at Cardiff East Dock shed. Later rebuilt as pannier tanks, a process that produced quite an attractive locomotive, they survived intact into British Railways ownership. Few Cardiff Railway locomotives lasted that long however. The six Kitson-built 0-6-0Ts of 1889/95 vintage did not survive the late 1920s although four 0-6-0STs of the thirteen built by Parfitt & Jenkins, a local engineering firm, for the Cardiff Railway's predecessor the Bute Trustees, survived to the grouping. They finally became extinct when the final two, GWR Nos 694/5, were withdrawn in 1926, the former having had a working life of fifty-four years.

The traffic arrangements at Swansea docks were singular among the South Wales ports. Here the Swansea Harbour Trust managed the docks until 1923

Rhoose station on the Barry Railway well illustrates the spaciousness of the stations built by the Vale of Glamorgan Railway in the closing years of the last century. (L&GRP)

independently of the local or national railways. In the early years of this century they took over the operations of haulage contractors who had been operating the loading and unloading of colliers and other vessels before this. They then proceeded to build up a fleet of powerful and compact, if somewhat heterogeneous, four- and six-coupled saddle tanks, numbering fourteen at the grouping. Eight survived nationalisation, and they, together with the engines of Powsland & Mason, a contracting firm which operated independently of the Harbour Trust within the Swansea docks until taken over by the Great Western in 1924, gave these docks a unique if somewhat antiquated flavour. The final survivor, 1151, a Powsland & Mason Peckett 0-4-0ST of 1916 vintage worked here for forty-seven years before being withdrawn in August 1963, having spent its final years shunting the fish quays at the South Dock. A memory I have, of over thirty years ago, is of these small engines one Saturday afternoon at Danygraig with 1142/3/ 5 and 1151, all 0-4-0STs, standing at the front of the shed, with its distinctive roof line and individual arched doorways to every engine road. Dirty and unkempt, resting after yet another week of unglamorous labour, they were dwarfed by the pannier tanks around them. At least they were until a friendly driver beckoned and I climbed aboard 1142 and found that the spell of a steam locomotive was not confined to a Castle or a King.

It has not been possible here to describe all the many locomotives that once worked in the South Wales docks or all the practices of train and coal handling that grew up over the years, and which up to the middle of this century were part and parcel of their operating procedures. These grew as the dock system grew, until refined into working methods that were the envy of the world, but unfortunately they are now only rapidly fading memories. Today only Barry Dock exports coal, using the land once occupied by the High Level and Gladstone sidings alongside the No 2 dock as a stocking area, but a conveyor system is now used for loading vessels, not the traditional high-level tippers. The last of these, at King's Dock, Swansea, ceased operation during April 1987, bringing to an end, after a lingering death, an era in South Wales.

On 19 August 1949 a selection of the locomotives that worked in and around the Swansea docks stand outside the Rhondda & Swansea Bay Railway shed at Danygraig. (L&GRP)

161

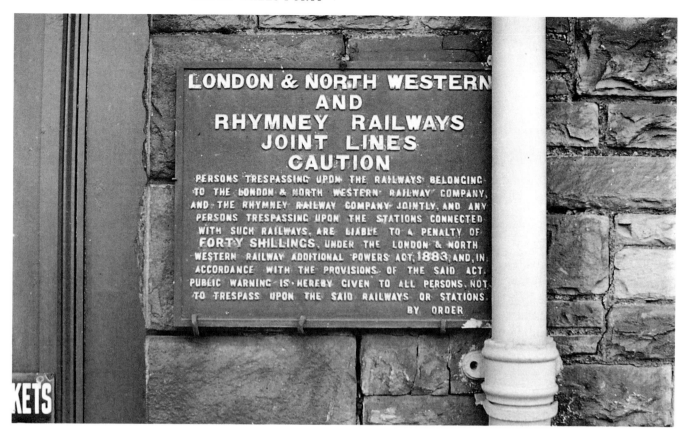

9
THE LMS

The inland traffic for South Wales iron, steel and above all coal, while never achieving the levels that were exported, were nevertheless large and were important commodities for other industrial areas of Great Britain. These needs were almost totally ignored by the local railway companies, and apart from the West Midlands the Great Western served no other major industrial area. Thus it is perhaps not surprising that local industrialists welcomed the interest shown by two major English companies, the London & North Western and Midland railways, in participating in this traffic. This was not a view shared by the Great Western or some of the local railways, although one at least, the Rhymney, had a successful relationship with the LNWR for over fifty years, although the LNWR's relationship with a near neighbour, the B&M, could best be described as 'shot-gun'.

In time these interlopers came to serve two major valleys, or at least a major portion of them, and penetrate short distances down five others. Running powers extended their sphere of influence even further resulting in their locomotives gaining access to Newport for passenger traffic, and the docks at Cardiff and Swansea (the former for goods traffic only, not mineral). The major valleys they served were the Sirhowy, a London & North Western preserve, and the Swansea which was operated by the Midland. The limited penetrations from the north were made by the LNWR and were into the Afon Llwyd as far as Talywain, the Ebbw Fach and Ebbw Fawr as far as Brynmawr and Ebbw Vale respectively, the Rhymney as far as that town, and finally the Taff into which the North Western majestically swept from the heights at Dowlais to reach Merthyr. Of these lines three were jointly owned and operated, that to Brynmawr with the Great Western, from Nantybwch to Rhymney with the Rhymney Railway, and from Morlais Junction to Merthyr with the B&M. Running powers from Nine Mile Point in the Sirhowy valley, and from Rhymney gave it the means of entering Newport and Cardiff respectively. The North Western's access to Swansea did not fall into any of these categories and was somewhat by the back door. Leaving the Great Western line at Pontardulais it headed across the base of the Gower peninsula to reach Swansea (Victoria) and the South Dock after running along the shore of Swansea Bay.

Entry to the valleys from the north was not easy. The Midland arrived at Swansea via Hereford and Brecon to reach the heights above the Swansea valley by running powers over the Neath & Brecon Railway, while the London & North Western arrived there by way of the Central Wales line from Craven Arms. Long and arduous though these routes may have been I believe that the most difficult, and certainly the most spectacular was the LNWR Heads of the Valleys line from Abergavenny to Merthyr. The climb began less than half a mile from Abergavenny (Brecon Road) station, well before the town was left behind. The resulting embankment lifted the line to the hillside south-west of the town and

London & North Western and Rhymney Railway joint lines trespass notice (D. K. Jones)

London & North Western Railway Webb Coal Tank 58902 at Abergavenny on 1 June 1953. (D. K. Jones)

even before Govilon was reached, at the entrance to the Clydach Gorge, the gradient had included nearly a mile at 1 in 34. Three and a half miles at 1 in 37/ 38, broken by a less steep section through Gilwern station followed, and the line now clung to the very edge of the gorge's precipitous side, piercing outcrops with tunnels at Clydach and Gellifelen, before the gradients eased to become a mere 1 in 60 at the approach to Brynmawr. The climb was neither as long nor quite as steep as the Brecon & Merthyr's famous seven-mile bank, but I defy anyone who has seen this stretch of line not to be impressed. Closed nearly thirty years ago it is still largely intact today. The narrow shelf cut into the hillside and following its every curve, and even underpinned by masonry at one point, is still clearly visible from the A470 Heads of the Valleys road.

Once beyond Brynmawr things improved but little as the line see-sawed across the top of the Ebbw Fawr, Sirhowy and Rhymney valleys before skirting Dowlais and finally tunnelling to reach the Brecon & Merthyr at Morlais Junction for a final spiralling descent at 1 in 45/50/46 to Merthyr (High Street) which it and the B&M shared with the Great Western and Taff Vale railways. As if these gradients were not enough the altitude reached made operation in winter a nightmare. From Brynmawr to beyond Dowlais the line was above 1,000ft. The highest point reached was at Waenavon on the Brynmawr to Talywain branch, which at 1,400ft made it the highest station in England and Wales. But Nantybwch on the 'main line' was only a few feet short of this altitude.

The only valley the London & North Western succeeded in dominating was the Sirhowy following its astute purchase of the Sirhowy Railway. However, its metals only extended as far as Nine Mile Point where it was obliged to make an end-on junction with the GWR (as successor to the Monmouthshire Railway Company), and access to Newport was only obtained from the valley for passenger traffic. Prior to the grouping this lack of running powers for freight traffic over the Great Western was responsible for the coal from the Sirhowy valley being routed by way of Bird-in-Hand Junction, at Pontllanfraith, and Ystrad Mynach to the sidings at Aber, near Caerphilly. Sirhowy valley coal destined for the docks at Newport was hauled from here by the Alexandra Dock Railway, via Machen and Bassaleg. After 1922 the LMS worked this traffic to Nine Mile Point, but here they handed over to a GWR locomotive, a minor concession only. The working of Sirhowy valley coal to Cardiff, Penarth or Barry remained, of course, unaltered after the grouping. It was worked forward with Rhymney valley traffic to Cardiff, tripped to Radyr Sidings for Penarth, or picked up by a Barry engine for that dock, and worked via Penrhos Upper and Tyn-y-caeau junctions to Cadoxton.

In the Swansea valley the Midland Railway had no such problems in entering Swansea docks. Its purchase of the Swansea Vale Railway virtually guaranteed this, and it consolidated its position with the construction of its own high-level coal tipper on the north side of the Prince of Wales Dock, sandwiched between ones owned by the GWR and R&SB, together with a second, low-level, appliance on the south side of the King's Dock. Access to both these coal tippers was via the Great Western, from an end-on junction on the eastern side of the Midland passenger station at St Thomas, and the Swansea Harbour Trust lines. The Midland also had its own goods shed a few chains on the dock side of its junction with the Great Western.

The character of the two valleys served by these constituents of the LMS were completely different. The Sirhowy is narrow and steep sided throughout,

The LMS at Merthyr

Working Passenger Trains. – Passenger trains will be run to either No. 1 or No. 2 platforms, and in all cases when the line is not clear up to the stop block, a train will be piloted by the foreman or shunter on duty. The train will be stopped at the Home signal to enable the pilotman to join it.

When it is necessary to allow a Train to run to No. 2 Platform immediately after a train has run to No. 1 Platform it may be allowed to do so before the Engine of the first train has run round its Train, but should a third Train be expected to follow the second the Engine of the first Train must be allowed to run round its Train and push back into the Station clear of the Cross-over Road leading to No. 2 Platform before the second Train is admitted.

As soon as the second Train has arrived and stopped at No. 2 Platform clear of the Cross-over Road, the Train standing at No. 1 Platform must then be drawn out on to the Down Main Line to clear the first arrival Line for the admission of the third Train.

Before a train is set back from either No. 1 or No. 2 lines into Taylor's Sidings (situated opposite the engine shed) the person in charge of the shunting operations must see that the proper signal is lowered before giving the driver a hand signal to set back.

The person in charge of the shunting operations at Taylor's Sidings is responsible for seeing that the converging lines at each end of the sidings are clear before shunting into these sidings from either end. Great care should be taken to leave the sidings clear at both ends after shunting operations. If from any cause this cannot be done the person in charge of the shunting operations must immediately advise the signalman.

When a shunt is required to be made out of Taylor's Sidings the person in charge of the shunting operations must advise the signalman what is required to be done.

Electric Bell Communication between Signal Box and Arrival Platforms. – In connection with the working of the Cross-over Road points near the stop-blocks at the end of Nos. 1 and 2 Platforms an Electric Bell is fixed between the Signal Box and the buffer stops at the end of the Arrival Lines.

The Cross-over points are worked by the appointed Shunter from the ground, but are electrically controlled from the Signal Box. All Trains must be brought to a stand clear of the Cross-over points.

When the Shunter requires to use the Cross-over points he must send the appointed Bell Code to the Signalman. When the Signalman can allow the Crossing to be used he must release the electric locks, and the Shunter must, if necessary, repeat the Bell Code at intervals until this is done. Upon completion of the work the Shunter must ask for the electric lock to be restored by sending the appointed Code to the Signal Box. *(LMS – August 1939)*

A passenger's-eye view of the down platform at Argoed station in the Sirhowy valley. This up working, headed by a Webb Coal Tank, is standing at the up platform, the staggered platform arrangement being dictated by the narrowness of the shelf on which the railway climbed the western side of the valley. (L&GRP)

A busy scene at Colbren Junction on the Neath & Brecon Railway, looking southwards. The line to the left is the N&B main line to the Dulais valley, while to the right is the connecting line, built jointly by the N&B and the Swansea Vale Railway, to the Swansea valley over which the Midland Railway gained access to Swansea. On the Dulais valley line an N&B saddle tank, probably one of their quartet of ex-GWR 0-6-0STs of the 1076 and 1854 classes, stands at the signal, while on the adjacent line is an N&B engine and van. On the line to Swansea both platforms are occupied. The rear of a down train is clearly visible, while on an up working a Midland Railway tank takes water before continuing northwards to Brecon. (L&GRP)

although surprisingly picturesque in its lower reaches, whereas the Swansea valley is broader and for most of its length the surrounding hills rise less steeply. Only above Ystradgynlais does the valley narrow, at which point the Midland used its running powers over the Neath & Brecon to climb up the eastern side of the valley and continue northwards to Brecon. At Gurnos the narrow Afon Twrch joins the Tawe, and it was westward up this valley that the Midland turned to reach its terminus at Brynamman.

LNWR metals in the Sirhowy valley began at Nine Mile Point, which in many ways was one of the odder South Wales stations. The name derived from the end-on junction, nine miles from Newport, that separated the tramroad of the Monmouthshire Railway & Canal Company and the Sirhowy Railway, there being no village or town of that name. However, long before the beginning of the present century the name ceased to have such a precise meaning following successive track modifications in the Newport area. The station had a Great Western signalbox at its southern end, and a North Western one at its northern. The change of ownership here was also underlined by the fact that the up starter was of LNWR design, whereas the corresponding down signal was pure Great Western. In tramroad days the horses were changed here, and the stables were subsequently converted into a house for the stationmaster. Leaving Nine Mile Point behind, the line climbed steadily up the already narrow valley, as a double-track formation cut into the western hillside as it headed towards Pontllanfraith and the complex Bird-in-Hand Junction with the GWR Pontypool Road to Neath line. Beyond here the valley narrowed even further and the climb steepened through Blackwood, Argoed and Hollybush. The heavily mined upper reaches of the valley were now approached and Pochin and Bedwellty pits were passed, the railway threading its way literally between the coal tips. The line which had been double tracked from Risca, singled just south of Tredegar station, and continued thus past its single platform and through the town to Sirhowy. From here it began its last and steepest climb which took it out of the valley to its junction with the Abergavenny to Merthyr line at Nantybwch.

The Midland line up the Swansea valley began at its St Thomas station, a two-platform structure on the opposite side of the Tawe from the North Dock. To the north of the station were extensive sidings, coal wagons were brought here from the mines served by the Midland for sorting before forwarding to the coal tippers. From here the line, which was double tracked, continued northwards along the eastern bank of the Tawe to Upper Bank where it divided into two single lines. The original Swansea Vale line continued up the eastern side of the valley to Ystalyfera and the valley of the Afon Twrch. This valley rises steeply western side through Morriston and Clydach to rejoin the original line at Glais Junction. From its opening this loop was used for the passenger services, the old line reverting to mineral traffic only. Beyond Glais the heavily industrialised lower Swansea valley was left behind and the railway continued as a single track through Pontardawe and on to Ynisygeinon Junction. Here the single line divided, the section to Colbren Junction climbing continuously for some seven miles at 1 in 50/55, the branch to Brynamman bearing west across the floor of the Swansea valley to Ystalyfera and the valley of the Afon Twrch. The valley rises steeply through Gurnos and Cwmllynfell, beyond which open moorland is finally reached as the wooded valley now gives way to bleak windswept upland as the line ran

Nine Mile Point station in the Sirhowy valley on 11 September 1939. The offset platforms can be clearly seen, together with the GWR signal box that controlled entry from the Risca direction. (L&GRP)

Nine Mile Point No 2 signal box dominates this scene in the Sirhowy valley taken on 11 September 1939. The pair of tracks adjacent to the signal box are the main running lines. The sidings on the left fed the Penllwyn branch, the junction for which is just behind the photographer. The loading gauge in the background stood on the sidings laid for the Pennant quarry that forms the backdrop for this scene, the gated entrance to which is visible to the right of the wagon, behind the shunter who has posed for this photograph. (L&GRP)

the last few miles to Brynamman (East). This Midland station was a single-platform terminus with no run-round facilities, and was separated from the GWR station, Brynamman (West), by the A4069 road. A connecting spur that by-passed the Midland station joined the Midland and Great Western tracks, but was only used for transfer of goods and mineral wagons. Only the rivalry of two major railway companies could give such a small town two unconnected terminal stations within sight of each other.

In the Sirhowy valley the passenger service provided by the LMS varied little from that which operated in the later days of the LNWR. In 1922 some ten up and the same number of down trains served the valley from Newport to Tredegar, with an additional return working from Risca. In the following decade the pattern remained essentially unaltered, with only minor variations in train timings, which were generally a few minutes slower, and the addition of an extra late-evening working. All but two of these trains ran through to Nantybwch and in addition there was a frequent shuttle from Tredegar to here which supplemented the through workings. Until more modern bogie stock arrived on the branch from about 1935, these services were worked by LNWR four-wheel stock.

Five-coach sets of these vehicles were operated up to about 1932 when, as an economy measure following a reduction in passenger numbers, the sets were reduced to four coaches. The make-up of the five-coach sets was a First/Second Composite, two Thirds and two Brake Thirds. The term 'modern' bogie stock is perhaps a little misleading as use was made of either downgraded main line stock, or that from other LMS constituent companies, such as the North Stafford, Furness, Midland and Lancashire & Yorkshire. To be fair, however, by the late 1930s LMS vestibule stock had begun to appear on the branch. The normal make-up of passenger trains with bogie stock was two coaches, with the occasional extra workmen's coach on certain trains.

In contrast the services in 1922 on the Midland branch to Brynamman were Spartan. Five up and six down workings only ran the full length of the branch from Swansea (St Thomas) from Monday to Friday, although there were additional trains on Saturdays as far as Pontardawe, which was the only station in the Swansea valley served by the twice-daily through services to Brecon. As in the Sirhowy the next decade saw little change in these services, both in their number and timings. The only change of note occurred in 1932, when following a traffic pooling agreement with the Great Western the through services to Brecon were withdrawn. In the later days of LMS control, and up to the time of withdrawal of the passenger service in 1950, the trains usually consisted of two-coach auto sets.

The services on the North Western's most arduous line in South Wales, that from Abergavenny to Merthyr, were by the 1920s surprisingly modest. Each of the eight up and seven down workings that ran between Merthyr and Abergavenny was, however, timed to connect at Abergavenny Junction with trains to or from Manchester, Liverpool, Shrewsbury or Hereford. An example of convenience and service, as well as an exercise in optimising revenue, that seems to have been lost in recent years. The operation of the services over LNWR metals on the short branches from the Merthyr to Abergavenny line were in the best traditions of the complex relationships of the railways of the valleys. Of the passenger services of the four branches the North Western only operated one, that from Brynmawr to Ebbw Vale, which saw a frequent service of fifteen trains daily in each direction. The remaining services were operated by the Great Western and Rhymney railways as part of the total service along the Afon Llwyd, Ebbw or Rhymney valleys from either Newport or Cardiff. Such a division of goods and passenger workings was not unique in South Wales however. The Riverside branch in Cardiff was built by the GWR but the passenger services were operated by the Taff Vale and Barry railways, while between Machen and Caerphilly the tracks belonged to the Brecon & Merthyr, but the passenger services were worked by the Rhymney, Alexandra Dock or Great Western at different periods.

The LNWR also provided excellent connections to and from Swansea over the

64xx class 0-6-0PT No 6412 with a single auto coach stands at Tredegar station (ex-LNWR) on 20 July 1959. The working is the 11.00am Nantybwch to Risca. (R. O. Tuck)

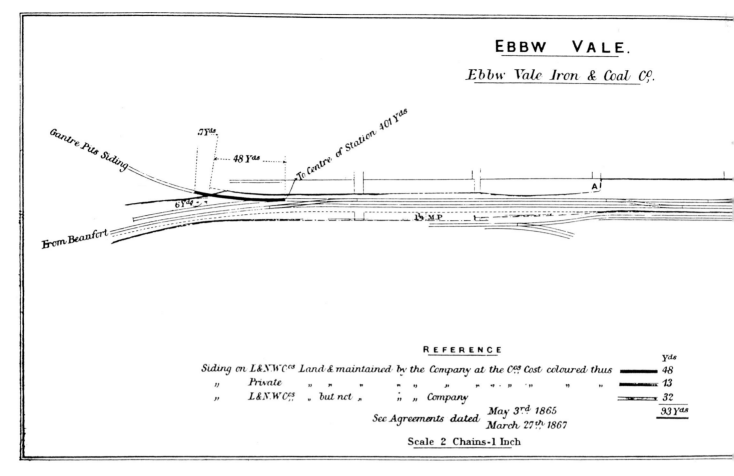

The railway clearing-house plan of Ebbw Vale (High Level).

Central Wales line as they did between Abergavenny and Merthyr. Through carriages were carried over the line not only to Liverpool and Manchester but also to Birmingham (New Street), Euston (twice daily), and York, certain services including a dining car. Locally on the section from Swansea (Victoria) to Pontardulais, a daily service of some ten motor trains operated each way, and a service of six return motor trains was also provided on the Gowerton to Llanmorlais branch, one of which was worked through from Swansea (Victoria).

The working of mineral traffic in the valleys over which it had control or access, presented the LNWR with some awkward problems of which that associated with the inability to work mineral trains into Newport docks from the Sirhowy valley has already been referred to. It also had a similar problem at Cardiff, for while it had access to the docks over the Rhymney Railway, with which company its relations were always cordial, its running powers were confined to merchandise traffic only. Despite this drawback however it built a 45 chain branch along the east and north sides of the East Dock, together with a goods shed and warehouse, and from 1875 until the grouping maintained a locomotive and crew at the nearby Rhymney Railway Dock shed for shunting there. The subsequent LMS presence in Cardiff survived until 1933 when through running over Rhymney metals ceased following a traffic pooling agreement with the GWR, although LMS engines continued to work Cardiff traffic as far as Ystrad Mynach. The practice of keeping a locomotive at Cardiff had ceased some years before.

But perhaps the most difficult problem faced by the North Western was the working of mineral traffic northwards. In the Sirhowy valley this meant from as

170

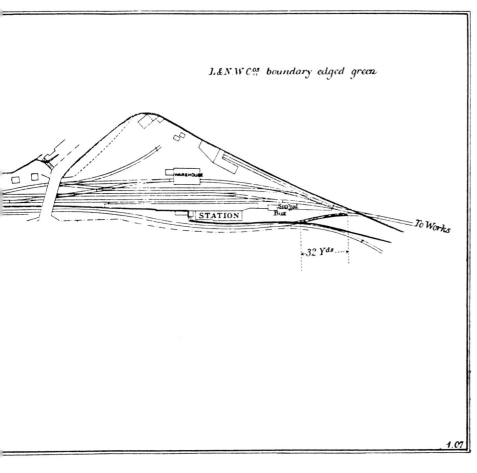

L.&N.W.C*os. boundary edged green

WAREHOUSE

STATION

Signal Box

To Works

-32 Y*ds*

1.07

Ebbw Vale (High Level) in the early 1950s. The station was near the centre of the town and while much more conveniently situated than the Great Western station (Low Level), suffered from the drawback that it only connected the town with Brynmawr and not the towns lower down the valley or Newport, the natural focus for the local population. The line running through the gate and to the left connected the LNWR to the Ebbw Vale steelworks, while the line running into the background to the left of the signal was the private railway running to the Trevil quarry. (B. S. Moone)

far as Nine Mile Point, a distance to Nantybwch, where the line to Abergavenny was joined, of some fifteen and a half miles. From the Rhymney valley, the Ebbw Fach (where it had running powers as far south as Rose Heyworth colliery), or the Talywain to Brynmawr line as far as Waenavon, while the distances were shorter they were up the severest gradients found in these valleys. The three miles or so from Rhymney to Nantybwch was at an almost unbroken 1 in 35, and between Sirhowy and Nantybwch the gradients varied between 1 in 42/37, while on the Talywain line the ascent to Waenavon was between 1 in 55/44, beyond which there was a descent of 1 in 40 to Brynmawr. Little wonder then that single-engine loads on this latter line and that between Rhymney and Nantybwch were restricted to some dozen wagons only, and that the *Instructions for LMS Servants working over the Great Western Railway*, relating to working away from Rose Heyworth colliery Signal Box, stated:

> . . . All LMS trains comprising more than eleven loaded wagons, or which have to take out more than eleven loaded wagons, must be worked on the up journey by two engines, viz one in front and one in rear, the rear engine being placed at the Newport end of the wagons while shunting is being performed on the main line . . .

Rose Heyworth colliery was of some importance to the LNWR since it supplied the railway with locomotive coal. How the North Western must have envied those companies that worked down, literally, to the docks, where sixty loaded wagons with a single engine was quite normal.

One should not forget the equally unfortunate Midland Railway on whose section of line between Ynisygeinon Junction and Devynock LMS regulations were later to stipulate that the brake vans to be used on mineral trains were to be either of twenty tons, or two of ten tons, and that the maximum load for two

---

Saturdays at Penclawdd

The Penclawdd branch, as it was generally called, was opened mainly for collieries in the district but a passenger service was also inaugurated. My recollection of this branch centres more upon the passenger working, especially the Saturday morning train from Penclawdd, which arrived at Gowerton about 07.50. This train was composed of seven coaches and on Saturday mornings always loaded above capacity, with passengers standing in coaches and guards vans and baskets and tubs of cockles piled high in every conceivable space. The cockle-women elbowed themselves in vigorously, or were pushed in unceremoniously from outside.

The engine, a Webb Coal Tank, was a game little nag, but seven coaches packed to capacity became a heavy load to lift up the bank from Elba Crossing into Gowerton station. Drivers usually hung back a little, whistling furiously for the crossing-gate distant, and when this was pulled off, the little engine 'got the works' to enable it to get a good swing along the short level track before arriving on the bank. A pious prayer would be muttered by the driver that the fireman, leaning through the gangway in strained attitude, would not miss the staff.

The length of Penclawdd station would not accommodate seven coaches and most drivers took it upon themselves to draw one coach over the platform which enabled the rear portion to be loaded without drawing-up. The front coach would not be on the platform slope but this inconvenience seemed to be ignored by the passengers – a buxom lot of young women and girls who, shouting with merriment, would clamber on to the footboards helping each other from behind and then in front, as some gained access into the compartments. Tubs of cockles would be handed in by the remaining by-standers, generally husbands and fathers who naturally had a stake in the cockle selling enterprise.

This doubtful but strategic move by the drivers did however enable the train to arrive at Gowerton Jct. in plenty of time to unload passengers and cockles and set back into the sidings without delaying the 07.40 from Swansea to Shrewsbury which would otherwise be held at Gowerton outer home signal.

(*T. Roper* R.O.)

locomotives was twenty-four 10-ton, wagons, which fell to twenty in fog or falling snow.

Once out of the valleys the troubles of the LNWR were not over, for traffic now had to be worked eastwards, and literally down, to Abergavenny. To facilitate these movements storage sidings were built at Nantybwch, which was the traffic control centre of the line until 1929 when it was moved to Abergavenny. Stops to pin and unpin brakes were mandatory at Brecon Boat siding, near Brynmawr, where the gradient briefly eased to 1 in 130, and at Llanfoist at the bottom of the last pitch of 1 in 40. In the reverse direction banking was of course normal. As if this were not enough for the operating staff, for the first few miles of their journey mineral trains from Abergavenny to the north frequently had to be assisted to the top of Llanvihangel bank.

While it will come as no surprise of course to learn that the main freight traffic over the Central Wales line was coal, in particular anthracite, the London & North Western section of this line from Pontardulais to Swansea served relatively few mines. The majority of coal moved in fact originated on the branches off the Great Western section between Pantyffynon and Tirydail, and the majority of this was worked to Llanelly, and following its run-down and closure, Swansea, but not over LNWR metals. Northwards movements of anthracite did of course occur, major customers being the breweries at Burton-on-Trent, but by the late 1930s these had been reduced drastically. Through mineral workings from Swansea were latterly at 1.30am and 9.45pm, with a similar working from Llandovery at 2.40pm. These trains usually terminated at Shrewsbury. They were balanced by workings from Craven Arms at 8.40am and from Shrewsbury at 1.35pm. Through goods workings also ran to and from such places as Liverpool, Burton-on-Trent, Crewe and Stafford, while at 4.40pm a through fish train from the South Dock departed northwards. Routed through Pontardulais in pre-nationalisation days it was, in the last years of steam re-routed via High Street Junction away from the LNWR line as it was run down prior to closure.

To operate the traffic in these widely separated LMS enclaves locomotives were based at six sheds. In the Monmouthshire area were Abergavenny, Tredegar and Blaenavon, all LNWR establishments of course, while around the Swansea area were a further three, one North Western and two Midland, at Paxton Street (later known as Victoria), Upper Bank and Gurnos respectively. For decades, in fact until the closure of the through line from Merthyr to Abergavenny in 1958, services were operated by Webb 0-6-2Ts, the famous Coal Tanks. In 1919 some fifty-five were allocated between the LNWR's three Monmouthshire sheds, with Abergavenny totalling thirty-seven, Tredegar fourteen, and Blaenavon four. As late as 1950 there were still fourteen in the district, and as is well known 58926, in conjunction with 0-8-0 49121, headed the SLS special over the line in 1958. Mention of 49121, a LNWR G2a, is a reminder that, certainly from the years of World War I, LNWR eight-coupled tender engines were also constant workers over these lines. In fact 49064, the last LNWR locomotive in the area, was one of these. Allocated to Tredegar it was withdrawn in 1959. These were the only LMS engines in South Wales to wander far from their home bases, and became well known for their summertime cross-valley excursions to Barry. In later years they were the only LMS tender locomotives allocated to the Monmouthshire valleys, and it was their range as well as their power that made them ideal engines for such workings. They were not the first eight-coupled North Western engines in the area however, their compound predecessors, in fact, are known to have been allocated to Abergavenny some years before. Tender engines were not, of course, popular on these North Western lines, particularly when running tender first, and the attempt in early LMS days to improve the motive power position by the introduction of the Beames 0-8-4Ts has already been referred to. But perhaps forgotten now is the fact that they were preceded by the Bowen-Cooke 0-8-2Ts, all of which appear to have left the area shortly after 1919. Just as the 0-8-4Ts had a forerunner, so too did the Coal Tanks. These were the 0-6-0ST Special Tanks introduced by Ramsbottom in 1870, construction continuing during the early years of Webb's rule at Crewe. Reputedly built for the Merthyr, Tredegar and Abergavenny line they were not active here it appears until 1877

when a large number were allocated to the district. The last of them is believed to have been withdrawn from the Abergavenny area in about 1921. LMS locomotives never superseded those of the North Western on the Monmouthshire valleys lines. In fact they did not appear until 1936 when Stanier 3MT 2-6-2T, No 79, first arrived. But it was not until after World War II that the numbers increased when one of the first Ivatt 2MT 2-6-2Ts came to Tredegar to be followed shortly afterwards by three more.

Before leaving the Abergavenny district I recall an occasion at Abergavenny station in the early 1950s when, as they had done for many years, a G2a 0-8-0 was banker up to Llanvihangel. A goods, hauled by a Great Western Grange passed through the station with the G2a at the rear, and at first letting the Grange do all the work. As it neared the middle of the station however, its driver decided to join in the fun and opened her up. The resulting noise, a mixture of asthmatic bark, big-end play, and the unsynchronised knocking from what I think must have been all eight axleboxes, stunned the central nervous system. The sounds of the hardworking Grange immediately disappeared and so did the rumble of the train itself. I have heard many stories about the noise that could be emitted from a North Western engine when flogged, but only after that day did I really believe them.

From an enthusiast's viewpoint the LMS shed at Swansea (Paxton Street) was much more interesting than Abergavenny or its sub-sheds. Even before 1921 the North Western had provided a greater variety of motive power here than in its other South Wales domain. The Coal Tank and the 0-8-0 were prominent of course, but in addition the shed once supported such classes as Webb 2-4-2Ts, DX 0-6-0s, Newton 2-4-0s, Bowen-Cooke 2-6-4Ts and even a few Prince of Wales 4-6-0s, as well as a variety of four- and six-coupled saddle tanks. As the years passed by a gradual replacement of many of the old LNWR designs took place. Midland 0-6-0 side tanks appeared in place of the old saddle tanks, Fowler 4MT 2-6-4Ts arrived new to the area, and in the 1930s Stanier 8F 2-8-0s came to the shed, the latter classes remaining at Paxton Street until its closure in 1959. Shrewsbury-based Stanier Black Five 4-6-0s also came to the line at about the same time as the 8Fs, but the final years of the Swansea to Pontardulais section saw them largely replaced by Standard Class 5MT 4-6-0s on the remaining through workings.

On the Midland line Upper Bank shed had been the home of the 0-4-4Ts that manfully worked the through services to Brecon until the 1930s, and following World War II it and Gurnos were the haunts of Johnson and Fowler 0-6-0Ts until their demise with the influx of Great Western 57xx class pannier tanks in the mid 1950s. For a long period too Upper Bank stabled five of the six auto fitted LMS 3F 0-6-0Ts which, when the passenger service to Brynamman was withdrawn, were transferred to Paxton Street displacing the aged Coal Tanks on the local passenger services to Pontardulais.

The role, in South Wales, of the London & North Western and Midland railways, and their successor, was never a major one, and in the inevitable retrenchment of the 1930s the traffic rationalisation schemes between the LMS and the GWR, which curtailed many workings, were necessary operating adjustments in the ruling economic climate. But despite these events the LMS maintained a stubborn independent presence until nationalisation, following which the logic of managing these lines as an integral part of the Western Region was acknowledged, although many doubted the intentions of their long-time rival, and used the sequence of events that followed this integration in the middle 1950s to justify these doubts. As this, too brief, remembrance of the LMS now closes I make no apologies for returning to the Abergavenny to Merthyr line once more. In retrospect one can only applaud those whose daily job it was to operate a line where the winter weather conditions could be so appalling that to lose a train in a snowdrift was not uncommon, and where it was possible for metal signal arms to be wrapped around their posts.

Pontardawe station on the Midland line in the Swansea valley in 1906. The problems of siting stations in the steeply sided valleys of South Wales are well caught in this scene, with the steep hillside, retaining walls and approach ramps behind the down platform, the angle of the top of the road bridge in the background, beyond which can be seen Pontardawe North signal box, and the closeness of the goods shed to the up line just beyond the platform ramp. (L&GRP)

10
RURAL BYWAYS

The perceived image of the railways of South Wales is entirely one of industrial lines serving mines, steelworks, and an urban population. Such an image·is to a large extent justified of course, particularly in the valleys. But it does obscure the fact that in the Vale of Glamorgan, and to the north of the valleys, the railways that once existed here took on a more rural aspect, and could truly be called country railways. They had all the delightful attributes of such lines even though they were originally owned by the local railway companies whose main business was heavy freight movement.

Foremost among these lines was that from Llantrisant to Cowbridge and, until the early 1930s, Aberthaw. Its pedigree as a rural branch was impeccable. As the Cowbridge Railway it was born out of the frustration of the town being overlooked by the South Wales Railway, and it had, as was common with many such lines, the classical problem that a large part of its capital was still unsubscribed two years after its Act of Incorporation. In addition it suffered from a protracted construction period, blamed by the engineer on the traditional combination of bad weather and the unreliability of local labour. It finally opened to passenger traffic, after its second inspection and much criticism, on 18 September 1865, having been 'formally' opened with due ceremony (and to goods traffic only) the previous January – since all the arrangements had been made by the local Corporation! There then followed eleven years of increasing financial worries before it gratefully fell into the arms of the Taff Vale Railway in 1876, a move that ensured its survival into the present century. (It was closed in 1965, except for a short length at the northern end to the Llanharry iron-ore mine.) The story of the Llantrisant to Cowbridge branch is a classic of its kind.

The extension to Aberthaw owed its origin to the Taff Vale's attempts to outflank the Barry Railway, although surely nobody in their right mind could believe even then, at the height of Victorian speculation, that Aberthaw could be developed as a port. Never viable, the Cowbridge to Aberthaw line carried on a twilight existence until closure in 1932.

The loads carried on the first day of regular goods traffic to Cowbridge encapsulated the railway's purpose and underlines once again the vital role played at that time by the railways in the community. Inwards were wagon loads of household coal and slates, for the hearths and roofs of the town's houses. Outward was hay destined for Aberdare, to satisfy the need of pit pony and delivery horse, since much of the land that once produced this locally in the Cynon valley could no longer do so. As was common in country towns on the opening of the railway the effect on the price of coal was immediate, which of course further stimulated its use, and the similar effect on other goods greatly assisted the local economy.

In its heyday it was the lifeline of local trade and commerce, with private sidings at such places as St Mary Church Road and Beupre serving small lime works and quarries. Aberthaw also featured prominently, with its lime works on

Torpantau

To work at Torpantau a man needed to be 'a little mad' – or so it was said on the Brecon and Merthyr line. Even the sunshine of high summer does not dispel the loneliness of that place. To serve there in winter, with storms sweeping across a landscape of cold cast iron, demanded a measure of fortitude. A portent – the first to be recorded? – of what Torpantau would mean can be found in newspaper reports written less than two years after the formal opening of the railway. Snow caused a suspension of all traffic 'from Thursday until Tuesday' (i.e., 26–31 January 1865) – there is mention of drifts twelve feet deep, of 'five trains at a time' stranded along the track and of three hundred men labouring to clear the road at the tunnel (*Brecon Journal, Merthyr Telegraph,* 4/2/1865).

As to the signal-box at Torpantau – the men who worked there during the earliest years of the Brecon and Merthyr must have been of heroic endurance. Two minutes dating from October 1868 contain a few fragments of information. The box was remote and difficult of access, the hours of service long – and a letter from the Traffic Manager, Mr Thomas A. Henshaw, urged that sleeping accommodation be installed at Torpantau. The matter was reserved for future consideration. More revealing still – and born no doubt of complaints received from the men – was a second letter of Mr Henshaw, asking that a fire-place be built in the signal-box. Winter at Torpantau, with no adequate warmth – the mere thought evokes a sense of awe! This letter was given a prompt, if qualified answer, ordering that 'the same be done at the lowest possible cost' (B.R. Archives Royal Oak: BMR I, Piece 2 – 14/10/1868, 23/10/1868).

(*V. J. Parry*)

the foreshore beyond the station, together with the large cement works (although the majority of this traffic was worked over the Vale of Glamorgan line). For many years Ystradowen station was the centre for the dispatch of timber and cattle, but the heart of the branch was Cowbridge itself, the largest station on the line, and for many years its terminus. The station was conveniently situated on the eastern edge of the town, unlike many a branch where the town or village served could be a mile or more away. The approach from Llantrisant was through lovely open rolling countryside, and its spacious layout, complete with two-road engine shed, loading docks, goods shed, cattle pens, and yard crane, befitted its importance to the locality. Latterly of more than sufficient capacity, even for the traffic peaks, it was for many years, despite its size, a source of complaints at times of markets, fairs, and agricultural shows. The cattle facilities were particularly restrictive – in the opinion of local farmers. Despite this, it was the railhead for agricultural traffic – livestock, hay, lime, fertilisers, and machinery – for the central area of the Vale of Glamorgan. It was a hive of industry and provided work for about forty people before the closure of the engine shed in 1924 significantly reduced the numbers employed there.

Motive power and rolling stock were typical of the country branch, where economy was ever the watchword. TVR four-wheelers, which were reputedly very draughty, and which served for many years, were followed by old clerestory stock of Great Western origin, and later by matchboard-sided auto trailers converted from steam railmotor coaches. The continuous striving for economy, however, did bless the line with two unusual periods as far as motive power was concerned, the first during the later Taff Vale days, and the second in the final years of GWR ownership. The Taff Vale Railway was very forward-looking in the early years of this century. Quick to appreciate the success of the steam railmotor, that peculiar hybrid of combined steam engine and carriage, introduced on the LSWR in April 1903, it had built one of its own by October of the same year. Initially put into traffic elsewhere on its system, they were finally introduced on to the branch in the spring of 1905. As was found elsewhere they were not entirely successful. The branch itself was about twelve miles in length, and as the service was actually worked through from Pontypridd to Aberthaw it

South Wales pastoral. An unidentified 57xx class 0-6-0PT descends the famous seven-mile bank from Torpantau tunnel, the mouth of which can be seen in the background. Below the engine is the head of Glyn Collwyn which contains the Talybont reservoir. The bare moorland above separates the industrial valleys of Glamorganshire from the rural ones of Breconshire.
(Seaton Phillips)

also involved working over some heavy gradients north of Llantrisant. As a result they only lasted on this service until 1912. The interesting development by the GWR some thirty-seven years after the introduction of the steam railmotors, was the use of its own diesel railcars on the branch in 1942. From this date, with only one short break, one remained on the line until the passenger service was withdrawn in 1951.

There were many delights on the Cowbridge branch, and usually schedules that allowed the savouring of them. Blackberries could be collected in season, and from the morning goods at Cowbridge the smell of frying bacon and mushrooms, the latter picked from the lineside by the fireman only minutes before, would often drift across the line, fried of course on the shovel.

Life was not always so idyllic unfortunately. During the arctic winter of 1947 the engine of the Cowbridge goods, 57xx class pannier 9780, became derailed in a snowdrift near Trerhyngyll & Maendy Halt. Help could not be sent until the following day, which meant that the poor relief fireman at Llantrisant had the unpleasant job of spending a bitterly cold night in the nearby shelter of the Halt to ensure that the water in the boiler did not freeze and that no further harm befell either engine or train. But all was not well the next day either when eventually a relief engine could be dispatched from Llantrisant, as that too became stuck, although thankfully not derailed, in the same snowdrift. Rescue of 9780 therefore had to be delayed until the line was cleared and fitters could

179

Unusual motive power on the Brecon & Merthyr line. A rebuilt Taff Vale Railway 04 class 0-6-2T pauses at Pantyscallog with two four-wheel coaches. (Dowlais Library)

get through to re-rail her, and it was some days before she could be brought back up the branch to Llantrisant.

A feature of train-working on the branch for many years, up to the introduction of the railmotors in fact, was the running of mixed trains, although in its final years such workings were confined to the Cowbridge to Aberthaw section only. Would that someone had photographed this truly rural style service, with its one or two coaches, a handful of goods wagons, and of course a brake van, ambling up from Aberthaw in the early afternoon at a leisurely speed of little more than 4mph.

It might seem a little peculiar to describe that straggling westward extension of the Barry Railway Company, the Vale of Glamorgan Railway, as a rural byway, for it was certainly never conceived as such. Its purpose was to tap the Llynfi, Garw and Ogmore valleys as a source of additional revenue for the Barry company. But the mineral traffic never developed to the levels envisaged. As a result it was never heavy, by South Wales standards that is, although many a branch elsewhere in the country would have been more than content with a fraction of what was once carried. The standard of provision of facilities, double-track line, passing loops at many stations, exchange sidings at Bridgend, and storage sidings at Barry, were far in excess of what was required, and were never fully utilised.

Leaving aside the through coal workings, which of course did not originate on

180

the line, the staple freight traffic, like that of the neighbouring Cowbridge and Aberthaw line, was lime, cement from Aberthaw, stone from the Ewenny and Duchy & Lancaster quarries at the western end of the line, together with agricultural traffic. Not much to sustain a line of just over twenty miles in length. To cater for this traffic there were, just before World War II, three return workings from Barry to Aberthaw, all of which also shunted at Rhoose on both legs of the working, and a single goods train that called when required at the quarries on its down trip to Coity Junction, and at the lime works on its return. The latter ran non-stop to Gileston before working at every station between there and Coity Junction. Its return at 2.30pm from here was a classic all-stations affair in true rural style, with its eventual arrival at Barry sidings timed at 5.55pm. Livestock was handled, when required, on a Monday with a train to Llantwit Major which arrived at Barry sidings at 12.15pm and returned at 5.15pm.

This locally generated traffic was supplemented to a limited extent by the use of the Vale of Glamorgan route as an alternative to the South Wales main line. In the early morning and late evening two eastbound freights passed along it. The first was the 2.30am Swansea Docks to Penarth Curve working (Penarth Curve sidings were situated near Grangetown). This reached Bridgend at 6.45am, but did not clear Barry sidings until 10.00 o'clock, while the latter having left Llandeilo at 5.20pm, again for Penarth Curve, cleared Barry sidings at 1.00am the following morning. There was also an evening westbound through freight (to Llandeilo) at 7.15pm from Penarth Curve, which having departed from Bridgend at 10.15pm passed the up train probably at or near Stormy Down about fifteen minutes later.

There was also at this time a regular through passenger train from Newcastle to Swansea (High Street), which was the successor to the Port to Port Express of Barry Railway days. With a long and honourable, if somewhat chequered, history, in 1938 only the down working traversed the Vale of Glamorgan line, the 9.30am departure from Newcastle reaching Barry at 7.20pm, and after a non-stop run, which was the only one on the Vale of Glamorgan line, arrived at Bridgend at 7.53pm, and eventually reached Swansea (High Street) at 8.45pm. The corresponding up working was booked via the main line, leaving Swansea at 8.15am, and interestingly the down train also had a booked time via the main line as an alternative to its route by way of Barry. Such variations were a far cry from earlier years when, for example in 1922, the 9.30am from Newcastle and the then, 7.30am from Swansea (High Street), took in not only Barry but Penarth as well.

An unremarkable local passenger service, which while mainly based on Barry did include the occasional working to and from Cardiff General or Clarence Road, completed the traffic plying a daily trade along this largely coastal line, whose

---

The defence of Ponsticill

Not many South Wales stations could claim to have been as well defended during World War II (even if indirectly), as was Ponsticill on the Brecon & Merthyr line. The railway here ran along the eastern side of a reservoir of the same name, so closely in fact that the Bofors anti-aircraft gun, set up to deter the Luftwaffe, had it decided to emulate the efforts of the 'Dambusters', was sited at the northern end of the up platform. The boredom of such a duty for the gun crews can easily be imagined, but strict adherence to any 'Standing Orders' regarding the attention of civilians was set aside, and such is the friendliness of the South Walian that such boredom was frequently relieved as gun crew, passengers and railmen passed the time of day in the most beautiful of surroundings.

181

promise was always unfulfilled. Yet unlike the other rural lines of South Wales it has survived remarkably intact. The local passenger services have long since disappeared, as has the agricultural and stone traffic, but the construction of the coal-fired power station at Aberthaw and the Ford engine factory near Bridgend, served by a specially built spur, together with a still not inconsiderable cement traffic, have kept the line alive to the present day.

Never an easy line to operate, its switchback nature as it crossed the 'grain' of the rolling limestone hills that form the Vale was often a severe test for the mineral traffic that traversed it. This fact was recognised by the GWR when it transferred to Barry shed some of its heavier 2-6-2Ts of the 31xx and 3150 classes; 3129 of the former and 3163/4 of the latter were there in 1922. But to travel from Barry to Bridgend on a sunny afternoon in, say, late spring was a delight. No narrow valleys confined one's view, to one side the sea was in almost continuous sight to well beyond Aberthaw, while rolling fields and small woods delighted the eye on the other. The graceful viaduct at Porthkerry, which gave so much trouble in 1899, strode high across a wooded defile, while beyond Gileston broad green acres stretched away to the hills that guarded the valleys themselves. This was South Wales at its most delightful. Scenes such as these, perhaps set off by clean, neat and well kept stations, made a reality of the assertion that not all was dominated by the despoliation of coal and iron in South Wales.

To the north the same assertion held true. To travel on either of the two lines that climbed from the valleys to the heights above, and then descended from here to Brecon, was to sample the true beauty of rural Wales. Broad rolling uplands, lonely and treeless at their summits, guarded wooded and verdant valleys below through which rivers and streams sparkled in their courses. Above, the silence of the moor was only broken by hawk or kestrel, while below, green meadows echoed to the bleat of gambolling lambs or the lowing of grazing cattle.

Descending on Brecon from the west was the Neath & Brecon Railway. An overstretched and impoverished extension of the Dulais Valley Mineral Railway which had been renamed in 1863, its single line reached Brecon in 1867. Shortly afterwards, due to its precarious financial position it fell easy prey to the Midland Railway which was desperately seeking an outlet in South Wales and in 1874 purchased the Swansea Vale Railway. Three years later the Midland took over the running of the Neath & Brecon north of Colbren Junction, thus giving it a through route to Hereford, having leased the Hereford, Hay & Brecon Railway also in 1874.

For many years the Midland brought a touch of crimson to the railways south of Brecon, and since the Brecon & Merthyr livery was described as a 'brick red' colour, the ubiquitous Great Western green was not in evidence until after the grouping. A splash of red though remained for a number of years afterwards on the Neath & Brecon line, only giving way after the traffic agreement of 1930 between the LMS and GWR saw the former company's withdrawal from through passenger and freight services. From the commencement of through workings by the Midland Railway its 0-4-4Ts bore the brunt of the passenger service, the typical make-up of such a train for many years being two Thirds, a Composite, and a Brake Third, all of which were six-wheelers. A feature of these workings was the daily inclusion of an additional through coach for Birmingham (New Street), a service that ran until the commencement of World War I. The 0-4-4Ts remained on these trains until the LMS withdrew from the line in 1930.

Freight services were in the charge of either Kirtley 0-6-0s or, in later years,

Crossing at Torpantau, the lonely summit station of the B&M, circa 1963. The signalman stands ready to exchange tokens with the fireman of 57xx class 0-6-0PT No 3767 on a Merthyr to Brecon working, while sister engine No 9746 waits at the head of a Newport train, and as can be seen more than one photographer was present that day. (Glyn Davies)

Johnson 0-6-0Ts, and banking over the long and severe gradients to the 1,267ft summit of the line at Bwlch, from either Devynock & Sennybridge in the north, or Ynisygeinon Junction in the south, was common. So severe were these hauls that in Midland days it was normal for a brake van to be inserted after every nine loaded wagons. A delightful touch by the Midland was the locomotive that hauled the engineers' inspection train for many years. Despite the gradients, and the fact that it was basically only a single-line rural backwater, Johnson 'Spinner' 4-2-2 No 610 was allocated to this work.

Like all rural lines the N&B from Brecon to Colbren Junction could always surprise, and amuse. Between Aberbran Halt and Devynock & Sennybridge station there were two private halts for the use of nearby estates. These were Penpont and Abercamlais, and if a stop was necessary at either a special order had to be given to the driver before the train began its journey from either Brecon or Neath. The Summit signalbox at Bwlch was high on the moorlands and totally isolated some sixteen miles south-east of Brecon. So remote was this spot that a cottage was built for the signalman and his family. Self sufficiency was, of course, the order of the day, and in order to obtain a supply of fresh milk the last signalman to occupy the box kept no less than three goats that rejoiced in the names of *Up Train, Down Train,* and *Nanny Bell*, and were famed throughout the line. This lonely outpost was closed in 1931 when through freight traffic had ceased, leaving one pick-up goods daily between Colbren Junction and Brecon, and a passenger service that only amounted to some three up and three down trains daily.

The N&B line also had the patronage of a celebrity, who brought many distinguished visitors to the line, including King Edward VII. The celebrity was the world famous opera singer Adelina Patti, who in May 1885 bought the castle at Craig-y-Nos across the valley from the Neath & Brecon line, and converted it into her home. For her convenience, and that of her eminent guests, a special waiting room was built on what had been the bare down platform at Craig-y-Nos station. It was of wooden construction with large windows above the waist, and was very unusual in that it was hexagonal in shape. From photographs that have survived there appeared to be quite a Midland Railway flavour to its design. This is perhaps not too surprising since it is unlikely that the Neath & Brecon, which at that time was confined to working its original line in the Dulais valley only, would have had either the inclination or the money to pay for its construction. Today to go to such lengths may appear extravagant, but in late Victorian times no such inhibitions would have been felt, since to require a world renowned opera singer to stand on a bare station platform on a high and exposed hillside, to be lashed by wind and rain that has to be felt to be believed, would have been unthinkable.

Conversation piece at Neath Riverside. Driver and guard pass the time of day before the departure of the 4.10pm to Brecon on 2 May 1959. Motive power is provided by 57xx class 0-6-0PT No 3687. The overbridge carries the South Wales main line.
(Seaton Phillips)

*Bedwas station, Brecon &
Merthyr Railway, was set at the
top of the village's main street,
and was typical of what could be
termed the industrial section of
the B&M, of which the term
Spartan would be the kindest
adjective. The restrictions of the
site here (it was on a hillside
shelf) forced the construction of
the signal box onto the platform
itself. The bridge in the
background is of some interest, it
stands today, and cast into the
girders are the words 'Rumney
Railway – 1863', a reminder of
the line's tramway origins.
Bedwas colliery is just out of
sight beyond the bridge.
(L&GRP)*

The principal goods traffic arising on the Neath & Brecon line north of Colbren Junction was timber, which when felled was brought to Devynock & Sennybridge station for shipment, the N&B owning a number of bolster wagons for this traffic. A similar product also supported the N&B's neighbour the Brecon & Merthyr Railway, which in contrast to the N&B had been built southwards from Brecon, not northwards to it. Not that that made any difference to either railway as the traffic arising north of the valleys could sustain neither. Their support came from the mining valleys to the south, and it is no coincidence that among the railways of the South Wales valleys these two, that stretched beyond their narrow confines, were constantly beset by financial difficulties. Unlike the N&B however the B&M retained its independence, although it did suffer a period of receivership, to serve the scattered communities north of Dowlais for many years. But like the N&B its very remoteness and absence of bustle gave it a unique character among the South Wales railways.

At Talybont the quiet passing of the day was for many years punctuated just half a dozen times by Newport and Brecon trains, although on summer Saturdays, as already described earlier, there were additional through services to Moat Lane and Llandrindod Wells. Life was to a large extent governed by the rhythm of their passage, housewives finding the 10.20am to Brecon and the 12.05pm return from there, which brought them home in twenty-five minutes, particularly convenient for shopping. The farming community relied on the daily goods. In 1938 this left Talyllyn Junction at 9.45am and arrived at ten o'clock, shunted and returned just over an hour later, while earlier in the day through goods trains to both Merthyr and Bassaleg called here briefly too. The regular engine on the Talybont pick-up working immediately after World War II was Dean Goods No 2468.

Talybont was the most important intermediate station on the Brecon section of

Stopping train to Brecon

The rural branches in South Wales could be as delightful, and their operation as unhurried, as any of their more celebrated West Country cousins. David St John Thomas recalls one such example of this way of life in Breconshire (now Powys) that typifies this unhurried attitude. The passenger service provided on the Neath & Brecon line was never noted for its frequency or speed. But on one such train, at a time near the end of the passenger services, David discovered at Cray, a diminutive station at the edge of an isolated village in the uplands south west of Sennybridge, that he had run out of film. On enquiring where he could obtain a new one he was told by the Guard – 'Try the village shop. We'll wait for you. It's not far.' More than a little surprised by this gesture he hurried down the road into the village, found the shop, and attempted his purchase. But as is common in village shops, local news and gossip precedes any purchase, so it was not easy for a stranger to rush in and demand instant attention. He only obtained this, and a fresh film, after he had breathlessly explained the reason for his urgency. After which, not only was he served with some dispatch, but everyone present, including the shopkeeper, followed him back to the station to see the truth of his statement for themselves, awed by the man who had held up the train to Brecon!

the B&M, and had attractive stone buildings, which included the stationmaster's house, on the down platform together with the usual offices. It was situated literally at the foot of the infamous 1 in 38 Seven Mile Bank, that formidable feature of the line commencing right at the end of the platforms, a situation which coupled with the sharp curve, always made starting a southbound train a tricky job. Not that working north was much easier as only a few hundred yards beyond the station there began another incline only slightly less steep at 1 in 40, and which continued at this inclination for about one and a half miles, a mere trifle compared to its neighbour. Naturally there were always restrictions on the working of the Seven Mile Bank. Following a 'wild run' in 1868 that resulted in a fatal collision at Talybont, no train was allowed to proceed from Talyllyn Junction to Talybont if there was a train on the section from Torpantau, and vice versa. It was also stipulated that the maximum load for an unassisted engine was twelve full or twenty empty wagons. Generally freight trains of this period were worked with at least two engines, one in the front and the other at the rear, and with two brake vans, one at each end of the rake of wagons. Pinning of the wagon brakes was mandatory at the north end of Torpantau tunnel before beginning the descent, and in the early days of the line, despite the threat of dismissal due to the extra expense that would be incurred by the company in replacing worn wheels, 'spragging' of the wheels was frequently resorted to as an additional precaution.

None of these precautions completely prevented such 'wild runs' however, the most spectacular of which was that of 2 December 1878. At about 9.30pm a northbound goods, consisting of twenty-two loaded coal wagons, eleven empties, three goods wagons, and a single brake van only, with two engines leading and one coupled behind the van, did not stop at the tunnel for the brakes to be pinned down. So in the pitch darkness of a bitterly cold December night over three hundred tons (excluding the weight of the engines) came hurtling down from the summit of the incline to its inevitable destruction. As a result of this accident the maximum load for a single locomotive was reduced to ten full wagons, and the practice of coupling two trains together ceased. Sixty years later these restrictions had altered but little. Single engines of Great Western Power Group A, the most common type using the line right up to its closure, were restricted to nine full mineral wagons only, while for general goods traffic the limit was no higher than fourteen.

But on a fine spring or summer's day one could easily forget such things, a local paper remarking in June 1868 that 'travellers remember this long curvilinear descent with pleasure'. And a pleasure it once truly was with beautiful views across the valley that were enhanced considerably after the construction of the Talybont reservoir in the 1930s. Situated almost at the half way point of the bank, the isolated station of Pentir Rhiw was opened in the early years of this century to serve the remote farms and homesteads of Glyn Collwyn, which were subsequently flooded on the opening of the reservoir. It was manned by a signalman only, whose job it was, in addition to his normal duties, to sell tickets from his box, the majority of passengers being hikers following the flooding of the valley. One can only admire the train crews whose task it was to start their trains here on this 1 in 38 climb when working to Newport or Merthyr.

South of Torpantau there is a second reservoir at Pentwyn, built as early as 1862 for the Merthyr and Dowlais area. This delightful stretch of water soon became a source of income for the Brecon & Merthyr, following the letting of boating and fishing licences (only 'fair angling' was allowed, the use of otters was expressly forbidden). The reservoir became immensely popular, a pleasure steamer plying its waters for a number of years despite sinking shortly after its first summer season; and from as early as 1863 regattas were held annually. Dolygaer was the station for the reservoir and such was the success of these regattas in drawing crowds to the line that the station had to be enlarged in 1869. Rowing crews would compete in these events from as far away as Bristol, and in 1867 it was estimated that over six thousand people attended.

But these exciting events were an exception, and they have long ago disappeared leaving the line to carry on its lonely existence. Never was this loneliness more in evidence than at Torpantau, where it was said by those who worked on the B&M, that to work at Torpantau a man had to be 'a little mad'. Not only that perhaps but also extremely hardy. Midwinter snowdrifts would frequently block the line, the winds were incessant, and long periods could be spent trapped in the signalbox. In B&M days requests had to be made some five years after the opening of the signalbox to build a fireplace in it. To work under those conditions without heating of any kind is almost beyond comprehension, and reveals how the financial situation forced economies on the running of the line which were continuously penny-pinching, frequently ingenious, and occasionally bizarre. In 1881 the B&M was selling grass cut from its embankments. The following year the Midland Railway requested the means for supplying footwarmers at Brecon station. The Brecon & Merthyr only agreed to this after the Midland had stated that it would install the boiler to produce the hot water at its own expense. Ten years earlier, in order to recoup some of the claim of £33 for a flock of sheep run down by one of its trains, the B&M sold the carcasses for £3.7s.7d (£3.38p).

Such parsimony was, of course, not unnoticed by the general public, and the

Abercamlais and Penpont Private Platforms.

When passenger trains are required to call at these platforms to pick up passengers an extra stop form will be handed to the guard and driver as under :—

For up trains	At Devynock & Sennybridge.
For down trains	At Aberbran.

In the case of passengers returning to the platforms from Brecon the extra stop form will be given to the guard and driver by the Brecon Station Master.

Private platforms on the Neath and Brecon Line. From Instructions affecting LMS servants when working over the Great Western Railway, published in 1939 by the LMS.

On 14 August 1949, 57xx class 0-6-0PTs Nos 3671 and 3783 rest outside the then recently rebuilt Neath (Riverside) shed. This brick building, built in 1946, replaced the earlier four-road Neath & Brecon structure. (L&GRP)

B&M was the butt of many jokes in local music halls. However, following the Great Western take-over things at last changed for the better. Under GWR control the motley collection of four- and six-wheeled coaching stock had disappeared by 1930 being replaced firstly by Great Western clerestory stock, the first bogie coaches on the line, and after about 1940 by standard GWR corridor stock. The latter usually worked as a two-coach set, although occasionally this would be strengthened to three. The Brecon & Merthyr engines were quickly relegated to freight work only and largely confined south of Dowlais. They were replaced by Dean Goods, Cambrian, and after 1936, 2251 class 0-6-0s, ably assisted by 57xx class 0-6-0PTs, and 45xx 2-6-2Ts. From early in 1953 LMS Class 2MT 2-6-0s began working from Brecon to Newport and were well liked, their increased coal and water capacity being much appreciated. It was one of the idiosyncrasies of the line that while there was a water column at Talybont station, there was not one at Brecon station.

But the abiding memories of those who still remember the line are of that infamous bank, of short goods trains double-headed down the banked back up, and brave little panniers barking their defiance as with two coaches trailing behind they struggled manfully to the heights above Glyn Collwyn before disappearing from view into Torpantau tunnel.

Beyond, of course, the valleys were reached, and the little train would drop below their enclosing hills and thread its way to the coast. It was a part now of a busy and complex network built up when South Wales was famous throughout the world for the quality of its products, and which drew thousands to live and work in these same valleys. The fortunes of this network have changed considerably since the passing of steam. Its reliance on coal movements is now much reduced following the closure of mines in the last few decades. Whole valleys now have no rail links at all, and in others it is tenuous. But in those that have survived there is a new hope. Passenger numbers have risen steadily over the last few years, and new stations have been built. A completely new service has been introduced from Radyr to Cardiff (Central – as General is now known) and beyond, using the old Taff Vale mineral line from Radyr. So it looks likely for the foreseeable future that the rails in the valleys will continue to serve the area as they have done for nearly a century and a half.

188

ACKNOWLEDGEMENTS

An account of the activities and operation of the railways of South Wales cannot be written from the knowledge of a single person. I am therefore grateful to those who have given their time, searched their memories, confirmed facts, and badgered friends and relatives to help and provide much valuable information. In particular I am indebted to Hadyn Shadbolt, Jim Dewar, and Gordon Chard, but in saying so I do not wish to diminish the assistance given by J. Aitcheson, J. Bowring, R. J. Caston, G. Coles, D. Jones, R. Page, H. Phillips, T. Pritchard, R. Shadbolt, and W. R. Veryard.

I would also like to thank the staff of the Central Reference Libraries at Cardiff and Newport who each answered many questions and provided much information, and to Mr A. Burton and Miss Brooks of Pontypridd Library, Mr D. Watkins of Dowlais Library, and Mr R. Arnold of Aberdare Library, who provided access to their photographic collections. In addition I am also grateful to British Rail, Western Region, for permission to quote from their publications, and to the British Steel Corporation for permission to publish the photograph of the river wharves at Newport.

INDEX